THE LIBERAL REPUBLICAN MOVEMENT

THE LIBERAL REPUBLICAN
MOVEMENT

BY

EARLE DUDLEY ROSS

A THESIS SUBMITTED TO THE FACULTY OF THE GRADUATE
SCHOOL OF CORNELL UNIVERSITY IN PARTIAL
FULFILLMENT OF THE REQUIREMENTS
FOR THE DEGREE OF DOCTOR
OF PHILOSOPHY

AMS PRESS
NEW YORK

66689

Reprinted from the edition of 1919, New York
First AMS EDITION published 1971
Manufactured in the United States of America

International Standard Book Number: 0-404-05407-2

Library of Congress Catalog Number: 71-137286

AMS PRESS INC.
NEW YORK, N.Y. 10003

PREFACE

This study was prepared in 1915 as a doctoral dissertation in the Graduate School of Cornell University. The aim has been to contribute something to the history of political parties and of party government by tracing the development of a movement that came at a time of readjustment in both party issues and party organization. The investigation of a nation-wide movement, the sources of which are to be found in the local party organizations, involves many complexities and frequent opportunities for error. The years 1873–1876, in particular, have presented a tangle of party interests from which it has been most difficult to ravel the Liberal thread. Much assistance has been derived from monographs on the political history of the individual states during the Reconstruction era, and in this connection special mention should be made of the studies prepared under the master guidance of Professor W. A. Dunning, of Columbia University.

The writer has endeavored very consciously and, he trusts, very concientiously to avoid the besetting sin of monograph writers, that of exaggerating the importance of their problems. He has nevertheless been convinced, as a result of his investigation, that the Liberal Republican Movement was something more than a mere "spasm of political enthusiasm of the negative character" which "passed away as quickly as it came," as a writer on political parties has characterized it.[1]

Grateful acknowledgments are made to the Cornell University Library, to the Harvard University Library, to the Library of Congress, to the State Historical Society of

[1] S. D. Fess, *History of Political Theory and Party Organization in the United States*, 253.

Wisconsin, to the Minnesota Historical Society, to the State Historical Society of Missouri at Columbia, to the Missouri Historical Society at St. Louis, to the Iowa State Library at Des Moines, to the New York State Library at Albany, to the New York Public Library, and to the Boston Public Library.

The investigation has been carried on under the direction of Professor Charles H. Hull, of Cornell University, who has been throughout a patient, understanding, and undictatorial counselor. My indebtedness to him is too great to be expressed adequately in any formal acknowledgement. Professor Julian P. Bretz, of Cornell University, has rendered most generous and effective service in the critical reading of the manuscript. Both the manuscript and the proof have profited greatly by the careful readings of my wife.

E. D. R.

Illinois Wesleyan University,
  Bloomington, Illinois.
    December, 1918.

CONTENTS

THE LIBERAL REPUBLICAN MOVEMENT

CHAPTER I

ORIGIN OF THE LIBERAL FACTION IN THE UNION REPUBLICAN PARTY

The Civil War, which tried so severely all of the institutions of the American Nation, created an anomalous situation in the party system. The Republicans had arisen and come into power as a distinctly sectional party. The Democratic organization, held together almost to the last by its politicians, had been forced asunder by the sectional conflict. The northern Democrats then divided among themselves. One portion supported the administration for the time being, and the rest maintained a moderate or extreme opposition. During the war the administration Unionists and the opposition Democrats completely filled the political field; the all-dominating issue of the preservation of the Union left no room for the activities of third parties.

Reconstruction inevitably brought readjustment in party organizations and issues. The chief problems of the Democracy, discredited by their connection with the war, were to regain the country's confidence and to secure positive, forward-looking issues. The Republicans, despite their seeming security, had the grave tasks of becoming a genuinely national party and of amalgamating the diverse elements that during the war had rallied under the party's banner. The composition of the Union party,[1] at first a

---

[1] See Dunning, "The Second Birth of the Republican Party," *American Historical Review*, XVI, 56 ff.; Greene, "Some Aspects of Politics in the Middle West," *Proceedings of the Wisconsin Historical Society for 1911*, 60 ff.; Julian, *Political Recollections*, 330.

source of power, was now becoming a cause of instability. While national integrity was at stake differences over other issues had been suppressed, but with the cessation of war old-time constitutional views reasserted themselves. The inevitable result was a disintegration of the party. There was a pronounced difference of opinion between the extreme or "radical" nationalists and the moderates or "conservatives" as to the conditions and method of restoration of the seceded states. Although Johnson's "National Union" movement of 1866 failed in its immediate aims, it forced the two factions of the Union Republican party into a struggle which was renewed with increasing bitterness in the impeachment contest and culminated in 1872 in open rupture.[2] For the time being, the Republicans were united in support of the war amendments; but it was becoming evident that all attempts to continue extreme restrictive and punitive policies would meet with an active opposition within their ranks. Furthermore the Republicans were suffering from the demoralizing effects of an impotent opposition. Their party had not been kept on its mettle. Internal dissension was one of the consequences and by 1869 several of the state organizations were weakened by bitter factional contests.[3]

The political situation in the Reconstruction era was further complicated by economic and social problems. Governmental abuses, long tolerated or condoned, were now being challenged and thus were coming within the cognizance of political parties. A reform influence was developing that threatened Republican unity almost as seriously as did contentious constitutional lawyers in Congress or factious politicians in the state organizations.

[2] Johnston-Woodburn, *American Political History*, II, 585; De Witt, *Impeachment of Andrew Johnson*, 516 ff.; White, *Trumbull*, 286, 312–326; Salter, *Grimes*, 357–362; Schurz, *Reminiscences*, III, 292.

[3] See, for instance, Julian, 302 f.; McClure, *Old Time Notes of Pennsylvania*, II, 203–217; Stebbins, *Political History of New York*, 412 f.; Dilla, *Politics of Michigan*, 99; Morehouse, *Fell*, 96–97.
```
```

In the late sixties there began, in the East and Middle West, the more or less definite activity of a group of reformers, composed largely of editors and scholars, who during the past decade had been for the greater part faithful supporters of the Republican party, but who from this time down to 1900, with some changes in personnel, endeavored to oppose abuses and secure reforms by concerted independent political action. In ability, in sincerity of purpose, and, all too often, in impracticability of method these men have a unique place in American history. But, although they were keenly alive to political and economic evils and honestly desirious of bringing about reformations, some of them at times seemed to be mere destructive critics.[4] Certain of their number, too, as their activity in the Liberal movement was to show, were speculative theorists, following unworkable theories, rather than efficient, pragmatical reformers. They remind us of Colonel Roosevelt's "people of means" who "will get together in a large hall, will vociferously demand 'reform,' as if it were some concrete substance which could be handed out to them in slices, and will then disband with a feeling of most serene self-satisfaction, and the belief that they have done their entire duty as citizens and members of the community."[5] Nor was their manner of appeal calculated to attract a wide following. Choate's characterization of Godkin's editorials as making virtue repellent was a pertinent criticism of many of these would-be reformers. In the East the views of this group were best voiced by Godkin in the *Nation*, Bryant and Godwin in the *Evening Post*, Ottendorfer in the *Staats Zeitung*, Bowles in the *Springfield Republican*, Arthur George Sedgwick in the *Atlantic Monthly* (1872–1873), and a number of writers, especially the Adams brothers, D. A. Wells, and Edward Atkinson, in the *North*

[4] See, for example, Rhodes' comment on Godkin in *Historical Essays*, 276.

[5] Roosevelt, *American Ideals* (Standard Library Edition), 79.

American Review. In the Middle West the spokesmen were Horace White in the *Chicago Tribune*, Murat Halstead in the *Cincinnati Commerical*, Fred Hassaurek in the *Cincinnati Volksblatt*, W. M. Grosvenor in the *Missouri Democrat* (until 1871), and Schurz in the *Westliche Post.* The rise of independent journalism in the years following the war is a factor always to be taken into account in the political development of the period, although its influence on the great mass of the voters was but gradually extended.[6] Most of these men had a regard for the Republican, or Union Republican party, the organization that, in spite of all its falterings and blunderings, had preserved the Union; but they desired that the party should be progressive, that it should face the new issues and not merely rest upon its past achievements. If the old party should fail to meet the pressing needs of the day they were ready to leave it for any organization that might appear more worthy of support.

It was natural that one of the first of the new issues to be championed by this group was civil service reform, as some of their number had been persistent advocates of the merit system since the introduction of Jenckes' bill in 1865.[7]

[6] See Merriam, *Bowles*, II, 132–134. For the ideas of this group, in addition to the editorials in the journals mentioned above, see Schurz's *Reminiscences* and his *Writings;* Lowell's *Letters;* Norton's *Letters;* C. F. Adams' *Autobiography;* Bigelow's *Retrospection;* Brinkerhoff's *Recollections;* Koerner's *Memoirs;* Austen's *Letters and Diaries of Moses Coit Tyler;* Ogden, *Godkin;* Godwin, *Bryant;* Merriam, *Bowles;* Cary, *Curtis;* White, *Trumbull;* Lloyd, *Lloyd;* Adams, *C. F. Adams;* Rhodes' essays on Godkin and Cox in *Historical Essays;* writings of Godwin, Godkin, Lloyd, Wells; publications of the American Free Trade League. Charles Francis Adams, Jr., in a speech during the campaign of 1872, said: "Meanwhile, for a long time past, and especially during the present campaign, I have acted in close sympathy with the class whose feelings now find vigorous expression through the columns of the N. Y. *Evening Post* and the *Nation,*—a class insignificant in numbers only, and one not safely to be disregarded." *Springfield Weekly Republican*, Oct. 4, 1872.

[7] Fish, *Civil Service and the Patronage*, 209–212.

Tariff reduction was another of their projects. To further this cause, the American Free Trade League was established in 1869, with Bryant, Godkin, Schurz, J. D. Cox, George Hoadly, Horace White, David A. Wells, and Edward Atkinson as leading members.[8] In the basic reconstruction measures they had generally supported the party, but, as anyone who understood the character of such men should have known, they would inevitably oppose the continuance of illiberal policies for partisan or other unworthy ends.

In the campaign of 1868 the Republicans relied most effectively upon their control of the South and the continuing popular distrust of their opponents. But while from a superficial reading of the election returns the Republican strength seemed overwhelming, a more careful analysis of the figures revealed serious weaknesses. The Democratic candidates had carried three northern states, including New York, they had been defeated by small majorities in three others, and with a "solid South," of which there were already serious portents, they would have won the election.[9] To be sure, most of the dangers that confronted the party were still latent. Wise, tactful leadership might prevent serious divisions; but it would have required no great gift of political prophecy to foresee the results of false moves by the Republican chiefs.

The Liberal Republican movement, coming in the midst of this period of party readjustment, combined something of all these complex, divisive forces in the Union Republican party. It marked the first deliberate attempt to meet the new political problems. The present study, while dealing to some extent with all phases of the movement, is concerned especially with its influence upon the reorganization of national parties.

[8] Lloyd, *Lloyd*, I, 24. Garrison started a "Revenue Reform League" in Boston in 1869. Garrison, *Garrison*, IV, 262.

[9] Cf. Dunning, *Reconstruction*, 134; Blaine, *Twenty Years of Congress*, II, 408.

As the foregoing suggestions indicate, President Grant, at the beginning of his first term, was confronted with many delicate problems which, both as politician and statesman, he must solve in order to keep his party intact and to retain the country's confidence. For the General the situation was one of peculiar opportunity. Had Grant but possessed the statesmanly capacity to formulate sound policies and the political skill to discipline recalcitrant factions he might well have become the real leader of his party and of the nation. He had not been chosen by reason of any party connections. The Republican managers had turned to him not as a Republican, but as the sole candidate whose success was reasonably assured.[10] The rank and file, adoring the great hero of the war, looked forward to his achievements "with an almost superstitious hope."[11] The reformers also cherished high expectations concerning him. Lowell, in a letter to his friend, Leslie Stephen, shortly after the election, well expressed the prevailing cheerful view: "If you write about American politics remember that Grant has always chosen able lieutenants. My own opinion is (I give it to you for what it is worth), that the extreme Republicans will be wofully disappointed in Grant. At any rate, if he should throw away his opportunity to be an independent President, he is not the man I take him to be. No man ever had a better chance to be a great magistrate than he."[12] And, in fact, if few presidents have had such great difficulties to face, few have enjoyed, at the outset, so general and enthusiastic a support.[13]

But it was very soon apparent that the General was

[10] Rhodes, *United States*, VI, 159; White, 332.

[11] Hoar, *Autobiography*, I, 246; Schurz, III, 285–303.

[12] Lowell to Stephen, Thanksgiving Day, 1868, Lowell, *Letters*, II, 7. See also editorials in the *Nation*, May 28, June 20, Oct. 29, 1868; Godwin, *Bryant*, II, 274, 276; Norton to Curtis, Jan. 29, 1869 Norton, *Letters*, I, 319.

[13] Cf. Rhodes, VI, 236.

peculiarly ill-adapted for a rôle which would have tried the
skill of the most experienced and tactful political leader.
He was at this time as ridiculously ignorant of party politics as he was of the duties of his high office.   Having
had the refusal, apparently, of both party nominations, he
had consented to lead the Republicans only after stipu-
lating that he should receive a renomination.[14]   He had,
however, no conception of his responsibilities and obligations as party leader.   He looked upon the presidency as
a just reward for his services to the country, and incident-
ally to the Republican party.   A soldier first and last, he
brought his military ideas into the White House, regarding
the relations of civil officials as he had those of officers in
the army.[15]   In his appointments, too, he felt entirely free
to pay personal debts of friendship, regardless of party
claims, to say nothing of the interests of the public service.[16]
With no more trepidation over his responsibilities in managing the party than in managing the government, upon which
he entered "without fear," he began by ignoring acknowledged party leaders.   Urgent requests from a prominent
Republican editor for inside information on proposed policies were completely ignored.[17]   The identity of the members of his cabinet, whom he considered as a personal
"staff," was not divulged beforehand, even to his bosom
friends.[18]   An influential Pennsylvania politician, who ventured to present the claims of his state to a portfolio, was
given to understand that the President would select a cabinet entirely in conformity with his own wishes.[19]   His unusual method of choosing advisers[20] produced a cabinet which,

[14] McClure, II, 216; *Schurz's Writings* (Bancroft ed.), II, 415.
[15] Schurz, III, 306; Garland, *Grant*, 391.
[16] Garland, 393; Sherman, *Recollections*, I, 474; Schurz, III, 308-310;
Hoar, I, 305.
[17] Badeau, *Grant in Peace*, 156.
[18] Wilson, *Dana*, 405; Blaine, II, 424.
[19] McClure, II, 221 f; *Nation*, Mar. 4, 1869, p. 164.
[20] For details, see Badeau, 161-166; White, 334-337.

when finally announced, proved to be equally anomalous.[21]
Obscure friends without official experience or definite party
standing were associated with men of marked ability and
with some of pronounced reform sentiments.[22] But in no
case, apparently, was the good of the party organization
considered in the original selections, and in one instance, at
least, the President gratuitously created ill-feeling in a friend
whom he had sought to please.[23] Other important appointments were equally unfortunate for party harmony. The
President's immediate assistants, as well as many other
important officials, were drawn from army officers. At the
beginning of the term they were his closest advisers[24] and
constituted a sort of "Kitchen Cabinet."[25] The traditional
rights of congressmen in respect to appointments were at
times disregarded in a way that no executive with experience in political usages would have ventured.[26] The slighting manner in which Charles A. Dana's claims to the
collectorship of the port of New York were ignored undoubtedly helped to create a most dangerous critic at a
highly strategic point.[27]

This policy of holding aloof from the councils of party
managers did not long continue. The soldier President,
most tenacious in carrying through his pet projects, soon
felt the need of loyal supporters in Congress. Such adherents, in accordance with Grant's ideas of political fitness,
should be rewarded for their devotion by the control of the
federal patronage. The notorious congressional clique, of
which Butler, Conkling, Cameron, Morton, and Chandler

[21] Cf. Hinsdale, *Hist. of President's Cabinet*, 207.

[22] Rhodes, VI, 236–241; White, 337.

[23] Badeau, 165, 169.

[24] Badeau, 12–13, 158, 206; Wilson, 405 f.

[25] Hinsdale, 207.

[26] See, for instance, Cullom, *Recollections*, 176.

[27] Wilson, 406–409, 414–416. Wilson's opinion that Dana's opposition
was disinterested and impersonal was not generally shared by con-
temporaries.

were the leading spirits, furnished the desired band of dependable administration men.[28]

One of the first of the schemes upon which Grant had set his heart was the purchase of San Domingo, "the beginning of an Iliad of woes"[29] for the party. From this unhappy expansion project grew the administration's open and irreparable break with Sumner, marked on the side of the supercilious, egoistical Senator by bitterly exaggerated denunciations of the President and his advisers, and on that of the headstrong, vindictive Executive and of his defenders by the summary removal of Motley from the English mission and the displacement of Sumner as chairman of the committee on foreign affairs.[30] To secure the votes of carpetbag senators for the annexation treaty by the appointment of a southerner, Judge Hoar was also forced out of the cabinet.[31] Senator Schurz's opposition to annexation marked the beginning of the differences between the administration and the influential leader of western reform sentiment.[32] The President's obstinate and unreasonable course in this matter also caused much dissatisfaction among some of his close supporters. Morton was opposed to his chief's efforts to force the Senate's action on the treaty, foreseeing nothing but an ultimate defeat for the administration.[33] Henry Wilson warned Grant that Motley's removal would

[28] Rhodes, VI, 388 f.; Foulke, *Morton*, II, 265; Sherman, I, 474; Conkling, *Conkling*, 326.

[29] White, 342.

[30] For detailed arguments on both sides of this controversy, see Pierce, *Sumner*, IV, 433 ff., and Badeau, chs. 23–24. An impartial summary is given by Rhodes, VI, 349–354, 362 f. For Sumner's view of the episode, see Sumner to Morrill, Sept. 8, 1870, *Forum*, XXIV, 406–408.

[31] Cox, "How Judge Hoar Ceased to be Attorney-General," *Atlantic Monthly*, LXXVI, 162 ff.; Sumner to Bigelow, Aug. 7, 1870, Bigelow, *Retrospection*, IV, 402.

[32] Schurz to Grosvenor, Mar. 31, 1870, *Schurz's Writings*, I, 484; Schurz, III, 307 f.

[33] Foulke, II, 151 n. For Senator J. S. Morrill's opposition and the favor with which it was received, see *Forum*, XXIV, 405 f.

be likely to injure the party in Massachusetts.[34]   Senator
Cole, of California, a thick-and-thin organization man, wrote
from the senate chamber, when the confirmation of Motley's
successor was being held up, that the opposition was "in
favor of Motley" and added naïvely, "Grant often forgets
to act justly.   He is not always a wise politician."[35]   The
Republican defeat in the New Hampshire state election
in the spring of 1871 was regarded as a direct protest against
the administration's treatment of Sumner.[36]

The San Domingo fiasco was, in a sense, the President's
personal experiment, but in dealing with more pertinent
issues upon which Republicans differed Grant was no more
successful in promoting harmony.   The passage of the tariff act of 1870, with the President's full approval, was a
marked triumph for the protected interests.[37]   This was an
especially vital issue for the party at this time since the
sentiment for tariff reform among Republicans was coming
to be widespread.   In the Middle West there was a most
persistent opposition to the continuance of the war duties.[38]
In this section administration papers, otherwise loyal, were
avowed supporters of the free-trade movement,[39] and prom-

[34] Wilson to Grant, July 5, 1870, Pierce, IV, 446. See also on the indignation of prominent Massachusetts Republicans at Motley's removal,
Sumner to Morrill, Sept. 8, 1870, *Forum*, XXIV, 408.

[35] Cole, *Memoirs*, 333.

[36] Pierce to Sumner, Mar. 15, 1871, Sumner MSS.; *N. Y. Herald*, Mar.
15, 1871; Lyford, *Rollins*, 250.

[37] Tarbell, *Tariff in Our Times*, 62. When in the fall of 1869 John
Bigelow, then editor of the *N. Y. Times*, advised the President to recommend the removal of the war rates Grant replied: "Oh, we can't do
anything of that kind." Bigelow, IV, 317.

[38] Rhodes, VI, 278. Schurz, in denying that the Missouri Liberal
movement of 1870 was a plot of the revenue reformers, declared that
if the issue had been squarely on the tariff the majority against protection would have been more than double that received by the Liberal
candidates. *Schurz's Writings*, II, 32 f.

[39] Tarbell, 55; *Nation*, Mar. 3, 1870, p. 132; *Cincinnati Semi-Weekly
Gazette*, Apr. 14, May 5, and *passim* 1871.

inent Republican congressmen reflected the views of their constituents on this question.[40] Forty three of the Republican members elected in 1870 were classed as tariff reformers. Thirty five of this number were from the Middle West.[41] Even among the administration organs in the East there were protests against the injustice of the existing system.[42]

Advocates of civil service reform in Congress could get no better satisfaction from the administration. Leaders of the growing anti-administration faction, like Schurz and Trumbull, gave their hearty support to this cause.[43] Schurz, upon assuming his senatorial duties in 1869, thought that the "utter absurdity of our system of appointment to office has this time so glaringly demonstrated itself that even the dullest patriots begin to open their eyes to the necessity of a reform." For himself, he confided to a friend, he had "taken a solemn vow to pitch in for it next winter to the best of my ability."[44] General Cox in the cabinet was an equally relentless foe of the prevailing system of appointments.[45] But his efforts to take the offices under his jurisdiction out of politics naturally aroused the bitterest hostility from party managers, like Cameron and Chandler, and when, in 1870, Grant failed to lend his support the

[40] Rhodes, VI, 275–277; Tarbell, 67; Salter, 363, 364, 379, 383. Emery A. Storrs, of Chicago, a leading Republican "spellbinder" in the national campaigns of 1868–1884, was in 1870 a most pronounced advocate of free-trade. Adams, *Storrs*, 235 ff.

[41] Ill., 8; Ohio, 7; Ind., 6; Iowa, 6; Mo., 3; Mich., 2; Minn., 1; Wis., 1; Kan., 1. *The Free-Trader*, quoted in *N. Y. Tribune*, Dec. 24, 1870. The list as given by the *Free-Trader* is reprinted in *Evening Journal Almanac*, 1871, p. 43.

[42] For such examples, see *N. Y. Times*, Mar. 17, 1871; Boston *Commonwealth*, Feb. 4, 1871.

[43] Bancroft-Dunning, *Schurz's Political Career*, 317; White, 349, 376.

[44] Schurz to Taussig, Apr. 18, 1869, *Schurz's Writings*, I, 483.

[45] For Cox's views, see his article, "Civil Service Reform" in *North Am. Rev.*, Jan. 1871, pp. 81 ff.

Secretary resigned.[46] The President seemed mildly favorable to the reform measure enacted the following year and made some commendable efforts to secure its execution. But when the salutary innovation was assailed by the keenly interested machine politicians, he failed to give it the backing necessary to its permanent establishment.[47]

Furthermore, most serious cause of dissension of all, the conservative Republicans' hope of a liberal southern policy was doomed to sad disappointment as the President came more and more under the influence of the radicals.[48] Nevertheless the champions of amnesty and complete restoration of home rule kept up the fight persistently, despite all administrative indifference or hostility. In the spring of 1870, when the radical managers sought to keep control of Georgia by a further interference in her internal affairs, a strong and successful opposition was made by the conservative senators, led by Trumbull[49] and Schurz.[50] In the session of 1870–71 the same group made a gallant stand against the Enforcement Act. And in the next session, when after the launching of the national Liberal movement even the radicals saw the expediency of concessions, they practically won their fight for general amnesty.[51]

These policies, which created dissensions in official party circles, all tended to alienate the independent reform group

[46] Opposition to fraudulent land claims also entered into Cox's trouble with the politicians. Ewing, *Cox*, 24 f. Cox claimed later that his resignation was due entirely to the failure of the President to sustain him in his efforts at civil service reform. See Cox to Sumner, Aug. 3, 1872, Sumner MSS. Forney wrote to Sumner (Oct. 20, 1870): "Cameron is here. . . . He and Chandler have got Cox out of the Interior and got Delano in." *Ibid.*

[47] Rhodes, VI, 387–390; Fish, 213.

[48] Rhodes, VI, 390; Woolley, "Grant's Southern Policy" in *Studies in Southern History and Politics*, 182 ff.

[49] White, 298–300; *Cong. Globe*, 41 Cong., 2 Sess., 1925 ff.

[50] Bancroft-Dunning, 319; *Cong. Globe*, 41 Cong., 2 Sess., 2061 ff.

[51] White, 356–360; below, p. 176.

outside. Indeed, the militarist Executive was a sad disappointment to them from the outset. In the first place,
his personal tastes and habits were most objectionable.
His lack of social accomplishments,[52] his utter inability
to speak in public,[53] his close associations with financiers
of ill-repute,[54] and especially his dense ignorance of public
affairs must have provoked the impatience, if not the open
contempt, of men of their refinement and ability.[55] Policies
did nothing to remove these unfavorable impressions.
Instead of the independent progressive administration anticipated, they saw a strictly partisan conduct of affairs. The
first acts showed how greatly they had been disappointed
in their man,[56] and later developments could but deepen
their disapproval.[57] George William Curtis, though the
editor of a loyal administration journal, was so good an
independent in spirit that he was forced to write in private
correspondence in 1870: "I think the warmest friends of
Grant feel that he has failed terribly as president—not
from want of honesty or desire, but from want of tact and
great ignorance."[58] The presence of Hoar and Cox in the
cabinet had been one of the few ties that held the independents to the administration.[59] Their early resignations,

[52] *Letters of Mrs. J. G. Blaine*, I, 48, 90; Badeau, 171–174.

[53] Badeau, 175 f.

[54] (H. Adams) "The New York Gold Conspiracy" in *Westminster Review*, Oct., 1870, pp. 422 ff.

[55] See, at a little later period, the statement of David A. Wells at the Union League Club in 1873, quoted in Austen, *Tyler*, 79. Professor Tyler's own observations on Grant in 1871 are much to the same effect. *Ibid.*, 57–62.

[56] Bigelow, IV, 263, 284 f.; *Norton's Letters*, I, 352; *Nation*, editorials, Mar. 11, 18, 1869.

[57] For a most unfavorable review of Grant's first year, see H. B. Adams, "The Session" in *North Am. Rev.*, July 1870, pp. 29 ff.

[58] Curtis to Norton, June 26, 1870, Cary, *Curtis*, 213.

[59] Lowell wrote to Stephen in March, 1870, after a visit to Washing-ton: "He [Judge Hoar] and Mr. Cox struck me as the only really strong men in the Cabinet." *Lowell's Letters*, II, 56 f.

virtual dismissals, showed the growing domination of the machine element and the lessening regard for reform sentiments.

The action on the tariff seemed an especial challenge to the reformers. The forcing out of David A. Wells, a conspicuous figure in the reform group, from the position of special revenue agent was resented as a victory for the protected interests in Congress.[60] As a result the attacks on the citadel of protection became more persistent than ever. In 1870 the Free Trade League waged a most aggressive campaign. Lecturers were kept in the field in the East and Middle West and a great mass of literature was distributed.[61] Other measures, much less academic but more effective, were taken against the enemy. In April at a meeting of revenue reformers in Washington plans were laid, it was reported, to defeat prominent protectionist representatives.[62] .The Liberal Republican campaign in Missouri that fall[63] was in part a free-trade demonstration. Governor McClurg, the regular Republican candidate, was said to have been one of the objectionable high tariff men marked for defeat.[64] Grosvenor, of the *Missouri Democrat*, was an ardent free-trader (the author of the League's publication, "Does Protection Protect?"), and he put forward this issue so prominently in the Liberal program[65] that the *New York Tribune* characterized the whole Missouri movement as a free-trade conspiracy.[66] The tariff reformers

[60] *Nation*, July 7, 1870, p. 2. Atkinson wrote to Sumner (Dec. 1, 1870) of Cox's resignation: "I suppose Cox's retirement was forced . . . because he is a free-trader." Sumner MSS.

[61] Fifth Report of the American Free Trade League, printed in *N. Y. Herald*, May 31, 1871; Brinkerhoff, *Recollections*, 190–205; Lloyd, I, 25.

[62] N. Y. *Evening Post* and *Chicago Tribune*, quoted in *N. Y. Tribune*, Sept. 7, 1870.

[63] Below, pp. 28 ff.

[64] *N. Y. Tribune*, Sept. 6, 1870.

[65] White, 352; Brinkerhoff, 215.

[66] *N. Y. Tribune*, Sept. 6, 7, 1870.

were credited with the defeat of about a dozen Republican congressmen that fall,[67] and they planned to make the most of their power in pushing for an early reform measure. A meeting was held in New York soon after the election "to determine whether an effort may not with advantage be made to control the new House of Representatives by a union of Western Revenue Reform Republicans with Democrats."[68] Speaker Blaine, learning of the projected coalition in the House, promised to follow the wishes of the reformers in the composition of the committee on ways and means in case the free-traders would agree not to oppose his reëlection to the speakership. The proposition was accepted by the New York conference.[69] Blaine's manner of carrying out the agreement failed to satisfy the more pronounced reformers,[70] while it caused alarm in protectionist circles.[71]

The treatment of the civil service during the first two years could be nothing but a cause of offence to the independents. The *Springfield Republican* said of Cox's resignation that the President dealt with high offices as if they were "a presidential perquisite to be given away upon his mere whim, without regard to the claims of the country. . . . He has simply allowed himself to manage public affairs, as if he were our master and not our steward."[72] A meeting of leading civil service reformers at New Haven, in November, 1870, sent Cox a warm letter of appreciation.[73]

[67] *N.Y. Tribune*, Dec. 13, 1870.

[68] *Idem;* White, 353.

[69] White, 354; Brinkerhoff, 205. Of this gathering Godkin wrote thus enthusiastically to his wife: "All our people are in high spirits. The Lord is delivering the politicians into our hands." Ogden, *Godkin*, II, 100.

[70] *Springfield Weekly Republican*, Apr. 19, 1872; Brinkerhoff, 207. For a more favorable view of Blaine's action, see White, 354.

[71] See editorial in Philadelphia *Press*, Dec. 7, 1871.

[72] Quoted in Merriam, *Bowles*, II, 129. See also on Cox's resignation, *Nation*, Oct. 13, 1870, p. 232.

[73] Ogden, II, 95.

Amnesty and enfranchisement for those disqualified under the Fourteenth Amendment or by state constitutions came to be a leading policy of the independents. They had supported the main features of the party's reconstruction program, including the war amendments, but by 1870 they felt that the limits of legislative action in dealing with the southern problem had been reached. They were strongly opposed to the radical policy of continued coercion in the South for the purpose of retaining a party majority. When Georgia's case was before Congress the *Nation* denounced the tactics of the radicals, led by Butler and Morton, and commended the stand of the conservatives. "The South," it asserted, "ought now to be dropped by Congress. All that paper and words can do for it have been done. . . . Some men in Congress—notably Messrs. Trumbull and Schurz in the Senate—have urged all these considerations with a force and clearness which show that the statesmanship of earlier days is not extinct and that come what will the torrent of folly will never find us without strong manly thinkers to breast it."[74] The same journal, a little later, maintained that the only way of ending the evils of negro and carpet-bag rule was to pass an act of general amnesty and leave every community to its normal action, allowing the intelligent portion of it to take its proper place. Most of the political talent and experience of the South were possessed by the disfranchised whites and no settlement would be real which did not give them their natural influence.[75] The *Springfield Republican* considered Grant's "neglect to do anything important for the restoration of good feeling and loyalty at the South" the worst of his many mistakes.[76]

The President's inept and undignified conduct, the dictation of protected interests in tariff legislation, the prevalence

---

[74] *Nation*, Apr. 28, 1870, p. 266.

[75] *Ibid.*, May 19, 1870, p. 314.

[76] Editorial in April, 1871, quoted in Merriam, II, 127.

of scandalously unfit appointments, with the smothering of all serious attempts to establish an efficient merit system, and the continuation of a narrowly partisan and a cruelly unjust southern policy all tended inevitably to range the independent reformers with the opposition.

Thus by 1871, when plans for the next national campaign were under consideration, the Republicans were confronted by serious factional divisions in all parts of the country. The various influences that have just been noted as tending to alienate both politicians and reformers all entered into this result. Peculiar aggravations existed in certain sections, but in all there were to be found factions or leaders ready for revolt. A survey of conditions within the state organizations by 1871 will further support this conclusion.

The Massachusetts organization was stirred to the depths by the attempted domination of General Benjanim F. Butler. As a leading member of the congressional clique with a strong, mysterious influence over Grant,[77] this unscrupulous, ever-pushing demagogue had soon secured the lion's share of the state patronage.[78] In 1871, with the administration's backing and the support of the labor element, he put himself forward vigorously as a candidate for governor.[79] The ensuing contest threatened to divide the party. Prominent Republicans issued a "manifesto" denouncing Butler's candidacy, and leading organs assailed his pretensions with much bitterness.[80]   But, contrary to

[77] Hoar, I, 361 f.; Butler, *Butler's Book*, 853–855. Grant requested Badeau in 1870 to be sparing in his criticism of Butler in his military history. See Grant to Badeau, Oct. 23, 1870 and Badeau's comments on Grant's attitude towards Butler's military record. Badeau, 471 f.

[78] Hoar, I, 362 f.; Pierce, IV, 498.

[79] "The Butler Canvass" in *North Am. Rev.*, Jan. 1872, pp. 147 ff.; Poore to Sumner, July 3, Sept. 13, 1871, Sumner MSS.

[80] Rice to Sumner, Sept. 18, 1871, Sumner MSS; Robinson, "*Warrington*" *Pen Portraits*, 132–134, 439–450; Pierce, IV, 494 f.; *Mass. Weekly Spy*, Sept. 1, 8, 15, 1871; *N. Y. Herald*, Sept. 25, 1871.

expectation, Butler submitted with good grace to defeat in the state convention and the organization, much to the disappointment of the Democrats, remained united.[81]

In New Hampshire by 1870 open hostility to the "machine," directed by E. H. Rollins and W. E. Chandler, staunch administration men, had developed over the distribution of the patronage and the general conduct of party affairs in the state.[82]

The factional differences in New York, the most conspicuous and the most destructive to the party in the East, were promoted by Grant's unsteady policy towards the rival senators[83] from this pivotal state. Fenton, who had the support of the "Tammany Republicans,"[84] at first enjoyed the President's favor and disposed of most of the offices.[85] But in spite of all his adroitness, he soon lost to Conkling,[86] who seems to have been a man after the President's own heart.[87] The first open trial of strength between the rival leaders came in the Senate in 1870 over the confirmation of a close personal friend of the President for collector of the port of New York, for whom a Fenton man had been removed. Conkling now championed the administration, and after a heated debate, filled with scandalous personalities,[88] he was sustained by a decisive vote. This appointment, a disgracefully unfit one,[89] was followed

[81] Hoar, I, 349; Boston *Commonwealth*, Sept. 30, 1871.

[82] Lyford, 221–223, 232.

[83] For excellent contemporary estimates of Fenton and Conkling, see *Springfield Weekly Republican*, Sept. 15, 1871.

[84] Members of the Republican organization in the City who were supposed to be in league with the ring. *Nation*, Oct. 20, 1870, p. 251; Alexander, *Pol. Hist. of N. Y.*, III, 250 f.

[85] Conkling, 317, 329.

[86] For Conkling's version of this, see his Cooper Institute speech (July 23, 1872) in *N. Y. Times*, July 24, 1872, and for Fenton's reply, see his speech of October 14, 1872, in *N. Y. Tribune*, Oct. 15, 1872.

[87] Conkling, 326.

[88] Stewart, *Reminiscences*, 255–257.

[89] See Eaton's report, quoted in Rhodes, VI, 383 n.

by a wholesale proscription of Fentonites.[90] In the state
convention that fall, Conkling, after being advised by the
President,[91] overcame the opposing faction by a free use of
the patronage club.[92] In revenge, the Fenton men took an
indifferent, if not hostile, attitude toward the party's state
ticket.[93] The next year, to strike directly at the strength
of the opposition, the administrationists undertook the
reorganization of the New York City central committee of
which Greeley was chairman.[94] This was readily accomplished through the all persuasive argument of the federal
patronage and a committee entirely subservient to the
Conklingites was secured.[95] But the old committee refused
most emphatically to recognize the new city organization.[96]
This factious strife culminated in the state convention of
1871 with a complete victory for the administration forces.
The main issues were the selection of a temporary chairman
and the decision between the rival delegations from the City.
After an exciting contest, the Conkling candidate was
chosen chairman and the credentials committee made up
accordingly. By the direct interference of Conkling, a
compromise between the rival factions was prevented, and
both were allowed to take part in the convention, but the
reorganized committee only was to be recognized in future.
Thereupon the Fenton-Greeley delegation left the hall in

[90] Eaton's report, in Rhodes, VI, 383n; Alexander, III, 250.
[91] See Grant to Conkling, August 22, 1870, Conkling, 328.
[92] *Nation*, Sept. 15, 1870, p. 162.
[93] Conkling, 330 f.
[94] *N. Y. Times*, Jan. 6, Apr. 18, 1871.
[95] N. Y. *Evening Post*, quoted in *N. Y. Tribune*, May 30, 1871.
[96] At a meeting of the old committee, Apr. 6, resolutions were adopted
denouncing the state committee's action and refusing to submit to it.
Greeley at that time offered a substitute resolution that the committee
would submit for the good of the party, but it received little support.
Resolutions were also offered at this time, but were not acted upon,
condemning the leading administration policies and praising Senator
Fenton's work in the custom-house investigation. *N. Y. Times*, Apr. 7,
1871.

great wrath, and held an indignation meeting by themselves.[97]   Among those participating in this seceding gathering were a considerable number who the next year took a prominent part in the Liberal revolt.[98]   The action of the convention completed the factional breach; New York Republicans were now separated definitely into administration and anti-administration wings.[99]   The time, however, was not yet ripe for a new party movement.   The opposition wing gave the state ticket a moderate support[100] and the election, coming most opportunely for the administration just in the midst of the Tweed exposures, resulted in a good majority for the party.[101]   Still the old differences remained; the administration's organ continued to abuse the opposing leaders,[102] and the "outs" attributed all their woes to the direct interference of the President in state politics.[103] There was no real assurance that Grant could carry the state in 1872.

In Pennsylvania the Cameron-Curtin rivalry appears. Since the war, the contests of these leaders had kept their state organization perturbed.[104]   With the ascendancy of Cameron as a member of Grant's inner circle the followers of Curtin, who was then minister to Russia, were almost completely driven from office.[105]   Thus in Pennsylvania, as

[97] White, *Autobiography*, I, 164–167; *Nation*, Oct. 5, 1871, p. 217.

[98] *N. Y. Tribune*, Sept. 29, 1871, gives a full account of the proceedings of the bolters.

[99] Cf. *Nation*, Oct. 19, 1871, p. 249; Fish to Washburne, Oct. 7, 1871, Washburne MSS.

[100] *N. Y. Tribune*, Sept. 30, 1871.   Greeley and leading Tammany Republicans took part at a Republican mass meeting in the City on October 25, *N. Y. Times*, Oct. 26, 1871.

[101] Alexander, III, 275.

[102] See, for instance, the attack on Fenton in *N. Y. Times*, Nov. 16. 1871.

[103] Blaine, II, 520.

[104] McClure, II, 203–217; S. A. Perveance to Washburne, Jan. 5, 25, 1869, Washburne MSS.

[105] McClure, II, 270.

in New York, a large and dangerous anti-administration faction was fostered. Outcasts though they were from presidential bounty, they were able at times to exert a decisive influence in state politics.[106] By 1871 Governor Geary, having broken with Cameron, was an outspoken critic of the administration,[107] and there was developing a marked opposition in all sections of the state.[108]

In the Middle West there was manifested a growing discontent with the management and policies of the party and a marked tendency toward independent action. Ohio, as will appear,[109] was one of the chief centers of the independent movements of 1870–1871 which culminated in the calling of a national Liberal convention. Among the old and tried Republican leaders in Illinois and Wisconsin there was great dissatisfaction with the conduct of affairs at Washington.[110] In 1871 Governor Palmer engaged, somewhat unreasonably,[111] in a controversy with the President over the use of federal troops during the Chicago fire,[112] which seems to have been a chief cause of his joining the Liberals the next year.[113] The leadership of Senator Zachariah Chandler, always a right-hand man of the administration, had produced bitter feeling among Michigan Republicans. Former leaders, like Austin Blair, dissatisfied with party management and embittered by long thwarted ambitions, were well prepared for a bolt.[114] In Iowa, Senator Harlan,

[106] McClure, II, 257, 273.

[107] See interview in *N. Y. Herald*, Apr. 12, 1871.

[108] McClure, II, 333.

[109] See below, p. 47.

[110] Greene, "Some Aspects of Politics in the Middle West," 72 f.; White, 344, 349; Morehouse, 97–99.

[111] See editorials in *Atlantic Monthly*, Jan., Feb., 1872, pp. 128, 255.

[112] Palmer, *Recollections*, 366 ff.; Koerner to Trumbull, Dec. 28, 1871. Trumbull MSS.

[113] Moses, *Illinois*, II, 813; Cullom, 192.

[114] Dilla, 99–101, 114–115, 123–127; Stocking, *Rep. Party in Mich.*, 90; A. Williams to Sumner, Dec. 28, 1871, Sumner MSS.

an ardent and indiscriminate supporter of the administration, was defeated for reëlection in the winter of 1871–1872 under conditions of unusual personal bitterness.[115] An opposition faction, led apparently by the ostracized ex-Senator E. G. Ross, was developing in Kansas.[116] Senatorial contests[117] were also partially responsible for the trouble in this state. Nebraska Republicans had troubles of long standing. In 1870 a bolting faction, led by Senator Tipton, joined with the Democrats in opposing the reëlection of a Republican governor, and the next year this governor was impeached and removed from office.[118] In California a sentiment of opposition to the administration office-holding clique was developing within Republican ranks.[119]

In the South the partisan radical policy was fast driving native whites, whether of Democratic or Whig antecedents, into an opposition party,[120] while disputes over the patronage were causing disturbances among the carpet-bagger politicians. In Texas, in 1869, with rival Republican candidates in the field, the administration came out openly for Davis, the radical, against Hamilton, the conservative. Federal officials who supported Hamilton were promptly removed.[121] Florida radicals were never harmonious; they quarreled from the first over the distribution of federal and state offices.[122] So badly were they divided in 1870 that the conservative opposition was able to gain a clear victory in the state elec-

[115] Brigham, *Harlan*, 260 ff.; *Nation*, Jan. 18, 1872, p. 34.

[116] Ross to Trumbull, Feb. 21, 1872, Trumbull MSS.

[117] Crawford, *Kan. in the Sixties*, 345–347.

[118] Watkins, *Hist. of Neb.*, III, 53–55, 62.

[119] F. M. Pixley to Trumbull, Dec. 22, 1871, Trumbull MSS.

[120] Cf. Hamilton, *Reconstruction Period*, 541.

[121] Ramsdell, *Reconstruction in Tex.*, 267–282. *N. Y. Tribune*, Sept. 6, 1869. The Sumner MSS. for this year contain a number of letters from Texas radicals to Sumner, regarding the removal of conservative office-holders, and other campaign details.

[122] Davis, *Reconstruction in Fla.*, 542, 610; Wallace, *Carpet-bag Rule in Fla.*, 126.

tion.[123]   While sharp practices kept the carpet-bag crowd
in office for the time being, it was evident that they could
not much longer retain their grip on the state.[124]   Native
Republicans in North Carolina, like the Helper brothers[125]
and Daniel R. Goodloe,[126] were from the first opposed to the
radical tendencies.   Troubles over federal offices, as usual,
seem to have aggravated the discontent.[127]   Georgia
through radical abuses and dissensions had passed intò the
control of the Democrats in 1870.[128]   The Republicans in
Louisiana, where the abuses of carpet-bag and negro rule
reached their height,[129] were contending in violently hostile
factions.   In 1871 the faction led by the notorious Governor
Warmoth effected a coalition with the disfranchised Democrats against the "custom-house" administration faction.[130]
The strife for leadership between their Senators divided the
party in Mississippi.   Senator Alcorn, though elected
governor by the radicals in 1869,[131] was an ante-bellum
resident and an old-line Whig; and he scornfully resented
the pretentions to political ascendancy of General Ames, his
carpet-bagger colleague.[132]   The opposition in South Carolina, composed of Democrats and conservative Republicans,
in the "Union Reform" movement of 1870 made a hard but

[123] Davis, 618 ff.

[124] Ibid., 629.

[125] N. Y. Tribune, June 11, 1869, quoting Raleigh Standard; Bassett,
Anti-Slavery Leaders in N. C., 27 f.

[126] Worth to Goodloe, May 8, 1868, Correspondence of Jonathan Worth
(Hamilton ed.), II, 1196; Hamilton, "The Election of 1872 in North
Carolina" in South Atlantic Quart., XI, 144.

[127] Goodloe to Sumner, May 11, 1869, Sumner MSS.; Hamilton,
"Election of 1872," 144; Bassett, 56.

[128] Avery, Hist. of Ga., 468; the Sumner MSS. for 1869 contain much
correspondence on the patronage squabbles in Georgia.

[129] Cf. Rhodes, VII, 104.

[130] Phelps, Louisiana, 369; Annual Cyclopedia, 1871, pp. 472–474;
Fortier, Hist. of La., IV, 117.

[131] Garner, Reconstruc. in Miss., 243, 246.

[132] Ibid., 291.

unsuccessful attempt to wrest the state from utterly corrupt radical control.[133]   In Alabama in 1870 the Democrats and Conservatives triumphed, largely owing to the dissensions between carpet-baggers and native Republicans.[134]

It was, however, less the factional divisions in the lower South than the coalitions in the northern ex-Confederate and border states in 1869–70 that brought into being a new national party.   Here the racial problem was less acute, and military control was therefore earlier withdrawn, facilitating the political overthrow of the radical minority.[135]

In Arkansas the corrupt, violent, and proscriptive carpet-bag government [136] aroused a factional opposition with which leading Democrats coöperated in the hope of securing universal amnesty and reform.   In April 1869, certain members of the legislature, "old whigs and disaffected Republicans,"[137] taking the name "Liberals," adopted resolutions bitterly denouncing the state officers, repudiating the radicals as not truly representing the Republican party, and urging all citizens to aid the Liberals in purifying the party organization.[138]   Democratic leaders, like Judges Watkins and English and A. H. Garland, favored a coalition with this Republican faction.[139]   In October, Governor Clayton sought to forestall such a coalition by promising the earliest possible enfranchisement and a reform in expendi-

---

[133] *Annual Cyclopedia*, 1870, p. 681; Reynolds, *Reconstruc. in S. Car.*, 139–150; O'Connor, *O'Connor*, 35–37.

[134] *Annual Cyclopedia*, 1870, p. 15; Fleming, *Reconstruc. in Ala.*, 751.

[135] Cf. Hamilton, *Reconstruction Period*, 501 f.   In Kentucky the open break in the party did not come until the state convention in March, 1872.   Warden, *Chase*, 730 f.; *Annual Cyclopedia*, 1872, p. 429.

[136] See Hempstead, "Arkansas from 1861 to 1909" in *South in Building of the Nation*, III, 322–327.

[137] The characterization of the *N. Y. Tribune*.   See editorial May 25, 1869.

[138] *Annual Cyclopedia*, 1869, p. 30.

[139] Harrell, *Brooks and Baxter War*, 93.

tures.[140] Nevertheless a permanent Liberal organization
was formed in the same month.[141] In the election of 1870,
as a result of the division of the Republicans, the Democrats
made considerable gains and the Liberals elected nine members to the legislature.[142] Thereafter two openly hostile
Republican factions were recognized—the regulars or
"minstrels" and the opposition "Liberals" or "brindles."[143]
The latter faction was the basis of the Liberal Republican
party in the state in 1872.[144] The President followed his
usual course of removing from federal offices all supporters
of the opposition.[145]

Another local movement which helped to prepare the
way for a new national party was that of the Virginia
"True Republicans" in 1869. In this state strong opposition developed to the election of Wells, the radical
provisional governor, by reason of his support of the disfranchising clauses in the new constitution. He also in-
curred the enmity of rivals in his own party.[146] The
regular Republican convention nevertheless nominated
him in March, whereupon the dissenters, led by William
Mahone, effected a rival organization under the name of
"True Republicans" and placed a ticket in the field headed
by Gilbert C. Walker, then a moderate Republican · but
friendly with the Conservative leaders.[147] The Conservatives (the designation taken by the opposition in the state,

[140] Harrell, 94; *Annual Cyclopedia*, 1869, p. 30.

[141] *Annual Cyclopedia*, 1872, p. 25.

[142] *Ibid.*, 1870, p. 32.

[143] Harrell, 96; Johnson, "The Brooks-Baxter War" in *Pubs. of
Ark. Hist. Assoc.*, II, 122.

[144] Harrell, 123.

[145] *Ibid.*, 113 f.

[146] Eckenrode, *Pol. Hist. of Va. during Reconstruc.*, 116 f.

[147] *Ibid.*, 119 f. Walker, originally a Douglas Democrat, was a native
of Southern New York. He had served in the Union army and remained in Virginia after the war. See editorial in *N. Y. Tribune*, July 8,
1869; Smith, *Executives of Va.*, 387.

including the Democrats, following the war), who had already made nominations, reassembled in April and, after some opposition, decided to receive the resignations of their candidates and to take no further action. Later, in June, they issued an address urging support of the Walker ticket.[148] The coalition thus effected on the basis of opposition to white proscription and of political jealousy was most successful; the Walker ticket won by over 18,000, and the objectionable clause of the constitution was defeated by an overwhelming majority.[149] During the campaign the "True" faction maintained that they were loyal supporters of the administration, and the Conservative papers resented the efforts of northern Democratic organs to represent the result as a victory for their party.[150] For a time Grant seemed well disposed toward the new movement,[151] but all the influence of radical leaders, like Boutwell, was brought to bear against this as against all other anti-proscriptive coalition movements.[152] The Virginia movement was later held, probably with essential correctness, to be a real beginning of Liberal Republicanism.[153] Governor Walker was supported for vice-president in the Cincinnati convention on the ground that he was "the first to make a successful Liberal

---

[148] Pearson, *Readjuster Movement*, 21; Eckenrode, 123 f.; Goode, *Recollections*, 100 f.; Massey, *Autobiography*, 42. The changed attitude of the Conservatives was due to the decision of the President to allow the disfranchising clauses of the constitution to be voted on separately.

[149] Eckenrode, 125; *Annual Cyclopedia*, 1869, p. 713.

[150] See General Imboden's letter to *N. Y. Tribune*, May 22, 1869; also *N. Y. Tribune* editorial, July 16, 1869.

[151] Washington Correspondent in *ibid.*, Aug. 12, 1869.

[152] *Ibid.*, July 15, 16, 1869; Boutwell to Sumner, July 19, 1869, Sumner MSS. Conkling in the Senate debate, in January, 1870, on the admission of Virginia said that the result of the election in that state was due to the mistaken notion that the administration favored the coalitionists. *Cong. Globe*, 41 Cong., 2 sess., 383.

[153] Goode (*Recollections*, 101) and Smith (*Executives of Va.*, 387) in referring to the Walker faction at this time as "Liberal Republicans" are anticipating in name, at least.

movement,"[154] and during the campaign of 1872 Walker and other Liberal leaders in Virginia took every opportunity to claim the honor of priority.[155]   But whatever its direct relations to the national opposition movement, the result of the Virginia coalition was most significant at the time as showing the trend of sentiment against the continuation of radical control. "The Virginia election," wrote John W. Forney, "is the worst blow we have had since the failure of impeachment. . . . There is great danger that we shall lose the whole South; and if so, we are gone in the North."[156]   The *New York Herald* interpreted this election to mean that the conservatives had "developed a new party organization, which, if followed up by the anti-radical elements throughout the Union, may soon give us the dominant national party of the future."[157]

A similar movement followed in Tennessee. Here the Republicans were divided into conservative and radical factions over the pressing question of the time and extent of the removal of political disabilities.   In the election of 1869 the Democrats had an understanding with the conservative candidate, Senter, then acting governor, by which he was to have their full support in return for the exercise of his discretionary power in allowing them to register. The result was an overwhelming conservative triumph.[158]   The

[154] N. Y. *World*, May 1, 1872.

[155] See Walker's interview and speech at Fifth Avenue Conference, *N. Y. Tribune*, June 21, 22, 1872; report of Liberal mass meeting at Richmond, *Richmond Whig and Advertiser*, June 28, 1872. Senator Conkling in a campaign speech in 1872 said that Liberal Republican movements had first been tried in Virginia, West Virginia and Tennessee. Conkling, 442. The *Missouri Republican* said (Oct. 30, 1871) that Walker, Senter (of Tenn.) and Brown (of Mo.) were all Liberal Republicans.

[156] Forney to Sumner, July 16, 1869, Sumner MSS.

[157] *N. Y. Herald*, July 8, 1869.

[158] *Annual Cyclopedia*, 1869, pp. 662 f.; Folk, "Tennessee Since the War" in *South in Building of the Nation*, II, 537; Jones, "Reconstruction in Tennessee" in *Why the Solid South?* 214 f.

next year, in the first state election under the new constitution, the Democrats were firmly established in power.[159]

In West Virginia in the campaign of 1870 the Democrats
and conservatives, putting forward the plea of a "white
man's party" and taking full advantage of a favorable
interpretation of the Enforcement Act by a Democratic
judge, were able to defeat the radicals.[160]

It was in Missouri, however, that factional strife led most
directly to a national Liberal movement.   Party insurgency
here was due partly to an oppressively proscriptive radical
policy and partly to dissatisfaction over federal appointments.   Early in the war the Union party in Missouri
was divided into definite radical and conservative factions.[161]   The radicals, securing complete control of the
constitutional convention of 1865, instituted a sweeping
proscription of all those in any way concerned in the
rebellion.[162]   Such a policy was opposed to the political
interests as well as to the principles of conservative leaders.
At St. Louis, in December, 1866, the more liberal element of
the party, responding to the widespread complaints at the
restrictive clauses, set on foot a movement for universal
amnesty and enfranchisement.[163]   B. Gratz Brown, originally a Benton Democrat[164] and in the front ranks of the
Union and anti-slavery men during the war,[165] took the lead
in this opposition to radical policies.   With the coming of
Carl Schurz to St. Louis the next year the liberal cause in
Missouri secured another efficient champion.[166]   Schurz's
views in this matter were known.   In the last Republican

[159] *Annual Cyclopedia*, 1870, pp. 709 f.

[160] *Ibid.*, 751–753; Callahan, *Hist. of W. Va.*, 167.

[161] Harding, "Missouri Party Struggles in the Civil War Period" in
Rep. Am. Hist. Assoc., 1900, I, 98; Smith, *Rollins*, 34–38.

[162] Harding, 102; Switzler, *Hist. of Mo.*, 454–459, 464.

[163] *Annual Cyclopedia*, 1870, p. 517; Switzler, 460.

[164] Switzler, 277.

[165] Harding, 97.

[166] *Annual Cyclopedia*, 1870, p. 517.

national convention he had secured the adoption of a
resolution favoring the removal of rebel disqualifications
so soon as safe and practicable.[167]   Within two years he was
elected to the United States Senate, after a bitter contest
with the radical "boss," Charles D. Drake, as the representative of the liberal faction.[168]   By 1870 the differences over
enfranchisement had divided the party in the state into
distinct "Radical" and "Liberal" wings.[169]

The action of the state convention in August of that year
precipitated the party's disruption.   The Radicals, so their
opponents said, had used most reprehensible tactics,
packing the convention with their adherents by manipulat-
ing the negro vote and by holding "snap" caucuses.[170]
The main question before the convention was that of the
amendments to the state constitution, then before the voters,
for the removal of disabilities.[171]   After a heated discussion,
the Radical resolution, approving the submission of the
amendments and declaring for enfranchisement "as soon
as it can be done with safety to the State," was adopted by a
majority of ninety seven over the Liberal substitute, declaring "unequivocally in favor of the adoption of the Constitutional Amendments."   Thereupon the two hundred and
fifty Liberals withdrew and organized a separate convention.
An attempt by the regular convention to compose the differences by a conference committee failed, and the Liberals
named a ticket of their own, headed by Gratz Brown for
governor.[172]

The federal patronage was another influence creating
dissensions in the Missouri organization.   William McKee,
owner of the *Missouri Democrat*, the chief Republican organ

[167] Schurz, III, 284 f.
[168] *Ibid.*, 292–301; *Schurz's Writings*, I, 473–481.
[169] Switzler, 469.
[170] *Schurz's Writings*, I, 513 f.
[171] Switzler, 468 f.
[172] *Ibid.*, 470 f.; *Annual Cyclopedia*, 1870, pp. 519 f.

in the state, was so indignant at having his regular organization selections for federal positions passed over for the
President's personal friends, who had no other claim on the
party, that he championed the insurgent movement to show
his power.[173] The sentiment for tariff reform among
Missouri Republicans, as already noted,[174] was probably an
additional factor of some weight in producing the Liberal
bolt.

The Democrats, kept in a hopeless minority through the
operation of the test-oath clause, adopted at this time what
was termed the "passive policy," an abstention for the time
being from open party activity.[175] In the campaign they
heartily supported Brown, and their leading paper, the
Missouri Republican, finally declared for the Liberal
ticket.[176]

The Missouri campaign was conducted most vigorously
and aroused attention throughout the country.[177] The
Liberals issued an address, written by Schurz, in which they
unsparingly arraigned the Radicals for their illiberality,
party trickery, and corruption in office; and claimed them-

[173] McDonald, *Hist. of Whiskey Ring*, 28–32; W. M. Grosvenor's
letter to *N. Y. Herald* (Nov. 17, 1875) on the history of the whiskey
ring, also printed in McDonald, 39 ff. McKee, on the formation of the
ring the following year, took his paper back to the administration side.
Grosvenor, letter as above and quoted in McDonald, 40.

[174] Above, p. 14.

[175] The Democratic members of the legislature recommended such a
policy in March and it was officially proclaimed by the state committee
in August. Switzler, 469 f.; *Mo. Republican*, Aug. 14, 1870. The
Republican said editorially, June 30, that it thought that nine-tenths of
the Democrats of the state were opposed to the naming of a ticket.

[176] At first the *Republican* was an unfavorable critic of the Liberal
leaders, see editorials, Sept. 5, 6, 1870, but later it came out fully for
Brown, editorials Sept. 29, Nov. 3, 1870.

[177] Brown wrote to J. R. Doolittle, Oct. 17, 1870, that they had a most
bitter fight because it meant death to the "rings," and "because it has
its ulterior significance." Doolittle Papers, copy in Mo. Historical
Society Library and printed in *Mo. Hist. Rev.*, XI, 11 f.

selves to represent the true Republican party of Missouri.[178]
Schurz at the start evidently had hoped to prevent a break
with the administration. Before leaving the capital to
attend the state convention he had written to Grant a most
conciliatory note in which he expressed regret over their
differences on the San Domingo question and assured the
President that the Senator's personal attitude had been
misrepresented.[179]   Shortly after the convention, in a letter
to Secretary Fish, he made this comment on the local situation: "As to our bolt in Missouri, I send you our manifesto.
It was a necessary thing."[180]   Grant, however, could see
nothing but party treason in the action of the Liberals.[181]
The motives of the reformers he could not comprehend; but
he appreciated fully those of the politicians and put the
bolters all in this class.[182]   He had had quite enough of
bolting coalition movements and he brought to bear against
the present one all the weight of administration disfavor.
"I regard the movement headed by Carl Schurz, Brown,
etc.," he wrote to the collector at St. Louis, "as similar to
the Tennessee and Virginia movements intended to carry a
portion of the Republican party over to the Democracy, and
thus give them control. . . . I hope you will see your
way clear to give the regular ticket your support."[183]   Federal office-holders in Missouri were freely called upon for
funds for the Radical cause and those adhering to the Liberals were promptly displaced.[184]   In explaining why he
could not leave the state during the campaign, Schurz wrote

[178] *Schurz's Writings*, I, 510 ff.
[179] Schurz to Grant, July 17, 1870, *ibid.*, 509.
[180] Schurz to Fish, Sept. 11, 1870, *ibid.*, 520.
[181] Cf. White, 355.
[182] See Grosvenor's letter in *N. Y. Herald*, Nov. 17, 1875.
[183] *Annual Cyclopedia*, 1870, p. 520.
[184] L. U. Reavis to Sumner, Dec. 1, 1870, Sumner MSS. Senator
Drake, in defending the President's action in the Senate, Dec. 16, 1870,
declared: "I advised and asked for those removals, and would do it
again." *Cong. Globe*, 41 Cong., 3 Sess., 7.

to Senator Carpenter: "You do not seem to be aware that Grant has read me out of the Republican party and is vigorously chopping off the heads of those who are suspected of sympathizing with me. Under such circumstances I have to fight right here. Had not Grant given himself into Drake's keeping and interfered in our affairs, we 'bolters' would have swept almost the whole Republican party with us. But the President fighting us (and fighting himself too), we have to work for we not only want to carry the State, but to carry it heavily.

"So you may thank Grant for it if I have no time to devote to the outside world. Oh, there is much wisdom in high places.!"[185]

Despite all official interference in the campaign, the Liberal ticket was elected by over 40,000 majority and the suffrage amendments were adopted overwhelmingly.[186] The new congressional delegation was composed of four Democrats, three Radicals, and two Liberals.[187] In the legislature the coalitionists had complete control,[188] the Democratic members alone having a majority on joint ballot. The Democrats secured the election of their candidate for speaker, and that of their redoubtable champion, F. P. Blair, Jr., to fill a vacancy in the United States Senate.[189] Schurz's speech in the Senate in December,[190] in which he presented an elaborate exposition and defense of the "Missouri movement," made it clear that his break with the

---

[185] Schurz to Carpenter, Oct. 20, 1870, *Schurz's Writings*, I, 520 f.

[186] *Annual Cyclopedia*, 1870, p. 521; Switzler, 468 f.

[187] *Annual Cyclopedia*, 1870, p. 521.

[188] The membership was as follows: Senate—Democrats 13; Fusion (elected by the united votes of Dems. and Libs.) 3; Liberals 6; Republicans 12. House—Dems. 77; Fus., 12; Libs. 20; Reps., 24. Switzler, 471.

[189] *Ibid.*, 471 f.; Smith, *Rollins*, 56 f.

[190] *Schurz's Writings*, II, 2 ff.

administration was complete,[191] and that he regarded party ties very lightly.

So by the end of the second year of Grant—the President of whom the Republicans had had such high expectations—the party was confronted by dissensions or actual divisions in every section of the country. The leading Democratic organ thus graphically and gleefully pictured the situation of the enemy: "Greeley and Fenton against Grant and Conkling, Butler and anti-Butler, Cameron and anti-Cameron, Sherman and anti-Sherman, Harlan and anti-Harlan, Schurz and haters of Schurz, Warmoth and Dunn, Hamilton and Davis—truly is not the Republican party a united band of brothers."[192] And an influential independent Republican editor warned the President that if he expected to be reëlected he should begin at once to make up with leaders like Sumner, Schurz, Trumbull, and Fenton, all of whom represented strong elements in the party.[193] Other keen observers, of Republican affiliations, expressed similar sentiments in private correspondence.[194]

[191] Senator Howe, of Wisconsin, wrote to Sumner (Oct. 25, 1870): "I fear Schurz is gone 'hook, line, bob and sinker.'" Sumner MSS. Schurz, in private conversation, thus defined his position in December, 1870: "I have taken my political life in my hand. I have resolved to act as if I were to end my career with this term in the Senate; to be independent, true to my real convictions, and not hesitate to say and do what I think to be right on account of any regard for a reëlection." Austen, *Tyler*, 53.

[192] N. Y. *World*, Sept. 30, 1871.

[193] *Cincinnati Commercial*, May 3, 1871.

[194] Various letters to Sumner, preserved in the Sumner MSS., express such views: Bigelow wrote from Paris (Oct. 2, 1870) that every one told him that Grant could not be reëlected; W. S. Robinson (Dec. 23, 1870) feared that the dissensions in Congress would lead to Republican defeat in 1872; George William Curtis (Jan. 14, 1871) thought that the party's supremacy was seriously threatened. If factional divisions in Congress and the state organizations were not soon healed "we are already beaten." Forney wrote (Aug. 24, 1871): "There is no doubt in my mind that the Republican opposition to President Grant can defeat his reëlection if organized under a separate flag." But he was equally certain that it could not prevent his renomination.

The weakening influence on the party of factional differences in state organizations and of independent opposition
to administration policies had been shown to some extent
in the mid-term congressional elections of 1870, as usual a
good test of the administration's standing before the country. The Republican majority in the House was reduced
from ninety eight in the Forty-first Congress to thirty seven
in the Forty-second [195] and the party lost in addition four
senators.[196] The Democrats gained sixteen of their representatives in the four border states of Virginia, Tennessee,
West Virginia and Missouri,[197] and their senators in Missouri,
Tennessee, West Virginia, and North Carolina.

With disappointed factions in nearly every state, whom
no sufficient means was taken to conciliate, and with the
independents agitating for reforms which were, for the most
part, inadequately supported or opposed by the administration, opposition to the President's renomination was
inevitable. During 1871 this opposition showed considerable strength.

The independent press was practically a unit in deprecating an extension of the military politician rule. The *New
York Herald*, viewing the political field "from our independent and impartial standpoint," presented a formidable
catalogue of Grant's failures as administrator and party
leader.[198] The *Nation* thought that the President's interference to secure Sumner's removal would give "a
serious, if not fatal, blow to General Grant's prospects of
renomination."[199] This indiscretion, however, was
trifling compared with the sins for which this journal held

[195] *Evening Journal Alamanac*, 1872, p. 48.

[196] *Ibid.*, 1870, p. 29, 1872, p. 43.

[197] Exclusive of the two Liberal Republican members from Mo.
Farther south the Democrats gained seven. Other notable gains were
the three New Hampshire members, five in Pa., and three in New York.

[198] *N. Y. Herald*, Jan. 6, 1871. See also editorial, Apr. 3, 1871.

[199] *Nation*, Mar. 16, 1871, p. 172.

the administration to account.[200]   Bowles, after hesitating so long as he could in the vain hope of better things from the President,[201] came out with telling impeachments of Grant's fitness to uphold the party's principles and traditions. The Republican party should have, he thought, a candidate "more in sympathy with its moral and intellectual tone, its reforming and progressive traditions, and more earnest, by temperament and associations, for the elevations and improvements in the offices of our government, and the character of its represenatatives which the people are so earnestly demanding, and the success of republican institutions so grievously needs." He was doubtful if a more suitable candidate could secure the nomination over Grant, but he pledged the *Republican* to work with those who were seeking that end.[202]   The *Cincinnati Commerical* predicted that after all the scandals and blunders that had thus far marked Grant's presidency there would soon be "evidences of a widespread conviction that he is the man whose candidacy in 1872 cannot be considered endurable."[203]

Factional opposition to the President's renomination was not lacking. Charles A. Dana in the *Sun*, almost from the start, had been condemning the administration's shortcomings with his peculiar virulence.[204]   Governor Geary in his message to the Pennsylvania legislature took occasion to denounce the President's southern policy.[205]   Summer, resorting to bitterest denunciation, used all his powers of persuasion to convince his friends of Grant's utter unfitness for office and of the impossibility of his reëlection.[206] Gree-

---

[200] *Nation*, June 8, 1871, p. 396.

[201] Bowles to Colfax, Jan 2, 21, 1871, Hollister, *Colfax*, 360.

[202] *Springfield Weekly Republican*, Nov. 17, 1871.

[203] *Cincinnati Commercial*, Mar. 18, 1871.

[204] Wilson, 413 ff.

[205] *N. Y. Herald*, Jan. 6, 1871.

[206] Sumner to Smith, Aug. 20, 28, Sept. 3, 1871, Frothingham, *Smith*, 318, 321, 323.   See also Austen, *Tyler*, 54.

ley's opposition to a second term for Grant will be noted presently in connection with the former's candidacy for the Republican nomination.[207]

Unfortunately for the anti-Grant movement, it seemed impossible to find a candidate who could unite all the opposition elements in the party. The *Springfield Republican* suggested as acceptable candidates Colfax, Boutwell and Hawley from those supporting the administration, and Adams, Greeley, Cox, Trumbull, Judge Davis, Gratz Brown, and Curtin, of those opposed to it. Any selection from this list, it contended, would provide a more available candidate and a far more capable president. "Indeed," it urged, "as it did not seem safe for the republicans to nominate any other than Grant in 1868, so it is hardly safe for it to renominate him now. It can elect next year almost any one of the men we have mentioned, more easily than it can reëlect him, and with a better promise of beneficient results to the country."[208]   Governor Geary of Pennsylvania, after his reëlection in 1870, developed some presidential aspirations, which designing friends encouraged.[209]   But the Governor seems scarcely to have been of presidential caliber, and, despite his strength with the labor element,[210] his candidacy never became formidable.   There was a considerable sentiment, extending even to the independent element, to elevate Colfax to the first place,[211] but the Vice-President, by all accounts, was loyal throughout to the head of his party.[212]

Certain of Greeley's especial admirers launched a boom for their favorite at this time which attained to some pro-

[207] See below.

[208] *Springfield Weekly Republican*, Nov. 17, 1871.

[209] McClure, II, 274.   Geary finally gave Grant a "luke-warm support."   *Ibid.*, 277.

[210] *Ibid.*, 276.

[211] Hollister, 348–355, 358–362.   But for Godkin's most contemptuous opinion of Colfax, see Ogden, II, 102.

[212] Hollister, 348–350, 355–358, 361–364; Austen, *Tyler*, 52.

portions. Greeley had been a hearty supporter of Grant
in 1868,[213] and, in the main, had sustained the administration's policies against its critics until after the state election
of 1871.[214] As a leading member of the Fenton wing, he
naturally was indignant over the use of the federal patronage in New York.[215] But he seems to have been most
desirous that the party organization should not be broken
up by factional strife.[216] Early in 1871 a rather definite
campaign was started to secure the Republican nomination
for Greeley. Cassius M. Clay, at odds with the administration after his recall from the Russian mission,[217] declared
for Greeley in January, either as the Republican or an
independent candidate.[218] Theodore Tilton was another
original Greeley man.[219] In April Greeley replied to the
solicitations of a Kansas correspondent, who purported to
speak for many Greeley supporters of that state, in a letter
made public in May, that, while in future he desired never
to be a candidate for any political position, he proposed
"never to decline any duty or responsibility which my
political friends shall see fit to devolve upon me and of which
I shall be able to fulfill the obligations without neglecting

[213] See, for instance, editorial in *N. Y. Tribune*, May 25, 1868. After
the election Greeley had been mentioned for postmaster general.
Nation, Nov. 12, 1868, p. 381.

[214] Ingersoll, *Greeley*, 512; editorial in *N. Y. Tribune*, June 21, 1870.

[215] *N. Y. Tribune*, Nov. 10, 1870; Nov. 9, 22, 1871.

[216] Reid to Bigelow, Apr. 10, 1871, Bigelow, IV, 488. In January,
1871, in a speech before the city general committee, after a cordial
defence of the administration, he ventured "to suggest that General
Grant will be far better qualified for that momentous trust in 1872 than
he was in 1868." *N. Y. Herald*, Jan. 6, 1871. Later in the year the
Tribune stated that while it was opposed to Grant's renomination, it
would support him in that event. *N. Y. Tribune*, May 6, 1871.

[217] Clay, *Memoirs*, I, 451–459.

[218] *Ibid.*, 502.

[219] Halstead, "Breakfasts with Horace Greeley" in *Cosmopolitan*,
XXXVI, 700–702. Greeley gave Tilton credit for "inventing" him as a
candidate. See Greeley's letter in *Golden Age*, Aug. 12, 1871.

older and more imperative duties."[220] The issue peculiar
to Greeley at this time was that of a single term for the
president. He had long been an advocate of this "principle,"[221] and he now brought it forward as a sufficient argument against the propriety of Grant's renomination. In
his letter to his Kansas admirer he stated that he had   not
yet formed a decided opinion as to the man who ought to
be our next Republican candidate for President, but it
seems to me advisable that he should be a steadfast, con-
sistent believer in the good old Whig doctrine of one
Presidential Term." Later in the year, when the *Tribune's*
opposition to Grant became more open, Greeley made much
of this argument.[222] As regards the more widely agitated
reform issues of the time, Greeley, the most conspicuous
protectionist of his day, was most hostile to all efforts for
tariff reduction, and neither in theory nor in practice had
he stood for civil service reform; but he had been the leader
in his party from the first in the movement for general
amnesty.[223] His position on this issue was especially emphasized this year by his southern trip. In May he went
to Houston, Texas, to deliver an address at the state fair,
and took the opportunity to visit the principal southern
cities. He was everywhere received well, generally with
enthusiasm.[224] In his speeches on public affairs, he pled
earnestly for the reconciliation of the sections and declared
for immediate and universal amnesty.[225] At a reception
in New York on his return, given by political friends among
whom the leaders of the Fenton faction were most promi-

[220] *N. Y. Tribune*, May 30, 1871.
[221] See his article, "The One-Term Principle" in *Galaxy*, Oct. 1871, pp.
488 ff.
[222] See editorials in *N. Y. Tribune*, Dec. 11, 16, 25, 1871.
[223] Cf. Linn, *Greeley*, 217; Ross, "Horace Greeley and the South,"
1865–1872, *South Atlantic Quarterly*, XVI, 325 ff.
[224] *N. Y. Tribune*, May 15, 20, 23; June 1, 1871; *N. Y. Herald*, May 22,
1871; Ross, "Horace Greeley and the South, 1865–1872," 333 f.
[225] *N. Y. Tribune*, May 22, 30, 1871.

nent, he set forth at some length his views on southern conditions.[226] Following his southern trip, Greeley was fairly before the country as a candidate to succeed Grant. His particular supporters now declared themselves openly. Tilton's *Golden Age*[227] and Leslie's *Newspaper*[228] were most ardent advocates, and C. M. Clay, in a Fourth of July speech at Lexington and in October at the St. Louis fair, presented Greeley's claims as the candidate best fitted to deal with the problems before the country.[229] Greeley's customary western lecturing trip in the fall was spoken of in some quarters as a "presidential tour."[230] In Chicago at a supper given in his honor by John Wentworth and Josiah B. Grinnell, both prominent in the Liberal movement the following year, Greeley's nomination by the Republicans was suggested.[231] Leading independent Republican papers also spoke of Greeley's nomination with favor.[232] But the pretentions of the editor of the *Tribune* were frowned upon by fellow editors of the administration press. His views of the southern question were held to be mistaken and dangerous, and in his relations with the opposition faction in New York he was charged with being merely a tool of Tammany politicians.[233] It may well be doubted if Greeley at this time had serious expectations of securing the Republican nomination. His public utterances on the subject certainly

[226] *N. Y. Herald*, June 13, 1871; *N. Y. World*, same date. The speech is also printed in full in Greeley's *Letters from Texas*, etc. An assembly district "Greeley Club" was formed the same night.

[227] *Golden Age*, June 3, 24; July 1, 15, 1871.

[228] *Leslie's Illustrated Newspaper*, July 15, 1871.

[229] Clay, I, 502 f; *Golden Age*, July 15, 1871.

[230] *Sunday Mercury*, quoted in *N. Y. Times*, Sept. 4, 1871; *N. Y. World*, same date.

[231] *N. Y. Herald*, Sept. 13, 1871.

[232] See, for instance, *Cincinnati Commercial*, Apr. 15, 20, 1871; *Springfield Weekly Republican*, June 16, 1871. For Bowles' high regard for Greeley at this time, see Hollister, 361.

[233] *N. Y. Times*, June 8; Nov. 19, 23, 1871; *Cincinnati Semi-Weekly Gazette*, June 2, 1871.

show no such attitude of mind,[234] and there is some evidence
that in allowing his candidacy to be considered at all he was
seeking merely to weaken Grant and to help to secure the
nomination of a more desirable candidate, like Colfax.[235]
But whatever his motives, there can be no doubt that the
movement started for Greeley at this time was an essential
factor in his nomination by the Liberals the next year.

It was soon evident that, no matter what candidate was put
in the field against him, opposition to Grant's renomination
was futile. The President being in full favor with the organization, all of its powerful machinery was set in motion
to insure a second term. The patronage was bestowed
where it would do the most good, and federal officials were
busily employed in seeing that the right sort of delegates
were chosen in their districts.[236] The Republican organization in the South was then, as it has been ever since, the
useful servant of the administration.[237] Morton in advocating Grant's renomination at a serenade given to the Senator
in April set the example for the faithful.[238] In some cases
Republicans of advanced views and not in sympathy with
many administrative policies, putting the continuation of
their party's control above other considerations, made the
best of the inevitable. George William Curtis, who was
in many respects one in spirit with the independents,[239] had
no illusions about Grant's shortcomings but felt, nevertheless, that it was best that he should be renominated.[240]

[234] See his letter in *Golden Age*, Aug. 12, 1871, and his speech on his
return from his southern trip, N. Y. *World*, June 13, 1871.

[235] Hollister, 355, 361.

[236] Cf. *Nation*, Sept. 14, 1871, p. 172. In July Senator Sherman wrote
to his brother that Grant would be renominated. *Sherman Letters*, 232.

[237] See editorial in N. Y. *World*, July 3, 1871.

[238] Foulke, II, 197.

[239] For a time evidently, Curtis was thinking strongly of supporting
the opposition faction. Harper, *House of Harper*, 301.

[240] Curtis to Norton, Mar. 4, 1871, Cary, *Curtis*, 215; Curtis to Sumner,
Jan. 19, July 28, 1871, Sumner MSS.

Gerrit Smith, admitting the President's errors of judgment, considered his renomination absolutely necessary to preserve the results of the war by preventing that most-to-be-dreaded calamity of a Democratic rule.[241]   Judge Hoar considered Grant "a pretty poor President,"[242] but his scruples and personal grievances were not sufficient to range him with the President's opponents.[243]   Certain Republican members of Congress who at times showed strong reform tendencies and were known to be averse to many of the ways of the administration failed to take action to secure a more acceptable candidate.[244]

The administration forces, on their side, in view of the threatening dangers to the organization from factional division and independent opposition, made some efforts to promote unity and harmony by endorsing reform projects and by attempting to conciliate disaffected party leaders. General Grant, during his first term, while taking up readily enough with some of the most objectionable features of organization politics, seems to have acquired little of the skill and tact so essential to the true party leader.   He was thoroughly disgusted with the factious majority in his first Congress, and thought, as he confided to his bosom friend, that fear of the Democrats was all that kept the party from losing the House,[245] but he apparently had no clear idea of leading and harmonizing his majority in their general policy.   When he expected the resignation of his Secretary of State in 1871, he thought that the country and party would be best served by the transfer of the Vice-President to that department.[246]   He apparently had slight fears for

[241] Smith to Sumner, Aug. 23, 31, 1871. Frothingham, 320, 322. See also Smith's "broadside," issued in August in defense of Grant, and the President's acknowledgment. *Ibid.*, 317, 329.

[242] Storey and Emerson, *Hoar*, 245.

[243] *Ibid.*, 229.

[244] See below, p. 53.

[245] Grant to Washburne, July 10, 1870, Grant, *Letters to a Friend*, 66 f.

[246] Grant to Colfax, Aug. 4, 1871, Hollister, 356 f.

the outcome in 1872. "Everything," he wrote in the summer of 1871, "seems to be working favorably for a loyal administration of the Government for four years after the 4th of March, 1873."[247] In November of the same year, he thought that the only serious danger threatening the party was from possible unfavorable awards at Geneva.[248] But that even the stolid General could not be entirely insensible to the demands for improvement in certain lines was evinced by his message to Congress in December, 1871. He favored certain tariff readjustments, a closer supervision of the public lands, the removal of southern disabilities, and reported the formulation under executive supervision of civil service rules.[249] "How completely," wrote Bowles, "our good President comes over to the advanced platform in his message! Really, it is pretty discouraging to those of us who are trying to have the convention nominate another man! If he would only practise as well as he preaches, he would not leave a single inch for us to stand upon. . . . Still, I insist he is the weakest candidate the Republican Party can nominate. And yet, again, I don't see how it is possible to nominate anyone else. And yet I hope!"[250]

Some efforts were made, too, by administration supporters to conciliate the leaders of the growing opposition. Senator J. S. Morrill begged Sumner, during the Missouri campaign, to use his influence to prevent Schurz from taking a stand which would lead to his break with the party.[251] Some of Sumner's colleagues tried hard to retain his support for the organization. After the adjournment of Congress in

[247] Grant to Colfax, Aug. 4, 1871, Hollister, 356 f.

[248] Grant to Badeau, Nov. 19, 1871, *Grant in Peace*, 473. Cf. a similar opinion of Boutwell in his letter to Washburne, May 9, 1871, Washburne MSS.

[249] Richardson, *Messages and Papers of the Presidents*, VII, 148, 152, 153, 155, 156–159.

[250] Bowles to Colfax, Dec. 14, 1871, Hollister, 364.

[251] Morrill to Sumner, Sept. 10, 1870, Sumner MSS., and printed in *Forum*, XXIV, 409.

1871, Morton wrote in a most conciliatory strain deploring the San Domingo dispute, as it was a "controversy among friends" and hoped that the memory of it would not be revived. He assured Sumner that he was still his "friend and admirer," and urged a mutual toleration of their conflicting views: "In the course I took I believed I was doing right, what was best for my country and party; and I give you credit for equal purity of purpose and patriotism. My earnest wish is now for the harmony of the Republican party for the sake of the country."[252] Henry Wilson, always a party peacemaker, later tried persistently to compose the differences between Sumner and the President, but all to no purpose.[253] In the fall of 1870 Greeley was sounded on the English mission, probably with no expectation that he would accept.[254] The President also tried to win over the influential editor by social attentions, but his efforts resulted in no better mutual understanding.[255] In New York the more discriminating party journals, while severely condemning the intrigues with Tammany of the opposition faction, freely censured the administration for its unfair distribution of the patronage, and urged a recognition of Fenton men, both from motives of justice and expediency.[256] Conkling protested to Sherman after the divided state convention that, in spite of the bitter complaints of the *Tribune*, the administrationists had "done nothing harsh to the anti-administration minority, but the least and mildest thing which would prevent a split in our organization with trouble for the future, and probably a double

[252] Morton to Sumner, Aug. 20, 1871, Pierce, IV, 488. See also Howe to Sumner, July 21, Aug. 30, 1870; Morrill to Sumner, Sept. 5, 10, 1870, Sumner MSS. (the letter of Sept. 10 is printed in the *Forum*, XXIV, 409); Fish to Morrill, Sept. 6, 1870, *Forum*, XXIV, 410.

[253] Pierce, IV, 497.

[254] Hollister, 359.

[255] *Ibid.*, 360; Andrews, *U. S. in Our Time*, 58.

[256] *Harper's Weekly*, Mar. 18, 1871; *Independent*, Oct. 5, 1871.

delegation in the next national convention."[257] Opposing
Republican papers were consolidated in New Hampshire
in 1871 as a means toward putting an end to the factional
fight in that state.[258] Late in 1871, favors were temptingly
held out to the leaders of the Curtin faction in Pennsylvania
to keep them from joining the opposition movement.
McClure declined a federal district attorneyship,[259] and an
offer, made through Senator Wilson, to permit the Curtin
men to name a cabinet member was not accepted.[260] No
compromise which involved the continuance of Cameron's
domination of the state organization would now be considered.[261] Early in 1872, when George W. Julian was suggested as a Republican candidate for Congress, the Morton
faction was ready, after years of antagonism, to call a truce.
But coming at this late hour, the cessation of factional strife
failed to keep this veteran Republican in the party fold.[262]

Appeals to party loyalty could not reconcile all the discordant elements; factional and reform opposition was
too deep-rooted. The hopeful observation of a western
organ that the "white heat of party dissensions in Massachusetts and New York seems to have ended in fusing the
discordant elements,"[263] was true only for the time being.
The fundamental causes of disruption remained and the
administrationists, while recognizing their existence, failed
to take the steps necessary for their removal; at the beginning of the presidential year the factions in the party were
unreconciled and the reformers were unsatisfied. All that
was needed for an open split was the organization of a
national opposition movement.

[257] Conkling to Sherman, Oct. 13, 1871, Sherman, I, 479.
[258] Gerrish to Washburne, Sept. 27, 1871, Washburne MSS.
[259] McClure, II, 328 f.
[260] *Ibid.*, 330 f.
[261] *Ibid.*, 329, 331.
[262] Julian, 335.
[263] *St. Paul Weekly Press*, Oct. 5, 1871.

CHAPTER II

DEVELOPMENT OF A NATIONAL LIBERAL MOVEMENT

By the end of 1871, when it had become evident that no influence within the party could prevent Grant's renomination, a movement for the formation of a new party was already under way. In 1870, some of the leading tariff and civil service reformers seem to have thought this the quickest and surest means for securing their ends, and the Missouri bolt gave a decided impetus toward a new reform party. The free-trade propaganda in the congressional elections was looked upon in regular party circles as a move toward a separate organization,[1] and such a course was for a time contemplated,[2] but it was postponed indefinitely after the election.[3] Probably a few only of the more advanced of the independent group thought it wise to leave the old party while there were hopes of better things from it. Bowles, who broke away from the Republicans with great reluctance only after he became convinced that the reform element could not get a fair hearing, felt at this time that the desired reforms could be better secured under the old banner.[4] Early in the year, when the new party question was already getting into congressional debates, the *Nation* thought that the formation of a reform party at this time would not be practicable, as no new organization could be built up which would unite both tariff and currency re-

[1] *N. Y. Tribune*, Sept. 6, 7, 1870.

[2] Merriam, *Bowles*, II, 135. A call for a national reform convention was actually drawn up at this time. See speech of C. F. Adams, Jr. at Quincy, Sept. 30, 1872. *Springfield Weekly Republican*, Oct. 4, 1872.

[3] *N. Y. Tribune*, Dec. 13, 1870; Morton to Fishback, Dec. 9, 1870, Foulke, *Morton*, II, 145 n.

[4] *Springfield Weekly Republican*, Nov. 25, 1870, quoted in Merriam, II, 135.

formers, since these issues appealed to different sections.[5]
But as the hopelessness of securing definite reforms from an
administration influenced largely by the congressional
clique became constantly more apparent, the sentiment
grew for the creation of a new reform organization before
the next presidential election. Godkin had reflected this
feeling the year before in his reply to an enthusiastic young
newspaperman in Chicago who sought his advice on the
political situation: "I think we may fairly look forward to
building up on the ruins of the Republican party a better
party than we have yet had, and I trust that in a year
hence we shall see our way to it more clearly than we do
now, having for its object Tariff Reform, Civil Service Reform and Minority Representation, and basing its action
on the facts of human nature and the experience of the
human race. We shall always have plenty of old hacks
and windbags to deal with, but the day will come when they
will simply amuse us."[6] In the South there was a desire
for the extension of the conservative coalition movement to
form a new national party.[7]

Senator Schurz was the most active and efficient promoter
of this movement for a new national party.[8] While defending the Missouri bolt of December 1870 in senatorial
debate with Drake, his radical antagonist, Schurz remarked
that every hint at the formation of a new party was treated
as a sort of high treason. For his part, he did not see anything especially criminal in such a move and frankly admitted that "things have a tendency in that direction."
He understood that parties and issues did not spring up

[5] *Nation*, Mar. 10, 1870, p. 151.

[6] Godkin to Cook, Oct. 6, 1870, Ogden, *Godkin*, II, 69.

[7] A. G. Magrath of S. C. to Chase, July 4, 1870, Chase MSS.; Fowler
to Johnson, May 15, 1871, Johnson MSS. Hinton R. Helper in May
declared that a new party must be formed. *Mass. Weekly Spy*, May 26,
1871.

[8] Cf. Adams, *Adams*, 390.

suddenly, but there was now a growing impression that the old parties had out-lived their usefulness. At the moment the necessary inspiration was lacking, but there was already the "preliminary fermentation" working in both parties. The Republican party was doomed, he warned, unless it realized at once the need of a progressive, reform policy. The party, he was sure, contained a regenerating element if it could but obtain control.[9]   "I have made up my mind," he wrote to Cox a little later, "to go on, without regard to my own political fortunes, preaching the doctrine that a party like ours cannot be successful without being honest. And I am confident we shall have a good many converts to that faith before the next Presidential election."[10]   There were soon evidences of such conversions.   In March, 1871, the reformers around Cincinnati—with whom Schurz had consulted late in the previous year regarding the formation of a new political organization of independent Republicans and Democrats[11]—formed the "Central Republican Association of Hamilton County."   The initial call professed full recognition of the achievements of the Republican party, but declared that, to continue, it must meet present issues. The signers, therefore, declared for general amnesty, a revenue tariff, reform in the civil service, and gradual but certain resumption.   General Cox, George Hoadly, and Stanley Matthews were among the signers.[12]   At a subsequent mass meeting the aims of the association were fully set forth by leading members.   The speakers asserted that the organization was composed wholly of Republicans and

[9] *Schurz's Writings*, II, 59–66.   In the same speech Schurz expressed the opinion that reform was much more likely from the Republican than from the Democratic party.   *Ibid.*, 66–69.

[10] Schurz to Cox, Feb. 3, 1871, *ibid.*, II, 176.

[11] See Judge Hoadly's speech at Avondale, Ohio, Aug. 23, 1872, in *Cincinnati Semi-Weekly Gazette*, Aug. 27, 1872.

[12] *Cincinnati Commercial*, Mar. 22, 1871.

strongly denied any desire to break up that party.[13] Schurz
was delighted with the organized activity of the Ohio reformers, expressing the hope that the association would be
extended to all parts of the state and that the promoters
might be able to "take care of Indiana too."   He thought
that similar organizations ought to be formed all over the
country.[14]

Early in 1871 when the movement against Grant's renomination seemed most promising Schurz had hopes of a
reformation within the Republican party,[15] but by September, convinced of the futility of all efforts against the
machine, he had begun to work definitely for a new party,
recruited, as he hoped, from the best elements of both the
old parties.[16]   In his Nashville speech, September 20, he
clearly forecasted the future policy of the reform group.
The pressing needs of the time, he pointed out, were general
amnesty, a return to local self-government in the South,
reform in the civil service, re-adjustment of the tariff, a
speedy return to specie payment, and the better control of
corporations.[17]   "These views of the condition of public
affairs, and the problems to be solved," he assured his
southern audience, "are shared by millions of people at the
North, especially the political school to which I belong,
called the 'Liberal Republican.' "[18]   He still had hopes,
he professed, of the ascendancy of the liberal, progressive
influences in the Republican party, in spite of the corruption

[13] *Cincinnati Commercial*, Apr. 6, 1871; *Cincinnati Semi-Weekly
Gazette*, Apr. 7, 1871.   At this meeting letters were read from George
William Curtis and Horace White.   Curtis expressed himself in sym-
pathy with the platform, but he considered the preservation of the
Republican party "indispensable."   White wrote that all the objects
of the association had his "warmest approbation."

[14] Schurz to Cox, Apr. 4, 1871, *Schurz's Writings*, II, 254 f.

[15] Schurz to Cox, Feb. 3, 1871, *ibid.*, 177; Schurz to Godkin, Mar. 31,
1871, *ibid.*, 253.

[16] Schurz to Sumner, Sept. 30, 1871, *ibid.*, 311–313.

[17] *Ibid.*, 258–260.

[18] *Ibid.*, 260.

and false partisanship that had so weakened its reforming energy. "But, if such hope should be disappointed, if the policy should prevail of securing party success by keeping fresh the old issues and by pushing the differences of the past into the foreground, if it should fail to appreciate its conciliatory mission, if it should place itself under the dominion of selfish and tyrannical interests—in one word, if it should not succeed in making the third party superfluous, then it seems to me the time would have come for a new organization to step forward, the truly National party of the future, of a composition and with a policy such as I have described."[19]   He was sure that the formation of such a party would not be difficult "as soon as the attitude of the old parties will have demonstrated its necessity. I apprehend it appears already desirable to a very large number of thinking men all over this country. It may be there all of a sudden, and, unless I am greatly mistaken, the tendency is breaking through the skin of the body politic in all directions."[20] As for himself, the party through which the desired ends were secured was "utterly indifferent, provided they are accomplished." If he thought the Democratic party would secure them he would join it regardless of the cry of 'renegade' and he should be glad to have the Republican party meet the need, as it would be utilizing an existing strong organization. "But if a new party does it better, my views of public interest and duty will not permit me to be long in choosing."[21]   Schurz at this time also secured the forma-

[19] Schurz to Sumner, Sept. 30, 1871, 299–300.

[20] *Ibid.*, 300.

[21] *Ibid.*, 301. This speech is entitled in *Schurz's Writings* "The Need of Reform and a New Party." The day after this speech a letter was addressed to Schurz signed by about two hundred "formerly Confederate soldiers" expressing admiration for Schurz's political course and full sympathy for the sentiments expressed in his speech. They wished, they wrote, to abandon all sectional and reactionary parties and to ally themselves with any progressive national party. For the letter and Schurz's feeling response, see *ibid.*, 306–308.

tion of reform associations beginning at Nashville and extending all over the South West and the lower South. He thought that through such associations or clubs, both North and South, the best men from both parties might be united under a central organization.[22] The character of the work in which Schurz was now engaged was pretty generally understood. On his visit to New York City in November the *Herald* referred to him as "the great political missionary, laboring for the defeat of General Grant next year."[23] The alarm of the party organs was evinced by the abuse which they heaped upon Schurz as the leading spirit in the projected revolt.[24]

In various quarters by the end of the year there were evidences of a growing sympathy for a new party movement. In addition to the original independent journals, Frank Leslie put forward his paper as the "pioneer" in a national reform movement,[25] and the *Atlantic Monthly*, in its political section, expressed unmistakable opposition to Grant and sympathy with the reformers.[26] Governor Walker of Virginia in his message in December came out strongly in denunciation of the administration's southern policy, and presented an extended program of reform. The *New York Herald* thought that the Governor, foreseeing a union of the opposition, had taken the initiative in furnishing issues for a struggle in the ensuing session of Congress, and characterized his message as the "key note of the campaign."[27] At the St. Louis Cotton Fair in October Cassius M. Clay, in the speech already mentioned in connection with his support

[22] Schurz to Cox, Sept. 27, Oct. 14, 1871, *ibid.*, 310, 314.

[23] *N. Y. Herald*, Nov. 19, 1871. The *Mass. Weekly Spy* discussed editorially (Nov. 3, 1871) Schurz's efforts to form a new party of discontented Republicans and Democrats.

[24] *N. Y. Times*, Dec. 28, 1871; Bancroft-Dunning, *Schurz's Pol. Career*, 347; *Nation*, Jan. 4, 1872, p. 1.

[25] *Leslie's Illustrated Newspaper*, Dec. 30, 1871.

[26] *Atlantic Monthly*, Jan. 1872, p. 126.

[27] *N. Y. Herald*, Dec. 7, 1871.

of Greeley, advocated the formation of a new party. On the platform with him were such representative politicians as James S. Rollins, F. P. Blair, jr., B. Gratz Brown, and General Beauregard, and his suggestion was received with much enthusiasm.[28] In the fall election in Ohio the Cincinnati independents supported the Republican state ticket,[29] but in the election of members of the legislature there was a marked tendency in different parts of the state to vote for independent candidates, largely with the view of securing a more satisfactory United States senator.[30] In the subsequent session of the legislature a project for a coalition of independent Republicans and Democrats to defeat Senator Sherman's reëlection was frustrated only by the failure to secure a suitable candidate.[31] The defeat of the devoted administrationist senator, Harlan, in Iowa at about the same time was a cause of rejoicing to the "Liberal Republicans of Iowa."[32]

By the beginning of the presidential year, with all these various manifestations of opposition, conditions seemed favorable for the launching of a national Liberal movement. This was effected through the only existing official Liberal organization, that in Missouri. The Liberal state convention at Jefferson City, January 24, advised by Schurz[33] and attended by a number of new party promoters from outside the state,[34] adopted resolutions calling for universal amnesty, a more equitable adjustment of the

[28] Clay, *Memoirs*, I, 503; Rollins to Clay, Sept. 11, 1871, *ibid.*, 588 f.

[29] Schurz to Cox, Sept. 27, 1871, *Schurz's Writings*, II, 310; *Cincinnati Semi-Weekly Gazette*, Sept. 29, 1871.

[30] *Cincinnati Semi-Weekly Gazette*, Sept. 15, 19, Oct. 6, 17, 1871.

[31] John Sherman to W. T. Sherman, Jan. 26, 1872, *Sherman Letters*, 335; Williams, *Hayes*, I, 362 f.

[32] J. M. McDill to Trumbull, Jan. 19, 1872, Trumbull MSS.

[33] Letter to Follenius, Jan. 20, 1872, *Schurz's Writings*, II, 315 ff.

[34] Scovel to Trumbull, Jan. 29, 1872, Trumbull MSS.; *Annual Cyclopedia*, 1872, p. 552; *Mo. Republican*, Jan. 25, 1872.

tariff, reform of the civil service, and the checking of federal encroachments on the rights of the states. All Republicans desirous of aiding in securing these reforms were invited to meet in national mass convention at Cincinnati on May 1.[35]

The independent Republicans in Congress, in the session of 1871–1872, contributed much toward launching the new party, both by exposing the most striking abuses in the administration and by defending the Cincinnati convention project. During this session the cleavage between the administration supporters and the Liberals became complete. It had been foreseen that the long-accumulating differences would be fought over at this time. "If we are to have a new party," wrote the Washington correspondent of the *Nation* in December, "it will grow out of the debates in Congress this winter."[36]   Independent senators like Schurz, Sumner, Fenton, and Trumbull were apparently in frequent consultation among themselves, and in close touch with the promoters of the Liberal movement outside.[37] At the beginning of the session probably none of the independents in Congress, except Schurz, were definitely connected with a new party policy.   Trumbull wrote only two weeks before the Jefferson City convention that he had not committed himself to an independent movement and that he did not mean to be drawn outside the Republican party, though there were some who would be glad to drive him

[35] Pamphlet of proceedings of the Convention; *Annual Cyclopedia*, 1872, p. 552. Letters were read from Senators Schurz and Fowler. *Mo. Republican*, Jan. 25, 1872. The printed proceedings of the convention contain endorsements from Cox, Matthews, Hoadly, and Stallo.

[36] *Nation*, Dec. 28, 1871, p. 415.

[37] Julian, *Pol. Recollections*, 333; Scovel to Sumner, Jan. 3, 10, 1872, Sumner MSS.; Fenton to Sumner, Mar. 6, 1872, *ibid.*; Trumbull to Flagg, Jan. 10, 1872, *Miss. Valley Hist. Rev.*, I, 106. Schurz consulted with Trumbull about his letter to the Jefferson City convention. See Schurz to Trumbull, Jan. 21, 1872, Trumbull MSS.

out.[38] But shortly after the appearance of the Missouri call, he expressed himself privately as favorable to the proposed convention, though he still hoped that it might enable the independents to control the regular Republican convention.[39] The rest of the avowed independents in both houses were known to favor the convention,[40] although in some cases they did not join the Liberals until after the campaign was under way.

There was still a hope among some of the independents that the more progressive of the organization men in Congress might be induced to oppose Grant's renomination, at least in order to prevent the disruption of the party. Bowles thought that an address from two or three dozen members of recognized standing, who had thus far been silent, demanding that the party have a change of candidate to prevent a division would forestall Grant's renomination and lead to the party's reformation from within. He asked Sumner if it would not be possible to secure such an address by April 15, signed by influential leaders like Dawes, Garfield, Buckingham, Wilson, the Morrills, and Logan.[41] But in the heated debates of the session, precipitated by the vigorous attacks on the administration, it soon developed

[38] Trumbull to Flagg, Jan. 10, 1872, *Miss. Valley Hist. Rev.*, I, 106. See also Trumbull's interview in December on the political situation, White, *Trumbull*, 369–370.

[39] Trumbull to White, Jan. 27, 1872, Trumbull MSS.

[40] *Idem.*

[41] Bowles to Sumner, Mar. 18, 1872, Sumner MSS. See also on the position of Wilson and Garfield, editorials in *Springfield Weekly Republican*, Feb. 2, Mar. 29, 1872. The Washington correspondent of the *Louisville Courier-Journal* wrote in April that the Liberal leaders were considering Logan for president. Quoted in *New Orleans Republican*, Apr. 7, 1872. Dawes came out definitely against the Liberals in a letter in March. *Nation*, Mar. 21, 1872, p. 177.

that the bulk of the Republicans in Congress would stick to their President.[42]

Throughout the session there was a sharp conflict between the Liberals and the administrationists in the Senate. Sumner's resolution limiting the presidency to a single term, while expressly excepting the next election, was interpreted by Grant's supporters as a thrust at his aspirations and was opposed accordingly.[43]   In the New York custom-house investigation, which unearthed a great mass of abuses in the "general order business," the lead was taken by the Liberal senators.[44]   The inquiry into the sale of arms to France, pushed to the limit by Schurz and Sumner,[45] seems to have had a considerable influence in increasing the disaffection of western Germans.[46]   The platform, candidates, and future course of the Liberals were freely discussed in these acrimonious encounters.   In a speech on February 23, Trumbull, while disavowing any knowledge of a Liberal Republican party "as a distinct organization from the Republican party," warmly defended the principles and policy of that faction.[47]   Morton, in reply, charged that the movement was directly in aid of the Democrats, and that Trumbull was seeking the Cincinnati nomination.[48]   By these debates in Congress and by the work of the Liberal pro-

[42] Eight senators and five representatives were apparently all the members of this (the 42nd) Congress ever identified with the Liberals. *Tribune Almanac*, 1873, pp. 28, 39–40; *Evening Journal Almanac*, 1873, pp. 31–35.

[43] Pierce, *Sumner*, IV, 498; N. Y. *World*, Dec. 22, 1871.

[44] White, 362–369.

[45] Pierce, IV, 504–513; Bancroft and Dunning, 333–337.

[46] Koerner to Trumbull, Feb. 19, 1872, Trumbull MSS.; Greene, "Some Aspects of Politics in the Middle West," 73; Foulke, II, 234; *Nation*, Apr. 4, 1872, p. 209.

[47] *Cong. Globe*, 42 Cong., 2 Sess., Appendix, 84 ff.

[48] *Cong. Globe*, 42 Cong., 2 Sess., 1179.   Trumbull's speech was interpreted in this way by the Republican press.   See *Boston Advertiser* Feb. 26, 1872.

moters in different parts of the country sentiment was created for the proposed Cincinnati Convention.

The response to the Missouri call during the next three
months, though rather hesitating for a time, showed a considerable enthusiasm for a new party among the leading independents and the disappointed politicians but no systematic organization for attaining that end.   The chief leaders
and organs of the independents were in full sympathy with
the platform and endorsed, at least qualifiedly, the project for a mass convention.   Bowles had clung to the vain
hope of a new Republican candidate.   But his observations
at Washington in March showed him the invincibleness of
the administration machine;[49] and thereafter his influential
journal strongly supported the Liberal cause.   The *Nation*
seemed hopeful of the new movement from the start and
commented on its developments prior to the convention
with unusual enthusiasm.[50]   The *Evening Post*, while fully
committed to the avowed aims of the convention, was fearful
of the machinations of the politicians connected with the
reform movement, and assumed at first more the position
of an impartial critic than an ardent supporter.[51]   The *New
York Tribune*, after it had become pledged to the cause,
complained that the *Post* gave the movement "any quantity
of advice, but no real sympathy."[52]   But as the Liberal
agitation developed even the cautious *Post* became cheerful
over the outlook for reform at Cincinnati.[53]   In the Middle
West the *Chicago Tribune* and the *Cincinnati Commercial*
were effective boomers for the Liberal convention.[54]

[49] Merriam, II, 178; Bowles to Sumner, Mar. 18, 1872, Sumner MSS.;
Springfield Weekly Republican, Feb. 2, 1872.

[50] See editorials in *Nation*, Feb. 1, 8, 29; Mar. 21, 1872.

[51] See, for instance, editorial in N. Y. *Evening Post* (semi-weekly
ed. cited throughout), Mar. 12, 1872.

[52] *N. Y. Tribune*, Apr. 15, 1872.

[53] *Evening Post*, editorial, Apr. 2, 1872.

[54] White, 372.

The attitude of Greeley and the *Tribune* was watched with especial interest. As successive congressional investigations had exposed abuses in the national government, Greeley's strictures on the administration had become more and more severe,[55] and in January he had refused as the New York national committeeman to sign the call for the Philadelphia Convention because he desired "to keep a position of independence."[56]   Nevertheless he hesitated for some time to give full support to the Liberal cause, as he wanted to be sure that the bolters would develop a formidable strength before venturing his political fortunes with them,[57] and, besides, the prominent place given to tariff reform in the Liberal program was naturally obnoxious to a life-long champion of protection.   Shortly after the Jefferson City Convention, he remarked that the 'bolters' were "almost certain to make hostility to Protection one of the planks of their platform, and that the *Tribune* can never abide no matter who may be rival candidates for President."[58]   And even when warming more and more to the Liberal cause he wrote: "Of course we shall ask to be counted out if the majority shall decide to make Free Trade a plank in their platform. The protection of Home Industry is of more importance, in our view, than the success of any party or ticket.   If it should be decided to make Free Trade a corner-stone of the Cincinnati movement, we ask only that we be not insulted by the assumption that any possible selection of candidates

[55] See, for instance, *N. Y. Tribune*, Dec. 19, 29, 1871; Jan. 5, 6, 18; Feb. 21, 1872.

[56] Greeley to Chandler, Jan. 15, 1872, *ibid.*, Mar. 7, 1872.

[57] J. M. Scovel wrote to Sumner, Jan. 3, 1872, that Greeley was waiting to see "what others do."   He had said that he might "have to go for Grant, though he did not wish to."   Sumner MSS. Reid informed Sumner, Jan. 25, that Greeley thought it best to let "present dissension fester a little longer."   *Ibid.* J. S. Morrill wrote to Greeley, Mar. 11, urging him most earnestly not to desert his old party.   *Forum*, XXIV, 411 f.

[58] *N. Y. Tribune*, Jan. 29, 1872.

would reconcile us to that decision."[59]   But as the prospects of a successful revolt improved, Greeley's grievances against the administration[59a] outweighed his doubts.   By March the *Tribune* was liberalizing rapidly[60] and Greeley was busily securing recruits for the convention.[61]

The responses to the call for the mass convention[62] were most encouraging in the Middle West.   Missouri Liberals, determined to represent fittingly the reputed home of the new movement, made preparations to invade Cincinnati in great force and in an imposing manner.[63]   Leading Ohio Liberals promptly issued a card urging all who favored the proposed reforms to attend the convention.[64] Dissatisfied Kansas Republicans met in February, two days after their regular state convention, issued an address, organized a "Liberal party" and called a convention at Topeka, April 10, to select delegates for the Cincinnati convention.[65]   This Topeka gathering attracted consid-

[59] *N. Y. Tribune*, Mar. 16, 1872.

[59a] See Greeley's bitter denunciation of Grant and declaration of relentless hostility in his letter to J. S. Morrill, Mar. 12, 1872, *Forum* XXIV, 412.   "You see that I am drifting into a fight with Grant   I hate it; I know how many friends I shall alienate by it, and how it will injure the *Tribune*, of which so little is my own property that I hate to wreck it: Yet . . . I should despise myself if I pretended to acquiesce in his reelection.   I may yet have to support him but I would much rather quit editing Newspapers forever."   Greeley to a Lady Friend, Mar. 13, 1872, Benton, *Greeley on Lincoln*, etc., 211.

[60] See editorials, Mar. 14, 16, 20, 21, 1872.

[61] Bowles to Sumner, Mar. 18, 1872, Sumner MSS.

[62] There was no uniform method of choosing delegates to the Cincinnati Convention, selections being made in the following different ways: by state conventions, by conferences of leading Liberals in a state, by those signing the response to the Missouri call, and voluntary delegations without special appointment.   All of these methods of procedure were held to be authorized by the Missouri call.   See editorial in *Mo. Republican*, Apr. 22, 1872.

[63] *N. Y. Tribune*, Apr. 25, 1872.

[64] *Chicago Tribune*, Feb. 6, 1872.

[65] Ross to Trumbull, Feb. 28, 1872, Trumbull MSS.; Wilder, *Annals of Kan.*, 574.

erable notice.   Gratz Brown was on hand with a stirring
speech, a platform was adopted, and 110 delegates for Cincinnati were selected.[66]   Western Liberals in other states,
though slower in their action, ultimately came into line.
The German Liberals at Milwaukee held a meeting, on
March 19, at which they endorsed the Missouri platform and
invited all similarly minded Republicans to attend their
national convention.[67]   Early in April, the Liberal promoters
in Illinois met at Springfield and drew up a call for delegates which was subsequently signed by many former
Republican leaders.[68]   Some twenty-five Indiana Liberals
urged the formation of county organizations and the selection of delegates in every part of the state.[69]   Michigan
Liberal managers held an informal meeting at Detroit,
April 18, and prepared their statement, issued two days
later, recommending that each town, city and county send
to Cincinnati mass delegations who should there select the
regular delegates to represent them in the convention.[70]
A mass convention at Davenport, Iowa, April 23, adopted
appropriate resolutions and selected 150 delegates.[71]
Late in April, a mass meeting in Nebraska City, Nebraska,
selected the Liberal delegates for that state.[72]   Minnesota
Liberals held no formal convention but were represented by
a voluntary delegation.[73]   From California only one or two

[66] *Kan. Commonwealth*, Apr. 11, 1872; Wilder, 576.

[67] *Milwaukee News*, Mar. 21, 1872; *N. Y. Tribune*, Apr. 6, 1872.

[68] Fell to Trumbull, Apr. 8, 1872, Trumbull MSS.; White to Trumbull,
Apr. 9, 1872, *ibid.;* Koerner, *Memoirs*, II, 536 f; *Chicago Tribune*, Apr.
18, 1872.

[69] *N. Y. Tribune*, Apr. 23, 1872.

[70] Dilla, *Politics of Mich.*, 135.

[71] Gue., *Hist. of Iowa*, III, 49.   This meeting was also addressed by
Gratz Brown.   *N. Y. Tribune*, Apr. 24, 1872.

[72] Watkins, *Hist. of Neb.*, III, 124.

[73] Holmes, *Minn.*, III, 51; Wilkinson to Trumbull, Feb. 20, 1872,
Trumbull MSS.

stragglers of little weight attended the Liberal gathering.[74]
Toward the latter part of April, Liberal meetings to form
local organizations and to select national delegates were
reported all over the Middle West.[75]

In the East New York took the lead. On March 30
twenty Republicans, including Greeley, issued a letter fully
endorsing the Liberal movement.[76] The Massachusetts
pronouncement, delayed to secure signers of the requisite
weight,[77] appeared on April 17 with a highly respectable
and even eminent list of endorsers.[78] Connecticut's call
followed on April 24,[79] and at about the same time a convention was reported at Rutland, Vermont[80] and the recruiting of voluntary delegations in New Hampshire[81]
and Maine.[82] The Liberal managers in Pennsylvania,
after considerable consultation,[83] sent out their call on
April 18.[84] An enthusiastic Liberal mass meeting at Cam-
den, New Jersey, April 22, chose twenty delegates to represent their state.[85]

But the crowning event of the Liberal agitation in the
East, before the convention, was the Cooper Institute mass
meeting on April 12. Schurz and Trumbull were the prin-

[74] *N. Y. Tribune*, May 3, 1872; San Francisco *Evening Bulletin*, May
7, 11, 1872.

[75] *Chicago Tribune*, Apr. 23–May 1, 1872.

[76] *N. Y. Tribune*, Mar. 30, 1872. About a dozen county meetings in
New York state to choose Liberal delegates were noted. *Ibid.*, April
11–27. See comments of exchanges on the N. Y. letter in *ibid.*, Apr.
1, 2.

[77] Atkinson to Sumner, Apr. 3, 1872, Sumner MSS.; *Springfield
Weekly Republican*, Apr. 12, 1872.

[78] *N. Y. Tribune*, Apr. 19, 1872.

[79] *Ibid.*, Apr. 25.

[80] *Ibid.*, Apr. 26, 30.

[81] *Ibid.*, Apr. 25.

[82] *Ibid.*, Apr. 29.

[83] McClure to Sumner, Apr. 8, 1872, Sumner MSS.

[84] *N. Y. Tribune*, Apr. 19, 1872.

[85] *Ibid.*, Apr. 23.

cipal speakers.[86]   Senator Fenton, whose attitude up to
this time had been in some doubt,[87] sent a letter announcing
his full adherence to Liberalism.   Greeley, called upon for
an impromptu speech, bitterly assailed the administration
leaders in the state and declared that he would have nothing
to do with their convention for choosing delegates to Philadelphia.   "I put it aside now," he concluded amid great
applause, "and go forward with the non-office holding Republicans to the Cincinnati convention and its consequences."[88]   The *Tribune*, in its editorial comment, was
confident that this enthusiastic gathering meant nothing
less than that the coming convention was to be a "success
alike in numbers, representative character and general
purpose.   Let it be equally wise and it will name the next
President of the United States."[89]   The *Nation* found it
"as enthusiastic a meeting as was ever got together in this
city," and praised Trumbull's "strong, clear, but una-
dorned statement of the charges brought by the promoters
of the new movement against the administration," and
Schurz's "powerful and *telling* rhetoric."[90]   And, though
the censorious *Evening Post* complained that the meeting
neglected the fundamental questions of the protective
system and federal encroachment and sent forth "petty
resolutions . . . as the voice of New York,"[91] the
gathering was, on the whole, an imposing and auspicious
launching of the new movement in the East.

From the South much interest in the proposed convention
was reported.   The Tennessee Liberals issued a call for

[86] *N. Y. Tribune*, Apr. 13, 1872, *N. Y. Times*, same date.
[87] *N. Y. Times*, Apr. 9, 1872.
[88] *N. Y. Tribune*, Apr. 13, 1872.
[89] *Idem.*
[90] *Nation*, Apr. 18, 1872, p. 249.
[91] N. Y. *Evening Post*, Apr. 16, 1872.

delegates early in March.[92]   In April the Louisiana bolters
published a lengthy "manifesto" with over five hundred
signatures,[93] and the committee invited the delegates from
Alabama, Mississippi, and Texas to unite with the Louisiana delegation in chartering a special train to the convention.[94]   During the same month conventions and mass
meetings for the selection of delegates were reported in
Texas,[95] North Carolina,[96] Maryland,[97] Mississippi,[98] South
Carolina,[99] Florida,[100] and Kentucky.[101]   West Virginia,[102]
Virginia,[103] Alabama,[104] and Georgia[105] evidently had voluntary delegations of considerable size; and the Arkansas
delegates were chosen by the Liberal central committee.[106]

The pre-convention agitation revealed in the Liberal
personnel a combination of the dissatisfied of all shades of
ability and integrity.   The most striking feature was the
large number of free-soilers and founders of the Republican
party among the bolters, whereas many foremost supporters
of the administration were newer recruits.   A political

[92] *Chicago Tribune*, Mar. 11, 1872.
[93] *N. Y. Tribune*, Apr. 19, 1872.
[94] *Idem.*
[95] *Ibid.*, Apr. 10.
[96] *Ibid.*, Apr. 10, 30.
[97] *Ibid.*, Apr. 22, 25.
[98] *Ibid.*, Apr. 23.
[99] *Ibid.*, Apr. 26, 29.
[100] *Ibid.*, Apr. 27.
[101] *Ibid.*, Apr. 30.
[102] *Ibid.*, Apr. 19.
[103] *Ibid.*, Apr. 27, 30.
[104] *Ibid.*, Apr. 30.
[105] *Ibid.*, May 3.
[106] *Annual Cyclopedia*, 1872, p. 25.   Delaware had no delegates in the
convention but George Alfred Townsend, who had gone to the convention as a territorial delegate from the District of Columbia, acted for
the State and cast her six votes.   See his letter to the Philadelphia *Press*
quoted in *N. Y. Tribune*, May 10, 1872.

writer in a Chicago magazine strikingly called attention to
this situation:

> "The men whose courage, eloquence, and statesmanship furnished the
> party with the means of its earliest victory are, with few exceptions, ob-
> noxious to the President, and are regularly belashed through the columns
> of his organs; while the party is led by men who first perceived the good-
> ness of the cause when it achieved success, or men always distrusted by
> the people supported by a few timid souls deterred by dread of change
> in political associations from plain political speaking."[107]

The surviving members of Lincoln's cabinet[108] were on the
side of the insurgents as were three of the four surviving Republican senators who had voted for Johnson's acquittal.[109]
Sumner, while not openly committed to the Liberal cause,
was generally reported to be a warm sympathizer.[110]   Thus
both prominent moderates and radicals among the original
Republicans were joined in the new movement, along with
a variegated band of political adventurers.   A brief consideration of the chief supporters of the movement in the
different sections of the country makes this clear.

Throughout the Middle West there was a marked defection of veteran Republicans.   In Ohio such men as Cox,
Stallo, Hoadly and the Brinkerhoffs[111] were arrayed against
the administration.   In Indiana George W. Julian[112] and

[107] Wheeler, "President Making" in the *Lakeside Monthly*, Mar. 1872.
Cf. Greene, 73–76.   Julian says, with evident rhetorical exaggeration,
that "troops of the old Free-Soilers of 1848 and 1852" were in attendance at the Cincinnati Convention.   *Pol. Recollections*, 337.

[108] Chase, Welles and Blair.   Seward apparently made no public
declaration before his death in October.   See Seward to Conkling,
Aug. 12, Conkling, *Conkling*, 445.   The *N. Y. Tribune* (Sept. 3, 1872)
called especial attention to this support.

[109] Trumbull, Ross and Fowler.   Henderson was at first reported for
the Liberals (see *Wis. Weekly State Journal*, May 7, 1872) but later in
the year was the Republican candidate for governor of Missouri.

[110] *Nation*, Mar. 21, 1872, p. 177.

[111] Judge Brinkerhoff's letter to Stallo in February, strongly endorsing
the new movement, is printed in *Chicago Tribune*, Feb. 12, 1872.

[112] See his letter in *N. Y. Tribune*, Apr. 25, 1872.

John D. Defrees[113] were likewise opposed to the old party.
The defection in Illinois was still more pronounced. Of the
leading ante-bellum Republicans, Trumbull, Browning,
Davis, Palmer, Koerner, Swett, Herndon, four of the state
officials under Yates and all but one of the existing officials
were numbered with the opposition.[114] Austin Blair, the
war governor, and other prominent Republicans of that
period led the bolters in Michigan.[115] Minnesota adherents
included such staunch free-soilers as Morton S. Wilkinson,[116]
Charles Sherwood,[117] and, a little later, the erratic Ignatius
Donnelly.[118] Josiah B. Grinnell assured Sumner early
in April that the 'old guard' of Iowa were in the new movement, and that the best men of the party would be found at
Cincinnati.[119] Senator Tipton of Nebraska, a radical "of
approved and superabundant loyalty"[120] when he entered
the Senate in 1867, was foremost among the prominent
Republicans of his state now in revolt.[121] In California,
where the Liberal defection never reached threatening pro-
portions, an administration paper commented thus on the
designation of Frank M. Pixley as Liberal national committeeman: "Mr. Pixley was one of the most zealous and

[113] For Defrees' career, see *ibid.*, Apr. 30; N. Y. *Evening Post* editorial,
Apr. 26, 1872. He was at this time a resident of the District of Columbia
and attended the Liberal Convention as a delegate from that territory.

[114] Greene, 73 f.; Moses, *Illinois*, II, 811; Lusk, *Eighty Years of Illinois*, 228.

[115] Dilla, 140.

[116] Holmes, III, 86.

[117] *Ibid.*, 105.

[118] Donnelly's support had been sought by leaders of both parties in
his state and he was apparently considering the Republican congressional nomination at one time. See letters during June and July 1872
in Donnelly MSS. See his letter in July, *Chicago Tribune*, July 18, 1872.

[119] Grinnell to Sumner, Apr. 9, 1872, Sumner MSS. Cf. on Liberal
personnel in Iowa the list given in *Clinton Age*, Sept. 13, 1872, quoted in
Haynes, *Third Party Movements*, 27.

[120] DeWitt, *Impeachment and Trial of Andrew Johnson*, 174.

[121] Watkins, III, 124.

efficient men in organizing the Republican party of California. He will now have a chance to show what he can do toward breaking it up."[122] But the Kansas Liberals with such promoters as Preston B. Plumb,[123] Edmund G. Ross,[124] Marcus J. Parrott,[125] Pardee Butler,[126] Samuel J. Crawford,[127] Samuel N. Wood,[128] and Charles Robinson[129] could probably present the most imposing exhibit of dyed-in-the-wool free-soilers.

In the East the movement showed equally notable converts. In New England no names had been more respected in Republican circles than those of F. W. Bird, Edward Atkinson, W. S. Robinson, Elizur Wright, F. B. Sanborn, and General Banks in Massachusetts,[130] Lafayette S. Foster, David Clark, Samuel C. Fessenden, and David A. Wells in Connecticut,[131] and Henry O. Kent in New Hampshire.[132] New York Liberals could place along with the names of Greeley and Fenton those of Henry·R. Selden, Henry A. Foster, William Dorsheimer, F. A. Conkling, Hiram Barney, D. C. Littlejohn, Thomas G. Alvord, and many others who "cradled" the party in the state.[133] In Pennsylvania the discontented found such

[122] San Francisco *Evening Bulletin*, May 11, 1872. See also on Pixley and his connection with Liberals, T. Gray to Trumbull, Apr. 7, 1872, Trumbull MSS.

[123] Connelly, *Plumb*, 224,

[124] Blackmar, *Cyclopedia of Kan. Hist.*, II, 608 f.

[125] *Ibid.*, II, 444.

[126] *Ibid.*, I, 265; Wilder, 584.

[127] Blackmar, *Cyclopedia of Kan.*, I, 475 f.

[128] *Ibid.*, II, 933.

[129] Blackmar, *Robinson*, 300.

[130] See more complete list in the Mass. letter in *N. Y. Tribune*, Apr. 19, 1872. Banks did not come out openly for the Liberals until August *Nation*, Aug. 8, 1872, p. 82.

[131] See list of Conn. Liberal leaders in *N. Y. Tribune*, Apr. 19, 25, 1872.

[132] Lyford, *Rollins*, 291.

[133] See list of signers of the N. Y. letter in *N. Y. Tribune*, Mar. 30, and the long list of prominent N. Y. Liberals in *N. Y. World*, Sept. 2, 1872.

leaders as A. K. McClure, John M. Hickman, David Barclay,[134] and, later in the campaign, A. G. Curtin and Galusha A. Grow.[135]

In the South prominent Republicans, many of them natives, were ranged on the Liberal side. A. W. Bradford of Maryland, who served as the "Union" governor during the years 1862–1865,[136] was the chief Liberal organizer in his state.[137] Ex-Senator Joseph S. Fowler, originally a Brownlow supporter,[138] directed the insurgent forces in Tennessee.[139] Franklin Stearns, the Virginia member of the Republican national committee, was a delegate to the Cincinnati convention, along with Governor Walker and other former Republicans who had put through the coalition movement in 1869.[140] Senator Alcorn of Mississippi, Joseph E. Brown of Georgia, H. H. Helper and D. R. Goodloe of North Carolina, ex-Governors Pease and Hamilton, Senator Hamilton and Judge Stribling of Texas, C. M. Clay of Kentucky and James S. Rollins of Missouri were other notable examples of unionists or scalawags converted to liberalism.[141]

But in addition to these respectable, and in many cases eminent, representatives, the new movement was hampered almost from the start by a set of supporters who could bring nothing but discredit upon any undertaking. The Liberal movement, inaugurated by the reformers, no sooner showed signs of success than the "practical" politicians schemed to exploit it for their own ends. As is always the case with

[134] N. Y. Tribune, Apr. 19, 1872; McClure, Old Time Notes, II, 333.

[135] Grow came out for the Liberals in August (Nation, Aug. 15, 1872. p. 97) and Curtin in September (ibid., Sept. 19, p. 177).

[136] Scharf., Hist. of Md. III, 457, 461; Biog. Cyclopedia of Md., 33.

[137] N. Y. Tribune, Apr. 22, 25, 1872.

[138] DeWitt, 534.

[139] Fowler to Johnson, Feb. 9, 1872, Johnson MSS.; Chicago Tribune, Mar. 11, 1872.

[140] N. Y. Tribune, Apr. 30, 1872.

[141] List of Southern Liberals in N. Y. World, Apr. 30, 1872; Fielder, Brown, 454; Smith, Rollins, 55.

6

such new party movements, disappointed office-seekers, members of broken rings and losing factions—political adventurers of all shades—hastened to join a chase which promised something in the way of the spoils of office. The large, if not determining, influence of differences over the distribution of patronage in bringing about the party revolt has already been explained.[142] In not a few cases the disaffection of some of the most active promoters of the new party movement can be traced directly to their disappointment in failing to secure office, or to their resentment at removal from office when their faction had gone out of favor. Thus, to cite a few of many possible examples of this sort, the Tamanmy Republicans removed from the custom-house and other offices during the Fenton proscriptions, or whose candidacy for office had been thwarted by their connection with the anti-administration faction, led by that ubiquitous political soldier of fortune, John Cochrane, [143] constituted a conspicuous element of the promoters of the movement in New York and in that state's delegation to Cincinnati.[144] George Wilkes, early among the opposition and active at Cincinnati, had been most deeply offended by the administration's refusal to reward his services for the ticket by a foreign mission.[145]   James M. Scovel, the chief organizer of New Jersey Liberals,[146] had supported the Johnson faction

[142] See above, pp. 17 ff.

[143] Alexander, *Pol. Hist. of N. Y.* II, 272; III, 90, 92, 259.

[144] See the long list of Tammany Republicans, including many removed from federal offices by Grant, in *N. Y. Times* editorial Apr. 15, 1872. The list of official delegates for New York in the convention contains the names of a number who had been removed from federal positions during the Fenton proscriptions, and of others who were notoriously disappointed office-seekers. *Ibid.*, May 2; *N. Y. Tribune*, May 2, 1872.

[145] Wilkes to Stanton, June 7, 1869, Sumner MSS.; Wilkes to Sumner, June 9, 12, 1869, May 15, 1870, *ibid.*

[146] Scovel to Sumner, Mar. 18, 1872, Sumner MSS.; *N. Y. Tribune*, Apr. 5, 1872 (item on N. J. Liberals).

in 1865 for the sake of the state patronage, but was later
"reconverted" by the radicals.[147]   Failing to get office under
Grant, after urgent solicitation,[148] he had become, early in
1870, a bitter critic of the administration[149] and took part
with alacrity in the efforts to start a new party.[150]   If the
fight were won he trusted, as he confided to Sumner, that
those would not be forgotten who had patiently borne the
administration's scorn and persecution for the sake of
"principle."[151]   J. M. Ashley, an active Ohio Liberal,[152]
had been associated with the ultra-radicals in Congress;
he had moved the impeachment of Johnson and had put
forth every effort to work up a case against the President.[153]
A little later, he had been intimately involved in land-
speculation scandals, but, largely through Sumner's influence, had been appointed governor of Montana territory
by Grant.[154]   His removal from that position late in 1869
had made him a bitter enemy of the administration.[155]
In the South carpet-baggers whose factions had lost in the
scramble for federal offices furnished most dubious recruits
for a reform movement.   Governor Warmoth and his
predatory crowd in Louisiana,[156] and the leading Liberals

[147] DeWitt, 79, 158.
[148] Scovel to Sumner, Feb. 5, 1870, Sumner MSS.
[149] Same to same, Feb. 7, 9, 1870; Mar. 11, 1871, ibid.
[150] Same to same, Nov. 28, 1871; Jan. 29, Feb. 12, 1872, ibid.
[151] Same to same, Mar. 21, 1872, ibid.
[152] Ashley was reported to have brought to the Cincinnati convention
a resolution on civil rights for the negroes, drawn by Sumner, N. Y.
Tribune, May 1, 1872 (item under "Convention Notes").
[153] DeWitt, 147, 152–157, 234.
[154] Nation, Sept. 12, 19, 1872, pp. 162, 178.
[155] Ashley to Sumner, Dec. 19, 1869, Sumner MSS. Ashley wrote
Chase (Aug. 29, 1871) that if the latter was nominated (evidently by
the Democrats) he would get a large Republican support. Chase
MSS.
[156] On the abuses of Warmoth's government see Sage, "Reconstruction in Louisiana" in Why the Solid South?, 403–410; Hamilton, Reconstruction Period, 372 ff.

in Arkansas[157] were typical of this class. There was obvious danger that supporters of this stripe might pervert the reformative purposes of the inchoate party.

The attitude of the Democratic party was a matter of prime importance to the Liberal movement, which could not hope to succeed without some form of Democratic support.[158] And such support the Liberals might reasonably expect, for the Democrats, owing to the discredited condition of their party, had been unable to profit materially by the dissensions and mistakes of their opponents. Their failure to show, either in platform or candidates,[159] any real change of heart in 1868, the unwise speeches[160] of ex-Confederates like Davis and Stephens, the still more unwise violence of persons identified with the party in the South,[161] and the Democratic opposition to the Fifteenth Amendment,[162] all lent color to the oft-repeated charge that the Democracy was still unreconstructed.

Under these unfavorable circumstances, certain of the more astute Democratic leaders concluded, even before 1872, that the party's best move was to renounce its past attitude toward the war and its results and make a new start. In the Montgomery County convention at Dayton, Ohio, May 18, 1871, Clement L. Vallandigham, the recognized

[157] Harrell, *Brooks and Baxter War*, 33, 45, 109 f., 123–124.

[158] The N. Y. *Evening Post* said in an editorial Mar. 1, 1872: "In order to succeed the Liberal Republican candidates must have very nearly the full vote of the Democrats, and the chief labor of the opposition canvass will now be to devise measures to unite them."

[159] *Harper's Weekly*, July 25, Aug. 8, 1868, and editorials in following issues during campaign.

[160] Editorial in *N. Y. Herald*, May 31, 1871; Hill, *Hill*, 353; *Harper's Weekly*, Apr. 22, June 17, 24, 1871. The *Mo. Republican* (Dem.) said (June 2, 1871)—"It would be difficult to imagine a more stupendous anachronism than the reappearance of Mr. Jefferson Davis upon the stump."

[161] For charges of connection of the Ku Klux with the Democratic party, see editorials in *Harper's Weekly*, Apr. 1, 15, Nov. 4, 1871.

[162] *Cincinnati Commercial*, Feb. 16, 1871.

leader of the peace Democrats, secured the adoption of resolutions fully accepting the war amendments.[163] These
resolutions were endorsed the next month, after a considerable contest,[164] in the state convention. The platform,
generally termed the "New Departure," was accepted by the
later state conventions of the year[165] and by leading party
organs.[166] The independent press, too, commended the
Democrats for at last taking the step that had so long been
urged upon them.[167]

But though ridding itself to some extent of the odium of
disloyalty, the party was still greatly hampered. Its
repentance was held to be insincere while the old leaders
remained in control.[168] The Tweed exposures in New
York, characterized by the administration press as typical
of Democratic rule,[169] were a serious set-back; the party
in this state, in particular, was saved from complete discredit only by the prompt and firm stand of such Democratic
leaders as Tilden and O'Conor in opposing the ring.[170]
As the time for another national election approached it was
thus natural that the Democrats, in view of their own impotence and the growing dissatisfaction among their opponents, should regard some sort of combination with rebellious Republicans as the most likely means of getting
into power. The successful coalitions in the border states

[163] Vallandigham, *Vallandigham*, 436–445.

[164] Powell, *Dem. Party of Ohio*, I, 197. Durbin Ward had made a
similar proposal the previous year, but his speech did not attract such
wide attention. Ward, *Ward*, 194 ff.

[165] *Annual Cyclopedia*, 1871, pp. 90, 392, 416, 482, 493, 517, 547, 556,
621, 775.

[166] N. Y. *World*, June 2, 3, 1871; Vallandigham, 447 f. The *Mo.
Republican* had strongly urged such a course a month before. See
editorial Apr. 27, 1871.

[167] See, for instance, *Springfield Weekly Republican*, May 26, June 9,
June 30, 1871; *Nation*, June 8, 1871, p. 396.

[168] See editorials in *Harper's Weekly*, June 3, 10, July 29, 1871.

[169] *Ibid.*, Aug. 19, 26, Nov. 25; *Mo. Democrat*, Sept. 4, 20, 1871.

[170] Alexander, III, 265–275.

in 1869–1870 had furnished precedents for such a policy
on a wider scale, and sentiment in favor of some such alliance was manifested in Democratic circles in 1871. The
Connecticut state convention in January[171] and that of
Pennsylvania in May[172] endorsed Schurz's position regarding disfranchisement as sound Democratic doctrine,
the resolutions of the former gathering referring to Schurz
as "this eloquent leader of the reformers." After the general party defeat in the fall elections, leading Democratic
papers advised, as the only means of defeating Grant,[173]
a union of the opposition, Democrats and Liberal Republicans, in which their party should maintain its identity
and be given its proportionate influence.

But not a few influential Democrats thought it expedient
for the party to play a still more humble rôle for the present.
They advocated the "passive policy"—the plan that had
worked so well in Missouri the previous year—refraining
from all action until after the independent Republicans had
placed a ticket in the field, and then, if the platform and
ticket were acceptable, uniting with them for the overthrow
of radicalism. The *Missouri Republican* came out strongly
for this course in October,[174] and, as the fall elections brought

[171] *Annual Cyclopedia*, 1871, p. 232.

[172] *Ibid.*, 621.

[173] N. Y. *World*, Nov. 18, 20, 24, 1871; western Democratic papers
quoted in N. Y. *Herald*, Nov. 14, 1871; editorials in *Harper's Weekly*,
Nov. 11, 18, Dec. 9, 1871 discussing coalition sentiment. George Wilkes
had a conference at Washington in December, 1871 with leading Democratic congressmen who expressed favor for a coalition movement in
which the "one term principle" and direct election should be leading
issues. *Spirit of the Times*, Jan. 20, 1872; L. D. Campbell to Wilkes,
Dec. 8, 1871, Sumner MSS.; Wilkes to Sumner, Dec. 9, 1871, *ibid.*

[174] See its editorial: "The Passive Proposition," October 23, 1871.
The *Republican* continued to urge this course up to the time of the Cincinnati Convention. In an editorial, Oct. 30, 1871, The *Republican*
said that a Democratic candidate would probably be defeated and the
fourth consecutive defeat would destroy the party. It thought that
the election of a Liberal Republican was the "most practicable" result
to be expected.

only continued defeat and discredit, a considerable sentiment for it developed.[175]   The New York *World*, the leading Democratic organ in the East, indignantly spurned the
proposal.   Such a policy would be contrary to the wishes of
the masses of the party.   Furthermore, the contention
was false that the party was losing ground, for, on the contrary, it had been steadily gaining since 1868 with the enfranchisement of the South.[176]   However, as the fortunes
of the new movement seemed constantly to improve and
those of the Democrats to become more hopeless with continuing defeats in the spring elections, there could be little
doubt how the party would act in case the platform
and candidates presented at Cincinnati were at all satisfactory.   The Nevada Democratic state committee hastened, on February 20, to advise the national committee
and convention to unite with the Liberals "for mutual
coöperation and action."[177]   Old-line Democrats in all parts
of the country were ready to join in such a movement,[178]
and Democratic congressmen were reported to be a unit in
favoring the endorsement of the Liberal nominees.[179]   In
the South the party sentiment seemed especially strong for
a union of the opposition.[180]   The *World*, most jealous for

[175] Montgomery Blair's letter in N. Y. *World*, Dec. 8, 1871; *Harper's
Weekly*, Dec. 16, 1871; Trumbull to Flagg, Jan. 10, 1872, *Miss. Valley
Hist. Rev.* I, 106; Ross to Trumbull, Feb. 21, 1872, Trumbull MSS.;
Doolittle's letter, Jan. 13, 1872 in *Southern Recorder*, Feb. 6, 1872;
Memphis Daily Appeal, Jan. 28, 29, 1872; *Milwaukee News*, Jan. 11,
1872; Iowa "Democratic leader" in *Burlington Hawk-Eye*, Nov. 2,
1871, quoted in Haynes, 23. The *Mo. Republican* said (Nov. 8) that
the result of the fall elections was "not encouraging to the uncompromising Democratic heart."

[176] N. Y. *World*, Dec. 8, 1871.

[177] *Annual Cyclopedia*, 1872, p. 567.

[178] See J. G. Jones to Trumbull, Feb. 24, 1872, Trumbull MSS.;
Brinkerhoff to Trumbull, Mar. 18, 1872, *ibid.*

[179] "Gath's" Washington letter in *Chicago Tribune*, Mar. 23, 1872.

[180] *Memphis Daily Appeal*, Jan. 18, Feb. 1, Mar. 9, 1872; *Southern
Recorder*, Feb. 6, 1872.

the integrity of its party's organization, deprecated at first any "dicker" between the Democrats and the Liberals[181] and continued for some time to treat the new movement coldly.[182]   But after the Cooper Institute meeting even the *World* declared that "If this great and spirited meeting is a foretaste of Cincinnati, the Democratic party can well afford to wait and watch."[183]

The organizers of the Liberal movement, on their side, had no desire for an alliance with the Democratic party as such.   Schurz, persistently distrustful of the Democrats,[184] was greatly chagrined when they secured the fruits of the Liberal triumph in Missouri.[185]   Governor Brown's speech immediately after the election was interpreted as committing him to the Democrats,[186] and the subsequent election of Frank Blair, of all men, to the United States Senate seemed to the administrationists indisputable proof that the Liberals were playing into the hands of the old enemy.[187] The other coalition victories in the border states were

[181] N. Y. *World*, Dec. 22, 1871.

[182] *Ibid.*, Feb. 24, Mar. 12, 1872.

[183] *Ibid.*, Apr. 13.   The *World* admitted (Apr. 6) in praising the New York Liberal letter that its criticism had been too emphatic.

[184] See, for instance, *Schurz's Writings*, II, 66–69, 296–299.

[185] Bancroft-Dunning, 341.   Schurz wrote to Grosvenor (Dec. 25, 1872) when Blair was a candidate for reelection: "Blair's first election was the first blow that staggered the Liberal movement.   You must have felt with me how severe that blow was.   That election appearing as the first fruit of our victory in Missouri deprived the movement of half of the credit it deserved, and placed us on the defensive." *Schurz's Writings*, II, 449.

[186] Schurz to Grosvenor, Dec. 13, 1870, *Schurz's Writings*, II, 2. Senator Drake said of Brown in the Senate, Dec. 16, 1870: "He has gone to the Democracy and may the Lord have mercy on his soul!" *Cong. Globe*, 41 Cong., 3 Sess., Appendix, 5.   See also Morton's speech on Feb. 23, 1872.   *Cong. Globe*, 42 Cong., 2 Sess., 1179.   *The Missouri Republican* (Nov. 10, 1870) called the election of 1870 a "Democratic victory."

[187] Forney to Sumner, Oct. 24, 1871, Sumner MSS.; *N. Y. Times*, Mar. 27, 1871.

rightly looked upon as resulting in the Democratic interest.[188] It was thus natural that the Liberals should
fear such gift-bringing allies. Bowles feared that the
"ghost of Democracy" would keep Republicans from the
movement and that it would be hard to establish a reform
party unless the Democrats would "formally throw up the
sponge."[189] Following the example of the Ohio Liberals
in the fall, the Liberals in New Hampshire and Connecticut
refused to support the Democratic candidates in their state
elections in February and March, in spite of earnest appeals
from Democratic papers and leaders[190] for such proofs of
their good will. The leading Liberal organs justified this
policy on the ground that defeat for the Democrats at this
time would tend to precipitate the much-to-be-desired dissolution of the old party and thus hasten the development
of the new.[191] The frequency and emphasis with which
these papers reported the death and final interment of the
ill-reputed organization of their prospective allies[192] show

[188] See Grant's letter to the revenue collector at St. Louis, Sept. 1870,
Annual Cyclopedia, 1870, p. 520.

[189] Bowles to Schurz, Mar. 22, 1872, *Schurz's Writings*, II, 353.
Ignatius Donnelly in reply to a request for his advice on the proposed
movement wrote that he had tried coalition with the Democrats in 1870
and had found a portion of them "intolerant, corrupt and treacherous"
and he had "no faith in them." See his answer endorsed on the back
of letter from W. L. Osborne, Apr. 11, 1872, Donnelly MSS.

[190] N. Y. *World*, Feb. 24, Mar. 22, 28, 1872; Doolittle to Trumbull,
Mar. 18, 22, Trumbull MSS.; Bowles to Sumner, Mar. 18, 1872, Sumner
MSS.

[191] *Chicago Tribune*, Mar. 30, 1872; *Springfield Weekly Republican*,
Mar. 29, 1872. Bowles' personal opinion of the result of Democratic
defeat in Connecticut seems not to agree with this. See his letter to
Schurz, Mar. 22, 1872, *Schurz's Writings*, II, 353. The *Mo. Republican*
urged that the spring elections proved that the Democrats could not
win in the national election and that the "passive" support of the Liberal ticket was the only hope of defeating the radicals. See editorials,
Mar. 14, 18, Apr. 6, 1872.

[192] See *Chicago Tribune*, Mar. 15, 24, Apr. 14, 1872; *Springfield
Weekly Republican*, Mar. 15, 1872; *Atlantic Monthly*, Jan. 1872, p. 125.

how greatly they desired such a clearing of the political
field. But that they realized that the party was still very
much alive and capable of upsetting their plans was shown
by their emphatic warning that the convention was for
Republicans only and was not to be subject in any way to
Democratic influence.[193]

For a time, no doubt, Liberal organizers like Schurz had
hoped to win over a large number, if not the bulk, of the
Democrats to the reform party organization. Senator
Chandler in a speech in the Senate on June 10, 1872, the
last day of the session, charged, on what he called good
authority, that early in November at a meeting in a New
York hotel an agreement was entered into between "a distinguished Democratic Senator and a distinguished Senator who had formerly been a Republican, with Samuel J.
Tilden and divers and sundry other Democrats that I could
name, that a new party should be organized to be called
the reform party." At this conference, Chandler continued, it was thought advisable that the Democrats in the
Senate should remain neutral during the session and allow
the discontented Republicans to do the talking, "and that
a certain Republican Senator, whom I will not name,
should be the nominee of this new party."[194] Fenton of the
Liberals and Casserly, Thurman, and Stevenson of the
Democrats promptly denied all knowledge of any such
agreement and Chandler refused to give the names of the
senators concerned.[195] While there is no definite evidence
available, it seems likely that some conference was held
between Democratic and Liberal leaders. Schurz was in
New York in November[196] and was probably the ex-Re-
publican senator referred to by Chandler. But that any

---

[193] *Springfield Weekly Republican*, Apr. 5, 1872; N. Y. *Evening Post*,
Apr. 15, 1872; Trumbull to Brinkerhoff, Mar. 20, 1872, Trumbull MSS.
[194] *Cong. Globe*, 42 Cong., 2 Sess., 4473.
[195] *Idem.*
[196] *N. Y. Herald*, Nov. 19, 1871.

real assurance of the abandonment of the Democratic organization could have been given by a Democrat like Tilden is unthinkable.[197]

In some quarters, however, there was a desire to come out definitely from the old party and unite with the new reform organization. This sentiment was manifested in the formation of the so-called Reunion and Reform Associations in 1871. These associations were formed in connection with the independent movement started by Schurz and the Ohio reformers, in order to include liberally-inclined Democrats, these organizations being open to Liberal Republicans and "Liberal Democrats" alike. The reform organizations started in the South by Schurz in the fall of 1871 were of this character. The first of the associations was formed in Tennessee in October, their platform being substantially that of the Missouri Liberals.[198] Some time later in the year, after being strongly urged by Schurz to take that step,[199] the Cincinnati reformers widened their organization to include persons from all parties.[200] The Reunion and Reform Association was in entire sympathy with the Cincinnati convention, but, as that gathering was to be confined exclusively to Republicans, it was thought best to keep the movements separate until a new reform party in which all might unite was definitely established. A call was therefore issued in March from the headquarters of the Cincinnati association for a Reunion and Reform national convention to meet at Cincinnati on the same day as the Liberals, but in another hall.[201] Mass meetings were

[197] The *N. Y. Herald* said editorially (Nov. 18, 1871) that it understood that Seymour and Tilden were much pleased with the new reform party project.

[198] *Annual Cyclopedia*, 1871, p. 720 f.

[199] Schurz to Cox, Oct. 14, 22, 1871, *Schurz's Writings*, II, 314 f.

[200] See account in *Cincinnati Commercial*, quoted in *N. Y. Herald*, Apr. 28, 1872, of the formation of the Reunion and Reform Association.

[201] *N. Y. Tribune*, Mar. 30, 1872.

reported in a number of states in the South and West to select delegates to this all-party convention.[202]   The organization was reported, in April, to be well-established in the South, but especially strong among Western Germans.[203] Certain influential Democratic papers in the South and West went so far as to urge the amalgamation of their organization in a new reform party, even to the surrender of its name.[204]

The interest which the whole country appeared to take in the discussion of their probable candidates may well have flattered the promoters of the Liberal convention. The availability of a considerable number of public figures was carefully canvassed, furnishing the press with no end of useful "copy."

Certain "perpetual" candidates were considered as a matter of course.   Judge Chase, who had long had the presidency "on the brain,"[205] after vainly hoping for the Democratic nomination,[206] "pulled some wires" for that of the Liberals.[207]   Some sort of an independent movement for Chase had been worked up in West Virginia,[208] and in April a conference of Liberal Republicans and independent Democrats met at Parkersburg and adopted resolutions instructing the Republican delegates to the Liberal

[202] N. Y. Tribune, Apr. 10, 25; Chicago Tribune, Apr. 22, 26, 1872.

[203] N. Y. Herald, Apr. 28, 1872, quoting article in Cincinnati Commercial; editorial in N. Y. Evening Post, Apr. 19, 1872.

[204] Madison Democrat, Apr. 3, 1872; Lakeside Monthly, Mar., 1872; Southern Recorder, Mar. 19, 1872.

[205] Hoar, Autobiography, I, 282.

[206] Halstead to Chase, Oct. 20, 1869, Chase Correspondence in Rep. Am. Hist. Assoc., 1902, II, 521 f.; Clay to Chase, Jan. 3, 1871, Chase MSS.; Fowler to Chase, Dec. 2, 1871, ibid.; also a number of letters from obscure correspondents in South and West, 1869–1871 in ibid.

[207] Hart, Chase, 413; Chase to Church, Mar. 26, 1872, Warden, Chase, 728; Chase to Ball, Apr. 8, 1872, ibid., 729.

[208] Church to Chase, July 19, 1871, Chase MSS.; Citizens of Clay township to Chase, Dec. 7, 1871, ibid.

convention and the Democratic delegates to the Reunion
and Reform convention to work for Chase's nomination.[209]
But the Judge's feeble health barred him from a contest in
which he might otherwise have been a strong competitor.[210]

Chase's colleague, Judge David Davis, proved a much
more formidable contestant. Davis was a man of wealth,
ambition and ability. He was nominally a Republican, but
was without strong party convictions.[211] He had been
mentioned the preceding year as a most suitable conservative for the Democrats to support, in case they selected a
candidate of that type,[212] and also as a possible coalition
candidate.[213] Now he was put forward by his supporters
as the best man to unite the opposition to Grant. As a
preliminary step apparently in securing the Liberal nomination,[214] he was named in February by the national convention of the Labor party to head their ticket, with Governor
Parker of New Jersey, a pronounced Democrat, as his
running-mate.[215] Davis was very generally regarded, with

[209] *N. Y. Herald*, Mar. 15, Apr. 20, 1871; *Annual Cyclopedia*, 1872,
p. 800.

[210] See Senator Hoar's opinion. *Autobiography*, I, 284.

[211] Monroe, "The Hayes-Tilden Electoral Commission" in *Atlantic
Monthly*, LXXII, 528; Northrup, "A Grave Crisis in American History" in *Century*, LXII, 927 f.

[212] *N. Y. Herald*, Apr. 19, July 21, 1871.

[213] *Ibid.*, Oct. 14; *Harper's Weekly*, Oct. 28, 1871.

[214] On Davis' attitude towards the labor nomination, see Grinnell,
Reminiscences, 196. The year before Davis had stated that he would
accept the Democratic nomination if tendered him with any degree
of unanimity. Interview in the *Chicago Republican*, quoted in *N. Y.
Herald*, July 21, 1871. Henry Watterson in his letter to the *Courier
Journal* from the Cincinnati convention wrote that the Democratic
congressmen as a preliminary move to Davis' nomination got up a convention at Columbus of a "gang of execrable dead-beats . . .
called Labor Reformers." Quoted in *Chicago Tribune*, May 9, 1872.
Wilson says (*Hist. of American People*, V, 123) that the labor convention
was "made up chiefly of trades union bosses and political free lances."

[215] *Annual Cyclopedia*, 1872, pp. 773 f.; Stanwood, *Hist. of the Presidency*, 335-338.

seeming truth, as the choice of the Democratic politicians.[216]
The leading Democratic congressmen seem to have been
committed to his candidacy[217] and other prominent Democratic leaders were reported as working to the same end.[218]
The "Bourbon" *Chicago Times* was the foremost Davis
organ,[219] and Democratic papers all over the country, with
but one notable exception, regarded the labor ticket as a
suitable one for the coalition.[220] The New York *World*,
in its solicitude for the dignity and integrity of the Democratic organization, strongly opposed Judge Davis' candidacy and denounced the tactics of the "cabal of Democratic
congressmen" who were backing the scheme.[221] The leading independent organs were most suspicious of any move
that threatened the interference of the malign Democrats
in their projects and served notice that Judge Davis, in his
present company, would not do at all to lead the Liberal
cause.[222]

[216] Trumbull to Koerner, Mar. 9, 1872, Koerner, *Memoirs*, II, 538;
Scovel to Sumner, Mar. 18, 1872, Sumner MSS.; White to Trumbull,
Mar. 17, 24, 1872, Trumbull MSS.; Dubois to Trumbull, Apr. 18, 1872,
ibid.; Watterson, "Humor and Tragedy of the Greeley Campaign" in
Century Magazine, LXXV, 33.

[217] See editorial in *Leslie's Newspaper*, Aug. 10, 1872; *Wis. Weekly
State Journal*, Apr. 16, 1872.

[218] McClernand to Trumbull, Apr. 24, 1872, Trumbull MSS.; Steiner,
Johnson, 261.

[219] *Chicago Times* editorials, Feb. 26, Mar. 7, 21, 1872, and following
issues.

[220] *Milwaukee News*, Feb. 25, 28, 1872; *Madison Democrat*, Feb. 27,
1872; *Clinton* (Iowa) *Age*, Mar. 8, 1872, cited in Haynes, 26; *Southern
Recorder*, Mar. 19, 1872 (quoting papers from various parts of the
South); *Memphis Appeal*, Feb. 17, 24, Mar. 11, 16, 1872; *Washington
Patriot*, quoted in *Memphis Appeal*, Mar. 17, 1872.

[221] N. Y. *World*, Mar. 14, 18, 19, Apr. 30, May 1, 1872.

[222] *Springfield Weekly Republican*, Mar. 8, 1872; *Chicago Tribune*,
Apr. 14, May 1, 1872; N. Y. *Evening Post*, Apr. 23, 1872; *Cincinnati
Commercial* and *Cincinnati Volksblatt*, cited in *Cincinnati Semi-Weekly
Gazette*, Apr. 30, 1872.

From the beginning of an active agitation for a coalition in the preceding fall, certain of Greeley's admirers, particularly in the West, had been bringing his name forward[223] and after his declaration for the Liberals he had become one of the stock candidates of the press.[224] At first, with his pronounced antagonism to certain Democratic principles, Greeley seems to have been not at all enthusiastic about the coalition nomination. To a Democratic admirer who in October had suggested his candidacy, he protested: "I am not the man you need. Your party is mostly Free-trade, and I am a ferocious Protectionist. I have no doubt that I might be nominated and elected by your help, but it would place us all in a false position. . . . You must take some man like Gratz Brown, or Trumbull, or General Cox . . . and thus help to pacify and reunite our country anew."[225] Again, in January, he returned this ultimatum to the labor people who were sounding him as to his desire for their support: "I heartily wish my name had never been connected with the presidency. I see plainly that it can only result in vexation and misapprehension. And I shall never shape and groove my opinions to make myself acceptable to any party. As far as the labor party seems to me right, I approve and commend its propositions, but no further for twenty offices."[226] This certainly has not the tone of the office-seeking maniac that Greeley has been so

[223] Clay, *Memoirs*, I, 503; Henry Reed's letters to *Cincinnati Commoner*, quoted in *Cincinnati Semi-Weekly Gazette*, Nov. 28, Dec. 5, 1871.

[224] See, for instance, *N. Y. Herald*, Apr. 27, 30, 1872; *Chicago Tribune*, Apr. 29, 1872; *Chicago Times*, Apr. 27, 1872. The *New York Times* contained some attack on Greeley's candidacy in practically every issue during the month of April. See especially editorials, Apr. 1, 11, 16, 21, 28, 29. The formation of "Horace Greeley Irish American Leagues" was reported in several wards of the city, *N. Y. Tribune*, Apr. 9, 1872; *N. Y. Times*, Apr. 10, 1872. Nast in his cartoon entitled "Cincinnatus" (*Harper's Weekly*, Feb. 10, 1872) forecasted Greeley's active candidacy.

[225] Ingersoll, *Greeley*, 545 f.

[226] Quoted in *Springfield Weekly Republican*, Jan. 12, 1872.

often represented.   But as the bolt spread in the Republican
ranks and the likelihood of success in union with the Democrats appeared reasonably assured, the veteran editor's
life-long desire for political recognition[227] seems to have
overcome his discretion.   He brushed lightly aside the
criticism of his inconsistency in signing the New York call
which strongly endorsed tariff reform.   His signature, he
held, while showing his general sympathy with the Liberal
movement did not commit him to everything contained in
its platform.   He was just as strong a protectionist as ever;
he desired simply that the convention leave this question to
the decision of the people in the congressional districts—
the position which the "Republican party has always maintained."[228]   Greeley's position on the tariff question at this
time foreshadowed a compromise in the convention.[229]

To the politicians, who were promoting a coalition movement in accordance with their own ideas, Greeley appeared
most available as a candidate for vice-president with Davis,[230]

[227] See on this characteristic, Blaine, *Twenty Years of Cong.*, II, 533;
Rhodes, II, 72.

[228] Editorials in N. Y. *Tribune*, Apr. 1, 4, 1872.

[229] See comment of the *Nation*, Apr. 4, 1872, p. 209.   See also Trumbull's correspondence with Sinclair Tousey on the tariff question in
April, 1872, Trumbull MSS.

[230] Defrees letter to Reid, mentioned in Ingersoll, 546 n.; McClure,
II, 334 f.   The Washington correspondent of the Savannah *Republican*
wrote: "Horace Greeley may be given the second place on the Davis
Reform ticket.   Many Democrats say they will vote for Greeley, although they would prefer to have him at the head of the ticket . . .
At present there seems to be no more available ticket for Liberal Republicans than Davis and Greeley."   Quoted in *Memphis Appeal*, Mar.
23, 1872.   W. S. Robinson wrote to Sumner (Mar. 18, 1872) that the
plan to run Davis and Greeley was "absurd."   Sumner MSS.   The
Chicago Tribune, on the contrary, in mentioning the report that Greeley
was to be candidate for vice-president spoke of his qualifications with
great praise.   "Mr. Greeley's name would be the strongest and most
popular that was ever submitted to the suffrage of the people for the
Vice-Presidency."   *Chicago Tribune*, Mar. 19, 1872.

and Greeley and his backers were evidently well satisfied with the assignment of the second honor.[231]   In reply to a definite proposal of this sort made early in March by Davis' manager, Greeley responded: "Very good. But let us have no bargains, no trades, no understandings, except that the Cincinnati Convention shall nominate that ticket which can get most votes, and be composed of worthy, capable men. We must have nothing cut-and-dried, but the genuine voice of the people."[232] Nothing could better show Greeley's political naïvete, in spite of all his experience with conventions and campaigns, than such a statement to the sort of politicians in whose keeping his candidacy rested.

"Favorite sons" were not lacking. Governor Brown in Missouri was reported to be exerting every influence at his command to become the national candidate of the movement which he had led so gloriously in his own state.[233] Sumner's name seemed to many a source of peculiar strength,[234] but his failure to declare his position definitely before the convention precluded any active effort in his

[231] McClure, II, 334; Dana to Clay, Feb. 23, 1872, Clay, I, 589 f. Greeley wrote to Grinnell at Cincinnati: "Leave my name out of the question as a candidate. We ought to unite on Judge Davis of Illinois, the old friend of Mr. Lincoln." Grinnell, 224. The *Washington Patriot* said in its report of the first day of the convention: "Greeley prefers Davis to himself and is decidedly opposed to Adams." *Patriot*, May 2, 1872.

[232] Greeley to Defrees, Mar. 10, 1872, Ingersoll, 546 n.

[233] J. A. Cochrane to C. C. Cook, Jan. 8, 1872, Chase MSS.; R. L. Lindsay to Trumbull, Jan. 19, 1872, Trumbull MSS. A conference of Liberal leaders in the interest of Brown was reported in Washington on April 2. Greeley was said to be the choice of the conferees for vice-president. *N. Y. Times*, Apr. 4, 1872.

[234] *Springfield Weekly Republican*, Apr. 26, 1872; Pierce, IV, 517; Bartlett to —— Apr. 21, 1872, Palfrey, *Bartlett*, 228. George Wilkes was a persistent Sumner advocate. See his editorials in *Spirit of the Times*, Jan. 20, Mar. 30, Apr. 20, 27, 1872.

7

behalf.[235]   Men like Curtin of Pennsylvania, Cox of Ohio, and Governor Palmer of Illinois were mentioned from time to time, both for first and second place.

The man in active public life whose candidacy made the widest appeal was Senator Lyman Trumbull.[236]   In spite of the strong rivalry[237] from Davis and Brown he had many loyal supporters all over the Middle West.[238]   He also had strong friends among the independent Republicans in the East.[239]

Charles Francis Adams was undoubtedly the choice of the majority of the independent, reform element.   In many respects Adams was an ideal candidate; his integrity, experience in public affairs, liberal views, and freedom from

[235] Pierce, IV, 527, 529. Wilkes claimed that Sumner told him a few days before the convention that he did not wish to have his name presented. *Spirit of the Times*, May 11, 1872.

[236] During the winter Trumbull received letters from more or less prominent persons urging his availability as a coalition candidate. See Joseph Brown to Trumbull, Dec. 12, Jan. 12, 1872, Trumbull MSS. Other letters of the same sort are given in White, 375. Trumbull replied that his avowed candidacy at this time would injure his work for reform. Trumbull to Joseph Brown, Dec. 25, 1871, *ibid*. Trumbull expressed the view until shortly before the convention that it would be· the best policy not to make nominations. Trumbull to Brinkerhoff, Mar. 20, 1872, Trumbull MSS.; Trumbull to Fell, Apr. 11, 1872, *Miss. Valley Hist. Rev.* I, 108.

[237] On the rivalry of middle western candidates, see B. C. Cook to Trumbull, Mar. 21, 1872, Trumbull MSS.; White to Trumbull, Mar. 24, 1872; Trumbull to Palmer, Apr. 8, 1872, *ibid.;* Trumbull to White, Apr. 24, 1872, *ibid.;* Dubois to Trumbull, Apr. 18, 1872, *ibid.; Cincinnati Semi-Weekly Gazette*, Apr. 30, 1872.

[238] Brinkerhoff to Trumbull, Feb. 8, 1872, Trumbull MSS.; Ross to Trumbull, Feb. 21, 1872, *ibid.;* Koerner to Trumbull, Apr. 5, 1872, *ibid.;* Dubois to Trumbull, Apr. 10, 1872, *ibid.;* Palmer to Trumbull, Apr. 13, 1872, *ibid.;* Magall to Trumbull, Apr. 16, 1872, *ibid.; Chicago Tribune* editorial Apr. 26, 1872.

[239] Lewis to Trumbull, Feb. 26, 1872, Trumbull MSS.; White, 375. *Leslie's Newspaper* (Apr. 20, 1872) put as its first choice Trumbull and Walker. The N. Y. *Sun* was also favorable to Trumbull. C. D. Hay to Trumbull, Jan. 3, 1872, Trumbull MSS.

recent party controversy, all fitted him to lead the new party movement.[240] The *Nation*, taking the stand that "the new candidate for the Presidency must be a first-rate man, a distinguished man, a man versed in affairs, and who has filled places of trust and difficulty with ability and fidelity, and who is as well known for the soundness of his judgment and the good repute of his associates as for the purity of his own character,"[241] put Adams at the head of its list of those having these qualifications.[242] The *Springfield Republican* was of the opinion that "the door is open wide enough when only Charles Francis Adams, Horace Greeley and Lyman Trumbull are admitted to the list from which successful nominations shall be made." While thinking highly of all these candidates, the *Republican* believed that Adams was the strongest, and that if the ticket was to be "double headed" Adams and Trumbull would present the most formidable combination.[243] Adams' candidacy also had the sympathy of eastern Democrats whose views were expressed by the *World*. Adams seemed to the *World* an entirely acceptable coalition candidate and it strongly intimated that a candidate of his type only would receive the Democratic endorsement.[244] He was almost the only available candidate of Republican antecedents who would not put the Democrats on the defensive, requiring apologies for his endorsement. His views ran counter to their party on no important question.[245] "If our next Pres-

[240] Cf. Adams, *Adams*, 390.

[241] *Nation*, Apr. 25, 1872, p. 269.

[242] *Ibid.*, Mar. 21, p. 181; Apr. 25, p. 265. Cf. N. Y. *Evening Post*, Apr. 23, 1872.

[243] *Springfield Weekly Republican*, Apr. 26, 1872. General W. F. Bartlett came out in the *Republican* with a strong letter for Adams, Apr. 10, which attracted wide attention. Palfrey, 226 f.

[244] N. Y. *World*, Apr. 23, 1872. But it promised to support Brown, Trumbull or Davis if adopted by the party, *ibid.*, Mar. 18, 23, Apr. 30, 1872.

[245] *Ibid.*, Apr. 27.

ident is to be selected on the grounds of fitness," it urged, "no man in the country is so well entitled to the office as Mr. Adams; and we believe this would be the judgment of three-fourths of the American people."[246] Shortly before the Liberal convention Schurz was advised by leading eastern Democrats, like ex-Governor Randolph of New Jersey, Manton Marble of the *World*, and August Belmont, the chairman of the national committee, that Adams' nomination would be the strongest possible and would insure the support of their party.[247] But Adams, in spite of his unquestioned integrity and high qualifications in many ways, did not prove to be altogether invulnerable as a candidate. His policy during the Fenian raids was used at this time, as later, to alienate the Irish support.[248] A couple of weeks before the convention he wrote to Wells of its possible action concerning himself in a rather cavalier manner[249] which was creditable to his political independence but likely to offend the dignity of the average delegate, even in a reform convention, and not likely to be fully appreciated by the average voter. The independent press gave its appreciation of his exalted sentiments,[250] and the *World* lauded the "high-toned, masculine letter . . .   the effusion of a statesman who scorns to weigh duty against advantage, who can descend to no unworthy compliances, and who desires no office except as a free, unbought mark of trust in his character."[251] His opponents, on the other hand, seized the opportunity to expatiate on the unpopularity of the Adams family and the utter lack of availability as a coalition can-

[246] N. Y. *World*, Apr. 24, 1872.

[247] White, 373; Bancroft-Dunning, 344.

[248] See correspondence in N. Y. *World* on this matter, Apr. 25–30, 1872; *Madison Democrat*, Apr. 26, 1872.

[249] *Annual Cyclopedia*, 1872, p. 777; *Springfield Weekly Republican*, Apr. 26, 1872.

[250] *Nation*, May 2, 1872, p. 281; *Chicago Tribune*, Apr. 26, 1872; *Springfield Republican*, quoted in N. Y. *Tribune*, Apr. 30, 1872.

[251] N. Y. *World*, Apr. 25, 1872.

didate of this member of it.[252]   But in spite of these possible weaknesses from the politician's point of view, Adams continued to be in the front rank of the possible candidates.

On the eve of the convention the situation as regards candidates was this: the "slate" of the managing, scheming politicians, among both the Liberals and Democrats, was Davis and Greeley; to most of the reform group, and to the conservative eastern Democrats, Adams and a prominent middle western Liberal like Trumbull, Cox,[253] or Palmer seemed to be the ticket best representing the aims of the opposition.

[252] *Washington Patriot,* quoted in *N. Y. Tribune,* Apr. 30, 1872; *Chicago Times,* Apr. 25, 1872; *Albany Argus,* Apr. 29, 1872; *Madison Democrat,* Apr. 26, 1872; *Richmond Whig and Advertiser,* Apr. 26, 1872. W. S. Robinson, the Boston correspondent of the *Springfield Republican* and a leading Massachusetts Liberal, wrote to Sumner (Apr. 9, 1872) that Adams' nomination "would in my judgment be a great mistake, for he and his family represent too much the anti-popular element—the sneering, sniffing element, which can never have permanent success in our politics." Sumner MSS. Cf. Bowles' comment on Adams' candidacy in the convention, below, ch. III, note 66. The *N. Y. Times* made good use of Adams' letter to cast discredit on the general character of the convention. See editorials, Apr. 25, 26, 27, 1872.

[253] The N. Y. *Evening Post* thought General Cox the most acceptable candidate for vice-president. See editorial on candidates, Apr. 23, 1872.

CHAPTER III

The mass convention that assembled at Cincinnati was
composed of most diverse elements, representing as it did
all shades of opposition to existing conditions.   Impractical
doctrinaires, constructive reformers, public men of tried
integrity, and political intriguers long-exposed were all in
evidence.[1] But with the exception of certain groups like
some of the Davis recruits from Illinois, Warmoth's hench-
men from Louisiana and the New York Tammany Republicans, the gathering was a respectable one and probably
compared favorably with most national conventions.[2]
Bowles thought that there were fewer manufactured delegations than at Philadelphia in 1856 and no more than at
Chicago in 1860.[3] The Davis men from Central Illinois
constituted the largest number of obtruding politicians.
The Judge's managers provided transportation for all whom
they could persuade to go to the convention in their candidate's interest.   Much Davis enthusiasm was stirred up
in that part of the state and several hundred joined the

[1] See Bowles' characterization in his letter from the convention,
Springfield Weekly Republican, May 10 (all dates when not otherwise
indicated are for the year 1872); Watterson, "Humor and Tragedy of
the Greeley Campaign," in *Century Magazine*, LXXXV, 30.

[2] White, *Trumbull*, 380; Julian, *Pol. Recollections*, 337. The correspondent of the *Nation*, probably Godkin, wrote of the convention:
"I doubt, indeed, whether a more respectable, honest, intelligent, public-
spirited body of men has ever got together for a similar purpose."
Nation, May 9, p. 303.

[3] *Springfield Weekly Republican*, May 10.

excursion.[4]   The New York and Pennsylvania delegations, a shrewd observer thought, contained more political experience than all the rest of the convention put together.[5] These political adepts, veterans of many a hard-fought campaign, directed by Senator Fenton for New York and Colonel A. K. McClure for Pennsylvania, were planning, as generally understood at Cincinnati on the eve of the convention, to join their skill to the numerical strength of the forces for Davis and nominate that candidate, with Greeley or Curtin for the second place.[6]

The boldness and pretentiousness with which these manipulators prepared to capture the convention brought upon them a decisive counter-stroke from the reform camp. Soon after reaching the convention city, four leading independent editors—Bowles, Halstead, White and Watterson—met together for consultation and formed a fellowship for united action which came to be termed in the campaign the "great quadrilateral."[7]   To these men Davis' candidacy, promoted as it was, seemed a complete travesty of the reforms for which they were working.   In consultation on the evening of April 29 they determined not to support the politicians' ticket under any consideration, and this ultimatum was wired to their various papers to appear the next morning as editorial leaders.   Fenton, as the recognized general of the Davis-Greeley forces, was promptly notified of this action.   The Senator admitted that the attitude of the independent press would be fatal

[4] Swett to Fell, Apr. 1, *Miss. Valley Hist. Rev.* I, 107; Stevenson, *Men I have Known*, 286; *Springfield Weekly Republican*, May 10.   It was said that 500, of whom half were Democrats, were brought to Cincinnati in Davis' interest.   Koerner, *Memoirs*, II, 544.

[5] Bowles in *Springfield Weekly Republican*, May 10.

[6] *Ibid.; Nation*, May 9, p. 303; McClure, *Old Time Notes*, II, 335; Trumbull to White, Apr. 24, Trumbull MSS.; Letter to N. Y. *Evening Post* (May 10) from a "Free Trade Revenue Reform Member"; Morehouse, *Fell*, 103.

[7] Watterson, 30.

to his candidate and left the following evening for Washington.[8] "The best men here," Bowles wrote to his paper, "are glad that Gov. Fenton has gone away. It leaves the result of the convention free from suspicion. The general feeling is that he left because of the failure of the Davis intrigue in which he was deeply engaged."[9]

But the triumph of the independents in this preliminary skirmish did not mean that the manoeuvres of intriguing politicians at the convention city had been suppressed. Greeley was the favorite candidate of the Tammany Republicans (with the exception of Senator Fenton) and of other eastern and southern politicians of a like caste,[10] and so soon as the Davis project fell through, they hastened to push forward his candidacy, some of the more enthusiastic supporters, as one reporter put it, "working for him like beavers."[11]

In accordance with the call for the mass convention, the persons in attendance from each state were to choose their

[8] Watterson, 33; *Springfield Weekly Republican*, May 10; *Nation*, May 9, p. 303.

[9] *Springfield Weekly Republican*, May 3. Bowles had written to Sumner (Mar. 30), "Fenton I take it will sell out if he can get his price. I am quite content that he should. He belongs to no true reform party." Sumner MSS. The N. Y. *Tribune* of May 1 thus mentioned Fenton's departure: "Gov. Fenton returned to Washington this evening [Apr. 30] in high spirits over what he believes the strongly probable success of the convention in candidates and platform." The *N. Y. Times* said (May 7) that he was "frightened away by the independent journalists."

[10] Trumbull to White, Apr. 24, Trumbull MSS.; Scovel to Sumner, Mar. 18, Sumner MSS.; interview of John Cochrane in N. Y. *World*, Apr. 29; Bowles' report of convention for April 30 in *Springfield Weekly Republican*, May 3.

[11] N. Y. *World*, May 1; N. Y. *Tribune*, May 1; *Albany Argus*, May 2. Bowles wrote of Fenton's sudden departure that "he did not like to stay and have the further odium of a failure in the now dominant Greeley movement." *Springfield Weekly Republican*, May 3. In the Pennsylvania gathering, April 30, McClure withdrew Curtin as a candidate for vice-president, and presented him as the state's first and only choice for president. *N. Y. Times*, May 2.

official delegates to act in the convention. The only delegations in which contest arose were those from the Illinois
between the Davis and Trumbull supporters, and from New
York between the Greeley men and the tariff reformers. The
Illinois people reached an amicable settlement the night
before the opening of the convention. The Davis adherents, though far outnumbering their rivals, conceded
them half of the delegates, and the caucus passed off most
harmoniously.[12] The differences among the New Yorkers
were more irreconcilable. In their meeting for organization, on April 30, it was soon apparent that the Greeley
men,[13] who were in a large majority, intended to secure a
delegation in their candidate's interest, while the representatives of the Free Trade League and other reform organizations[14] were determined to have a voice. The dominant
majority, to carry through their scheme, secured the appointment of a committee headed by Cochrane to report
the list of delegates, with the stipulation, finally conceded
to the reformers, that the district delegates might be named

[12] N. Y. Tribune, May 1; Morehouse, 103 f.
[13] Bowles thought that Waldo Hutchins was the real leader of the
New York politicians though John Cochrane as usual made himself
most conspicuous. Springfield Weekly Republican, May 10. Other
prominent Greeley men in the delegation were Ethan Allen, Sinclair
Tousey, Theodore Tilton, George Wilkes, William Dorsheimer, and
E. A. Merritt. N. Y. Tribune, May 1, 2. Evidently as an opening
thrust at the independents, a motion made by Tousey was adopted that
as it was reported that there were a number in attendance not fully
committed to the Liberal movement every man present should be compelled "to give his name, residence, and an assurance of sympathy with
the movement, and go on record as being in sympathy or leave the
room." Tellers were appointed for this purpose and the active participants duly qualified, no expulsions being reported. N. Y. Tribune,
May 1.
[14] Henry D. Lloyd was the chief spokesman for The Free Trade
League. A Mr. Bishop said that he represented the Young Men's
Municipal Association of New York City, 10,000 strong, who claimed a
representation in the convention. N. Y. Tribune, May 1.

by those in attendance from each district.[15]   The politicians openly showed their hand next day when a resolution was forced through providing that the delegation should vote as a unit for Greeley until twenty should request a consultation, after which the vote should go as directed by a majority, "provided the convention shall not direct a different method of procedure."[16]   The reformers in vain made bitter objections that in thus tying the delegates' hands, the same sort of tyranny was exercised against which the Liberal movement was largely a protest.[17]   The list of delegates[18] reported by Cochrane showed an almost complete disregard of the reform minority and a deliberate purpose to pack the delegation in Greeley's interest. Among the sixty-eight delegates but three tariff reformers were included, though that element had given the committee the names of twelve representatives whom they desired;[19] but the leading Greeley managers were all given votes. These tactics of the politicians in the New York caucus,[20] with their iron-clad unit rule and unrepresentative list of delegates, showed clearly enough that they meant to stop at nothing that long years of convention-manipulation could suggest to force their candidate upon the unwary reformers.

[15] *N. Y. Tribune*, May 1; *N. Y. Times*, May 1; Lloyd, *Lloyd*, I, 27.

[16] *N. Y. Tribune*, May 2.   The proviso was added at the instance of Judge Selden.   The resolution was finally adopted by a vote of 99 to 22.

[17] *Idem.*

[18] *Idem.*

[19] N. Y. *Evening Post*, May 3.   Henry D. Lloyd's openly-avowed opposition to Greeley led to his withdrawal as a delegate.   A motion made to substitute another delegate in his place was not adopted, but he declined to act.   *N. Y. Tribune*, May 2; Lloyd, I, 28.   David Dudley Field sent his name to the caucus, but the secretary refused to register him, probably by reason of his pronounced free-trade position.   *N. Y. Tribune*, May 1; Blaine, *Twenty Years of Cong.* II, 521.   After the caucus instructed for Greeley, Field said that he had no desire to act on the delegation.   *N. Y. Tribune*, May 2.

[20] For scathing criticisms of the New York caucus' action, see editorials in N. Y. *Evening Post*, May 3; *Cincinnati Gazette*, quoted in *N. Y. Tribune*, May 2, and *Cincinnati Semi-Weekly Gazette*, May 3.

At noon, on Wednesday, May 1, Colonel Grosvenor, as chairman of the Missouri state convention that had issued the call for the national gathering, called the convention to order, and Stanley Matthews of Ohio, as temporary chairman, set forth the short-comings of the administration and the responsibilities of the delegates in the usual style.[21] Liberals of a superstitious turn might well have considered that the later unhappy developments in their movement were a judgment upon them for the omission of the customary opening prayer.

The second day committees were named[22] and a permanent organization effected. The usual Republican rules, including the House of Representatives procedure, individual voting, and nominating by a majority vote, were adopted.[23] The failure to adopt a unit rule was due largely to the efforts of Theodore Tilton in the committee on resolutions, the Greeley leaders in the New York delegation considering that they had unnecessarily hurt their cause by suppressing the few free-traders in the delegation.[24]

The chief contest before the credentials committee came from the New York minority. Their protest, presented to the convention by Judge Selden, was promptly referred to the committee. The paper stated that the signers were opposed to Greeley's candidacy and that they protested against the high-handed manner in which the state's delegation had been packed in his interest. They cited cases where delegates actually selected by a majority from their district were excluded by reason of their opposition to

[21] *Proceedings of the Lib. Rep. Convention*, 4; *N. Y. Tribune*, May 2.

[22] Territories, whose delegates were allowed seats in the convention, were given representation on committees the same as states but their delegates were not allowed to vote for candidates. *Proceedings*, 6, 23; *N. Y. Tribune*, May 3, 4.

[23] *Proceedings*, 13-14.

[24] So stated in *N. Y. Tribune's* correspondence from the convention. See issue of May 3.

Greeley, and claimed that in the selection of delegates for districts not represented "all persons understood to be opposed to the nomination of Mr. Greeley were studiously ignored." The list of delegates as it now stood, they concluded, did not represent the true sentiment of the state's mass delegation.[25] In the hearing before the committee, Wilkinson, the New York member, a strong Greeley man, defended the action of the majority, while Mahlon Sands, the secretary of the Free Trade League, spoke for the contestants. After a heated discussion over the course of the reformers in case Greeley should be the choice of the convention (which Sands refused to state definitely), the committee by a vote of 28 to 12 decided against the contestants.[26] This report was subsequently adopted by the convention.[27]

Schurz, contrary to the general expectation,[28] took the chair as permanent president. In his "key-note" speech, "full of the loftiest aspiration,"[29] he exhorted the delegates to measure up to their opportunity "grand and full of promise." To disappoint the high expectations of the popular uprising against the abuses of the time would result not only in throwing away this opportunity but in discrediting for a long time to come all popular reform movements. Such would be the unhappy result, he warned, if they resorted to the "old tricks of the political trader," or frittered away their zeal "in small bickerings and mean,

[25] *Proceedings*, 8. Among the signers were Theodore Bacon, D. D. Field, Mahlon Sands, H. D. Lloyd, and William Dudley Foulke.

[26] *N. Y. Tribune*, May 3.

[27] *Proceedings*, 13. There was also some dispute over the casting of California's vote, the committee at first deciding that there was but one delegate present competent to act for the state, but later reporting that its information was erroneous as another delegate was present who claimed to be a bona fide California resident and promised to stump the state for the ticket. The convention adopted this modified report. *Idem.; N. Y. Tribune*, May 3.

[28] *N. Y. Tribune*, May 3.

[29] *Nation*, May 9, p. 303.

selfish aspirations." In making the platform he urged his
fellow delegates above all to "be honest and straight-forward
and not attempt to cheat those whom we ask to follow our
lead, by deceitful representations." For candidate no one
short of a real statesman, a man of "superior intelligence,
coupled with superior virtue" would measure up to the
Liberal standard. The end was not to defeat the existing
administration, but to secure a real political regeneration—
"therefore, away with the cry, 'Anybody to beat Grant'; a
cry too paltry, too unworthy of the great enterprise in which
we are engaged." "Availability" meant the finding of the
"very best men" and from that list selecting "the strongest." If such a man were selected the "insidious accusa-
tion" that the convention was "a mere gathering of disappointed and greedy politicians" would be completely
disproven, and its purity and patriotism of motive vindi-
cated. In view of the great things at stake, the delegates
were impressively besought to despise as unworthy the
"tricky manipulations by which, to the detriment of the
Republic, political bodies have so frequently been controlled," and for the common good to "rise above all petty
considerations" like personal friendships and local pride.
"We stand on the threshold of a great victory," he concluded, "and victory will surely be ours if we truly deserve
it."[30] The whole address was an earnest and eloquent plea
for the Liberal movement as conceived by its original insti-
gators. The speeches and tactics of the Tammany Republicans in the New York caucus had well reflected the
ideas and aims of the intriguing politicians in the convention; Schurz's speech was the best expression of the ideals
and aspirations of the reformers.

In the consideration of the platform the great and only
important source of disagreement was the tariff question.
At the one extreme were the radical free-traders from Mis-

[30] *Proceedings*, 9–12; *Schurz's Writings*, II, 354–361.

souri, Ohio and New England demanding a positive declaration for their principle,[31] and at the other Greeley refusing to lend his *Tribune* to the new party if such a policy were adopted.[32] Aside from the free-trade agitators, however, there was an evident tendency, even on the part of leading organizers of the movement, to consider the tariff as a question of not the first importance and to adopt a conciliatory attitude.[33] For three days before the opening of the convention conferences were held between the free-traders, led by Grosvenor, Hoadly, Atkinson, Wells, Godkin and Field, and the Greeley managers, especially Reid, Dorsheimer and Tousey. Efforts were made to secure a statement of the issue to which all would agree. Several proposals were offered by the reformers, ranging from the statement in the Missouri call, upon which the radicals insisted, to that contained in the New York letter signed by Greeley himself; but the Greeley spokesmen insisted as their ultimatum upon the non-committal proposal of

[31] For the attitude of the extreme free-traders before the convention, see Robinson to Sumner, Mar. 18, Sumner MSS.; Brinkerhoff to Trumbull, Mar. 23, Trumbull MSS.; Prime to Trumbull, Mar. 29, *ibid.*; Trumbull to White, Apr. 24, *ibid.*

[32] In an editorial, April 30, Greeley stated that in case the free-traders should secure the adoption of their plank he would have "increased respect for their courage, with a low estimate of their discretion." He asked only that they state their position clearly, as sooner or later the country must decide on the tariff issue. In a letter to a friend, May 1, Greeley complained that the free-traders wanted to force a platform on the convention that would probably defeat its candidate, but he was determined to thwart their plan. "They may make the candidate as they please, but not the platform if I can help it." Benton, *Greeley on Lincoln, etc.*, 214 f.

[33] *N. Y. Tribune*, Apr. 30, May 1. Bowles wrote from the convention (Apr. 30): "The fact is that most of the revenue reformers here are not tenacious of a radical declaration on this question. They see it is practically useless for their cause, while it would weaken if not defeat a great political movement through which all reform is to be moved forward." *Springfield Weekly Republican*, May 3.

their candidate—that the matter be referred to the people
of each congressional district for determination.[34]

The question was finally fought out in an all-night session
of the committee on resolutions. The committee contained a majority of protectionists, and some of the more
ardent free-traders threatened to bolt the convention if a
reform plank was not reported. Finally, however, to secure
harmony for the ticket, feeling certain at this time that
their candidate would be named, reform leaders like Wells,
Atkinson and Hoadly urged concession on this issue, and
a resolution identical with Greeley's formulation was
adopted.[35] This compromise was condemned by ultra free-
traders at the time[36] and has been characterized by the leading historian of the period as the one "resolution out of
keeping with the high aims and determined spirit of the
movement."[37] But this concession was considered by some
of the men who had the true interests of the Liberal movement most at heart as necessary to secure the greater ends,[38]
and it undoubtedly reflected the sentiment of a large
majority of the delegates.[39]

The other resolutions, embodying in the main the Missouri platform—equality before the law, acceptance of the
war amendments, universal amnesty, local self-government,

[34] *N. Y. Tribune*, May 1, 2; Watterson, 35; *Springfield Weekly Republican*, May 3; Reid's telegram to Greeley, May 1, printed in Benton,
Greeley on Lincoln, etc., 215 f.

[35] *N. Y. Tribune*, May 3; article by Isaac H. Bromley in *ibid.*, June 25;
Hoadly's speech quoted in *ibid.*, Aug. 26; Brinkerhoff, *Recollections*,
217.

[36] *Evening Post*, May 7; *Nation*, May 9, p. 300.

[37] Rhodes, VI, 419.

[38] Schurz to Greeley, May 6, *Schurz's Writings*, II, 362 f.; Bowles in
Springfield Weekly Republican, May 10; Trumbull to White, Apr. 24,
White, 379, and White's opinion in *ibid.*, 382.

[39] The *Nation* correspondent wrote of the tariff resolution: "It is right
to add that the sentiment of the Convention was overwhelmingly in
favor of this course." *Nation*, May 9, p. 303.

civil service reform—including the restriction of the president to one term, just and adequate federal taxation, denunciation of repudiation, a speedy return to specie payments, an expression of gratitude to the soldiers and sailors, opposition to land grants to railroads or other corporations, and just dealings with foreign nations—preceded by a statement of the manifold short-comings and complete failure of the existing administration[40]—were agreed to without dissent. The platform as thus constructed was received with enthusiasm when presented in the convention (on the morning of May 3) and was unanimously adopted.[41]

With the platform out of the way, the convention was ready, on the third day of its session, to proceed to its crowning work, the naming of the candidates to lead the new movement. Despite the confident assurances from the backers of the contestants, the choice remained excitingly uncertain. The organizers of this convention had no cut-and-dried program; the only definite "slate" had been largely broken up at the start. The politicians, to be sure, had continued to lay their plans and form new combinations, but with the diverse elements and influences at work in such a heterogeneous gathering it was still anybody's game.

Adams' prospects seemed to be constantly improving during the first two days.[42] Three of the quadrilateral of independent editors were his enthusiastic advocates.[43] Between his supporters and those of Trumbull entire harmony prevailed, and there was much sentiment for giving Trumbull the second place on the ticket.[44] Schurz's candidate of "superior intelligence, coupled with superior virtue" was

[40] Stanwood, *Hist. of Presidency*, 341–344.

[41] *Proceedings*, 18.

[42] *Springfield Weekly Republican*, May 3, 10; *Nation*, May 9, p. 303; Clay, *Memoirs*, I, 505.

[43] Watterson, 31; *Springfield Weekly Republican*, May 10.

[44] The Maine delegation circulated a card reading: "This ticket to win—For president, Charles Francis Adams, for vice-president, Lyman Trumbull." *Springfield Weekly Republican*, May 3.

generally understood to be Adams.[45] Colonel Grosvenor,
who had hitherto been regarded as a supporter of Brown,
now tried to persuade the Missouri delegation that the most
available nomination would be that of Adams with their
"favorite son" for his running mate.[46]

But this support was to prove costly to the Adams cause.
Brown's friends looked upon the preference of the Missouri
leaders for an easterner as rank treason.   Besides they were
becoming jealous of Schurz's position of supremacy in the
convention.[47]   Brown and his cousin Senator Blair, thought
to be a "good manager with considerable influence in
several of the delegations," were summoned and arrived on
Thursday night.[48] It was soon reported that, after conferences with delegations considered open to some mutual
arrangement, Brown had agreed to use his influence for
Greeley in return for the vice-presidency.[49] The *Commercial* announced next morning that the alignment of
candidates was now Adams and Trumbull against Greeley
and Brown.[50]

Such proved to be the case when the balloting began.
Adams led off on the first trial, fifty-six votes ahead of
Greeley.   But before the result was announced Brown, who
had been given ninety-five votes, secured the platform and
in a brief speech withdrew his name and strongly urged his
supporters to go for Greeley.[51]   The speech was greeted

[45] *Nation*, May 9, p. 303.

[46] *Springfield Weekly Republican*, May 10.

[47] *Idem.; Nation*, May 9, p. 303.

[48] Clay, I, 505.

[49] *Nation*, May 9, p. 303; White, 382. Bowles wrote to his paper at
midnight Wednesday that Gratz Brown was to come to the convention
next day and that it was understood that he would work for somebody
else's nomination. *Springfield Weekly Republican*, May 3.

[50] Editorial quoted in *N. Y. Tribune*, May 4.

[51] *Proceedings*, 21. The convention had decided to dispense with all
nominating speeches and merely to call the roll of the states when the
ballots were taken.

8

with cheers from the Greeley men and requests at once
came in for a transfer of votes.[52] This move put Greeley
two votes ahead on the second ballot, but thereafter up to
the last ballot Adams retained the lead. Brown's "combination" worked but imperfectly as he was not able to
transfer all of his own delegation to Greeley. Schurz,
alarmed by Brown's move, left the chair to urge the Mis-
sourians to support Adams.[53]

The nucleus of Greeley's support was the New York delegation which, with the exception of from two to six votes,
kept with him throughout. To this were added the votes
of New Hampshire, Vermont, most of those of New Jersey,
half of those from Pennsylvania, a good portion from the
South, and all from the far West. Adams' support in the
East, South and Middle West remained steady with an increase on every ballot. Trumbull never became dangerous,
and the strength of the others rapidly melted away after
the first vote.[54] The Illinois delegation, remaining equally
divided between Trumbull and Davis up to the last ballot,
really held the balance in the convention.[55]

In the face of Adams' increasing strength, the politicians
were forced to resort to strategy to snatch a victory from
the reformers. On the fifth ballot Adams was fifty-one
votes ahead of his competitor and within thirty-three of the
nomination. Illinois then retired for consultation and it
was generally felt that the end was approaching.[56] The
next ballot showed considerable gains for Greeley[57] and as

[52] *Proceedings* 21; *Nation*, May 9, p. 304; *N. Y. Tribune*, May 4.

[53] *Springfield Weekly Republican*, May 10.

[54] See the ballots by states in *Proceedings*, 22–29; *N. Y. Tribune*,
May 4.

[55] Cf. *Nation*, May 9, p. 304; Koerner, II, 556.

[56] *N. Y. Tribune*, May 4.

[57] The Illinois delegation returned after the stampede had begun.
Their vote of twenty-seven for Adams to fourteen for Greeley called
forth some applause from the Adams side. A few minutes earlier it
might have saved the day for them, but now it failed to stop the rush
to Greeley. *Nation*, May 9, p. 304; Koerner, II, 556.

REFORMERS VERSUS POLITICIANS

they were announced his managers, evidently thinking that the psychological moment had come, instituted one of the most remarkable stampedes ever seen in a national convention. From all parts of the hall changes for Greeley were now shouted in such rapid succession that they could barely be recorded and through it all a most confusing demonstration was kept up by the New York and supporting delegations.[58] An ardent young reformer gave this highly picturesque if biased description of the scene: "As the voting wore on, Adams strengthened, and by the time the fifth ballot was reached Greeley was plainly on the decline. Then came the spontaneous rally which had been carefully planned the night before. The Hall was filled with a mechanical, preordained, stentorious bellowing. Hoary-haired, hard-eyed politicians, who had not in twenty years felt a noble impulse, mounted their chairs and with faces suffused with a seraphic fervor, blistered their throats hurraying for the great and good Horace Greeley. The noise bred a panic. A furore artificial at first, became real and ended in a stampede."[59] Amid such confusion enough changes were made to give Greeley a majority. After that delegations hastened to get on the winning side.[60] Schurz, in desperation at the turn the proceedings were taking, ruled that the roll was defective and that a new call must be had. He was quickly shouted down by the New York crowd.[61] A motion to make the nomination unanimous was greeted from some quarters with most indignant

[58] *N. Y. Tribune*, May 4; *N. Y. Times*, May 4. Just before the sixth ballot, Judge Goodrich of Minnesota made a motion that no changes should be made in the record until the entire roll call was completed, but no vote was taken on it. *Proceedings*, 28.

[59] Henry D. Lloyd's speech at the Steinway Hall Conference, May 30, *N. Y. Tribune*, May 31.

[60] *Proceedings*, 29.

[61] *Idem.*; *N. Y. Tribune*, May 4.

nays and declared lost.[62]   Schurz, in his consternation, even forgot to make a formal announcement of the result until reminded of the omission by the alert General Cochrane.[63]

Brown easily secured on the second ballot the prize he had bargained for, after Senator Trumbull and General Cox had been withdrawn by their representatives.[64] This nomination also failed of unanimous adoption, such a motion being withdrawn after indignant protests.[65] The failure to comply with this customary formality of national conventions shows the complete lack of party feeling among the Liberal delegates.

Various causes, it is evident, contributed to bring about these nominations which seemed to mark the complete triumph of the politicians over the reformers. The result is to be attributed both to the weaknesses of Greeley's rivals and to his own peculiar elements of strength in the mass convention. Both of his leading rivals had serious handicaps. Adams' personality was of a sort to repel many westerners;[66] old-time political enemies of himself and his

[62] *Proceedings*, 29.   The *N. Y. Tribune* report stated (May 4) "that when the motion was made the element known as Free Trade and Revenue Reform manifested a disposition to mar the enthusiasm by dogged silence and an indignant and unanimous nay."

[63] *Proceedings*, 29; *N. Y. Tribune*, May 4.

[64] *Proceedings*, 29–30; *N. Y. Tribune*, May 4; Koerner, II, 556.

[65] *N. Y. Tribune*, May 4; *Proceedings*, 32.

[66] Cf. Morehouse, 103.   Bowles in his review of the Cincinnati convention wrote of Adams' position there that the chief objections urged against him were the tone of his letter to Wells, the fear that he might drive the Irish vote to Grant, and the feeling of westerners that he lacked the personal popularity to make a strong appeal. "Others recognized the historical capacity of the Adamses to disintergration rather than organization, and doubted whether Mr. Adams could successfully organize the elements of reform into a permanent power by his administration." *Springfield Weekly Republican*, May 10, 1872. Austin Blair in rejoicing over Greeley's nomination declared that Adams had no hold upon the laboring classes especially in the West. Dilla, *Politics of Mich.*, 137.

family from the South West were eager to secure his defeat;[67] and his opposition to the Free-Soil-Democratic coalition of twenty years before now brought him persistent opponents from his own state.[68] Trumbull was hampered by a divided delegation in his own state, the feeling becoming so bitter in the end that, probably out of spite towards the Trumbull men,[69] some of the Davis delegates turned to Greeley. The managers of these candidates, too, failed to unite their forces while there was opportunity. The supporters of either would have gone for the other in preference to Greeley,[70] but the continued support of both for first place scattered their forces. There was also no systematic effort on the part of Greeley's opponents to secure a more desirable compromise candidate, a policy that would have readily suggested itself to skilled political managers.

Greeley, on his side, found one of his best assets in his supposed weakness. At this time, as so often in the past, many had not taken his candidacy seriously.[71] The independent journalists in the convention, having little fear of their brother-editor's candidacy but greatly desiring the *Tribune's* support, failed to pronounce against him as they had against Davis.[72] Democratic papers which would have strongly

[67] Clay, I, 504; Linn, *Greeley*, 242.

[68] *Springfield Weekly Republican*, May 10. F. W. Bird boasted that he had defeated Adams' nomination. Bowles to Sumner, May 18, Sumner MSS. Bowles thought that Bird was acting in accordance with Sumner's wish in opposing Adams (*idem.*), but Pierce denies this. Pierce, *Sumner*, IV, 518 n.

[69] *Nation*, May 9, p. 304.

[70] Watterson's letter to the *Courier-Journal*, printed in *Chicago Tribune*, May 9; Julian, 339. Wells wrote to Trumbull (May 8) that he and Atkinson had been ready to change their votes from Adams to Trumbull at any time, but that the opportunity did not come. Trumbull MSS.

[71] Cf. *Nation*, May 9, pp. 297, 304; *Golden Age*, May 11; N. Y. *World*, May 4.

[72] Watterson, 31.

opposed his nomination, and no doubt with effect, if it
had appeared imminent at the start, did not give it much
consideration.[73]   In his wide popularity, especially in the
South[73a] and West,[74] the veteran editor had a more positive element of strength.[75] But the chief explanation of
Greeley's success is to be found in the efficient support of
the politicians.   All of the advantage of political scheming
and intriguing was on his side.   The Brown-Blair episode,
of which so much has been made, was but one of the politicians' schemes, very blunderingly executed and not at all
essential to the result.[76]   The utter inexperience of many of
the delegates with the ways of conventions[77] put them at
the mercy of the "old-timers" who made the most of their
opportunity.[78] This then is the real explanation—the
triumph of experienced political intriguers over inexpe-
rienced over-confident reformers.   Greeley in the past had

[73] Leading Democratic papers like the N. Y. *World* and *Washington
Patriot* had confined their discussion before the convention mainly to
Adams, Trumbull, Davis, and Brown.

[73a] See Ross, "Horace Greeley and the South," *South Atlantic
Quarterly*, XVI, 324 ff.

[74] Except with the German element.

[75] Cf. *Springfield Republican*, May 3; White's letter in *Chicago
Tribune*, May 4.

[76] Cf. Watterson in *Chicago Tribune*, May 9.

[77] Bowles wrote that the political experience of the leaders in the New
York and Pennsylvania delegations "gave them great advantage in
dealing with the novices and theoretical devotees from other states.
. . .   The venerable Judge Selden from Rochester was almost power-
less in the presence of so large a number of men more familiar with the
machinery of parties." *Springfield Weekly Republican*, May 10.
Edward Atkinson, after failing to get a motion before the convention in
its proper connection, remarked that "he was not familiar with the
usages of Conventions." Report of the convention for May 2 in
N. Y. Tribune, May 3.

[78] *Golden Age*, May 11. It was charged that on the last ballot New
Yorkers voted in the delegations of other states and unauthorized
changes for Greeley were made. *N. Y. Tribune*, May 11 quoting
Evening Post and giving Cochrane's letter denying the charges. See

many times been the victim of the schemes of political
managers; this time the "inside men" were for him and he
won.

The reformers, with characteristic petulence, were very
free in casting the blame on one another. The free-traders
blamed the organizers of the convention for permitting
protectionists to take part in it,[79] while they themselves
were blamed for not making concessions on that subject in
a way which would have insured their naming the candidate.[80] Schurz was criticized both for taking too conspicuous a part in the proceedings and for not exerting a
sufficiently strong influence privately in favor of some
reform candidate.[81] To the latter criticism he replied that
though frequently told he might exert a decisive influence
on the selection of candidates he had spurned to stoop to

also *N. Y. Times*, May 7; correspondent in *Evening Post*, May 10, and
Washington Patriot, May 4. The *N. Y. Times* charged (May 7) that
Fenton had been working for Greeley all along, and that his support of
Davis was only a blind. Bowles, however, held that Fenton had noth-
ing to do with Greeley's nomination though he was at the bottom of the
Davis movement. See his letter to the *Cincinnati Commercial*, May 4,
quoted in *N. Y. Tribune*, May 6. Bowles wrote to Dawes (May 21):
"Yes, Fenton was for Greeley in his way. But his way would have
killed him. It was not the men of the Fenton stamp who nominated
Greeley at all. . . . Fenton is neither a political idiot nor a political
buccaneer, and Greeley was nominated by a combination of these two.
The Theodore Tiltons and Frank Blairs, and not the Reuben E. Fen-
tons, did the business." Merriam, *Bowles*, II, 212. The *Evening Post*
said (Oct. 4) that most of the delegates were "as innocent as sucklings
of any political manoeuvres," and that the politicians had captured
them "like a bevy of quails under a net."

[79] Judge Hoadly's speech, *N. Y. Times*, Aug. 24; Brinkerhoff, 217.

[80] *Springfield Weekly Republican*, May 10.

[81] *Nation*, May 9, p. 303, Nov. 23, p. 328. Bowles wrote from the
convention, May 1, that Schurz's open advocacy of Adams, Trumbull,
or Cox "would insure immediate success." *Springfield Weekly Republican*, May 3. Joseph Pulitzer told Halstead years afterward that a
word from Schurz would have routed Blair and Brown. Watterson, 39.

the rôle of president-maker,[82] and as a foreign-born citizen hestitated to take too prominent a part in such matters.[83] Schurz, on his side, could take to task effectively the sort of reformer who, while speaking and writing for reforms and criticizing the failure of others to secure them, still would not give himself the trouble to attend a convention called in hope of bringing them about.[84] However, neither reproaches nor excuses could alter the fact: the national Liberal convention had fallen into the snare of the fowler.[85]

The Reunion, and Reform convention, with about two hundred delegates from eleven states, was called to order by Judge Stallo of Cincinnati on May 2 and formed a permanent organization with Judge Ranney as president.[86] It had been generally understood that this convention would endorse the Liberal convention's work if satisfactory. Some of the promoters had expected an invitation to unite with the main convention.[87] The president's address denounced both of the old parties impartially and advocated a union of all reform elements regardless of past differences.[88] Resolutions presented in favor of Adams and of Trumbull were referred to the committee.[89] The

[82] Schurz to Bowles, May 11, *Schurz's Writings*, II, 369.

[83] Schurz to Godkin, Nov. 23, *ibid.*, 446 f.

[84] Speech at Fifth Avenue Convention, June 20, *N. Y. Tribune*, June 21.

[85] The Liberals before adjournment appointed a national committee which organized with Ethan Allen of New York, one of Greeley's chief supporters in the convention, as chairman, and Daniel R. Goodloe of North Carolina as secretary. *N. Y. Tribune*, May 6. Senator Fenton was later chosen chairman of the Liberal congressional campaign committee. *Ibid.*, June 10.

[86] *Cincinnati Semi-Weekly Gazette*, May 3.

[87] *Wisconsin Weekly State Journal*, Apr. 16; Judge Collins' interview in *N. Y. Herald*, Apr. 28.

[88] *Cincinnati Semi-Weekly Gazette*, May 3.

[89] *Idem.* The resolution in favor of Trumbull (with a Southerner for vice-president) purported to be from "French speaking citizens representing twenty-two states, and 300,000 voters."

platform was essentially the same as that of the Liberals, with the important exception of a declaration for a tariff for revenue only.[90]   Greeley's nomination came as a most unwelcome surprise to this gathering.   Stallo denounced it as the result of treachery, declaring that the leaders of the Liberal convention lacked courage and honesty.   He had hoped, he said, for harmonious action between the two conventions.[91]   The convention was undecided how to act and after empowering its executive committee to call another national convention, at a time and place to be determined by them, it adjourned sine die.[92]   The further action of this group, as that of the other reformers, was uncertain.

[90] *Cincinnati Semi-Weekly Gazette*, May 7.

[91] *Idem.*   Stallo told a reporter before the convention that the western Germans desired Adams' nomination.   In case Greeley was nominated or overrode the convention on the tariff issue Stallo wished to be counted out.   *N. Y. Herald*, Apr. 28.

[92] *Cincinnati Semi-Weekly Gazette*, May 7.

CHAPTER IV

THE LIBERALS AND THEIR CANDIDATE

Greeley's nomination at Cincinnati presented a serious and unexpected problem alike to the reformers and to the Democrats. It will be the purpose of this chapter to explain the policy of the reformers both, prior to the meeting of the other national conventions, and during the campaign. The Cincinnati nominations were a hard blow to the reformers in the Liberal movement, but, aside from the more extreme free-traders, they endeavored to make the best of their embarrassing situation. The journalistic "quadrilateral" quickly came to the conclusion that they had gone too far in promoting the convention to back out when it named candidates whom they had not openly opposed.[1] They tried to assume a confident attitude in presenting the results of the convention to their readers. Watterson expressed the opinion that "Mr. Greeley has as many elements of strength within himself—as many of what the candidates call 'running qualities'—as any candidate who ever asked the suffrage of the American people."[2] Horace White wrote to his paper that "The opinion of the best judges this evening is that the ticket will sweep the country."[3] Bowles wired his assistants on the *Republican* to support the nominations but "not to gush."[4] Later, after reviewing the work of the convention and balancing the strong and the weak points of the ticket in a temperate, judicious

[1] Cf. White, *Trumbull*, 384; Merriam, *Bowles*, II, 187.

[2] Watterson's letter to the *Courier-Journal*, quoted in *Chicago Tribune*, May 9.

[3] *Chicago Tribune*, May 4. The *Tribune's* editorial next day on "The Political Outlook" asserted, "That Horace Greeley will be elected is beyond all doubt."

[4] Merriam, II, 187.

editorial, he frankly stated his disappointment at certain aspects of the situation, but concluded that while Greeley might be beaten, it would "not be an easy job."[5] Halstead made no secret of his disappointment at the defeat of the Adams-Trumbull ticket and at first gave the nominations only a qualified support, but he carefully indicated the strong points of the Liberal candidates and was soon championing them with characteristic enthusiasm.[6]

Other prominent independents promptly accepted the ticket. Senator Trumbull at once sent his congratulations.[7] Governor Palmer promised Greeley 75,000 Republican votes in Illinois.[8] Judge Chase wrote to his old anti-slavery friend: "The country has recognized emphatically your worthiness and ability and public services, and I am personally gratified that the choice of the Convention fell upon one to whom I am in such thorough agreement upon the great questions of amnesty and currency."[9] F. W. Bird indignantly repudiated the insinuation that Greeley's nomination had been secured by improper means.[10]

Schurz, the great Liberal organizer, withheld his final decision for some time. The outcome of the convention on which he had placed such high hopes of political regeneration filled him with sorrow and indignation. "I cannot yet think," he wrote a week later, "of the results of the Cincinnati Convention without a pang."[11] His disappointment

[5] *Springfield Weekly Republican*, May 10. See for similar expressions of confidence in private correspondence, Bowles to Schurz, May 8, *Schurz's Writings*, II, 368; Bowles to Allen, May 11, Merriam, II, 210 f.

[6] See editorials of *Cincinnati Commercial*, quoted in *N. Y. Tribune*, May 6, 7, 8, 11.

[7] *N. Y. Tribune*, May 4, 7; Greeley to Trumbull, May 3, Trumbull MSS. See also Trumbull's friendly letter of advice, May 20, *ibid.*, and Trumbull to Bryant, May 10, White, 386 f.

[8] *Schurz's Writings*, II, 366.

[9] Letter of May 4 in *N. Y. Tribune*, May 7.

[10] Boston *Commonwealth*, June 1. See also his letter to Sumner, May 7. Sumner MSS.

[11] Schurz to Bowles, May 11. *Schurz's Writings*, II, 369.

and misgivings were reflected in his correspondence with the Liberal candidate in which the Senator's tone of superiority in condemning the politicians was matched by the editor's outspokenness in criticizing the reformers. Schurz, while professing the fullest confidence in Greeley's personal honesty, denounced the "huckstering" in the convention by the "politicians of the old stamp." The "appearance of political trickery," he was convinced, "could not fail to shake the whole moral basis of the movement."[12] The great mass of the Germans, who had formed such a strong element among the Liberals, were entirely alienated and he doubted if even he could rally them again.[13] As to his own course, he was undecided. If the old moral force could be restored to the movement he would stop at no difficulties, but he doubted whether "those elements which in a moral sense formed the backbone of the movement" could be "brought into the foreground again so as to inspire confidence."[14] Greeley, in reply, spitefully denounced as "not Republicans, but frauds" the 'Revenue Reformers,' whom he desired Schurz to speak of in future as free-traders, since the other term was a "juggle." He expressed full confidence in his own success and advised Schurz not to be over hasty in his action. "I am confident," he wrote, "that the 'sober second thought' will bring us all into proper relations."[15]

[12] Schurz to Greeley, May 6. *Ibid.*, 363.

[13] *Ibid.*, 364–366.   See also Schurz's letter of May 11, *ibid.*, 371 f.

[14] *Ibid.*, 366–368.

[15] Greeley to Schurz, May 8, Bancroft-Dunning, *Schurz's Political Career*, 350 f.   In a letter, two days later, Greeley acknowledged his appreciation of Schurz's "position and services" and credited him with an intention "to do the right," though his "judgment on important points" differed from Greeley's. *Schurz's Writings*, II, 370 n.   Some weeks later, White got Greeley to admit that he had been wrong in the tone which he had assumed toward Schurz, and to authorize a statement (in the *Tribune*) that he could not answer any more political letters.   White to Schurz, June 9, *ibid.*, 382.

The free-traders, East and West, were generally disaffected. The *Nation*[16] and the *Evening Post*,[17] with their
strong free-trade and civil service convictions, found Greeley
an utter impossibility. The opposition of these papers
was stimulated by the hostility of the editors toward the
Liberal candidate. Godkin had long regarded Greeley
with deep contempt,[18] and Bryant and Godwin held him
in detestation.[19] The German leaders and papers, as
Schurz had informed Greeley, were almost unanimously
estranged.[20] Among the Ohio independents there was
great dissatisfaction. After the adjournment òf the convention the state's delegation, with some others, met at their
Cincinnati headquarters, where the "bargain and sale" of
the politicians was bitterly denounced by original Liberals
like Judge Hoadly. Two or three members, including
General Brinkerhoff, openly repudiated the ticket and resigned from the state executive committee. Others, like
Judge Spaulding, of Cleveland, would support the ticket as

[16] May 9, pp. 297, 300.

[17] May 7.

[18] Ogden, *Godkin*, I, 254–257, 292; II, 62. For Godkin's disgust at
Greeley's nomination, see Godkin to Schurz, May 19, *Schurz's Writings*,
II, 376.

[19] Ogden, *Godkin*, I, 167 f.; Bryant to Trumbull, May 8, White, 386;
Godwin to Schurz, May 28, *ibid.*, 392.

[20] Schurz wrote Greeley: "To the best of my information, my paper
is to-day (May 6) the only German journal in the country that has come
out for the ticket." He had received "piles of German papers which
all sing the same song." *Schurz's Writings*, II, 365. The quotations
in the *N. Y. Tribune* (May 7–11) show the hostility of the leading
German papers. On May 10 Schurz's *Westliche Post* was able to print
favorable comments on the ticket from about twenty western German
papers and a letter of endorsement from Gustave Koerner of Illinois.
See *N. Y. Tribune* editorial, May 11. See also list in *N. Y. Tribune*,
May 21.

a choice of evils, and a few warmly defended the Liberal candidates.[21]

The prestige of the Liberal ticket was further weakened by the outcome of the senatorial election in Connecticut, where the Democrats and Liberal Republicans combined to reëlect Senator Ferry over General Hawley, the choice of the Republican legislative caucus.[22] Liberal and pro-Greeley Democratic papers, counting on Ferry's adhesion, hailed his election as a good omen for a triumphant coalition.[23] But soon after, when Senator Ferry declared his unswerving loyalty to the Republican party and ridiculed the Greeley movement as a "mere mid-summer madness,"[24] the Republican press used the incident to disparage the projected opposition.[25]

Immediately following their defeat at Cincinnati, both in platform and candidates, the reformers, with characteristic confidence in their power to inaugurate an effective political movement off-hand, were planning to put in the field a new ticket that should truly represent their ideas and their standards of statesmanship. The Reunion and Reform convention, as already noted, had provided for a national nominating convention of its own, and this action was approved by leading western Liberals who hoped that the Democrats

[21] *Cincinnati Semi-Weekly Gazette*, May 7; *N. Y. Tribune*, May 6. Judge Hoadly and General Brinkerhoff wrote cards next day (printed in the *Cincinnati Commercial*), expressing the hope that a suitable candidate might be secured from one of the other conventions, especially that contemplated by the Reunion and Reform Association. *N. Y. Tribune*, May 6.

[22] *Annual Cyclopedia*, 1872, p. 222; *Nation*, May 16, 23, pp. 313, 330.

[23] *N. Y. Tribune*, May 15, 16; *Chicago Tribune*, May 16; *Milwaukee News*, May 10; *Mo. Republican*, May 16, 22.

[24] *N. Y. Times*, May 24; editorial in *N. Y. Tribune*, May 25; Schurz to Greeley, May 18, *Schurz's Writings*, II, 374.

[25] Editorial in *N. Y. Times*, May 24. See also editorial in N. Y. *World*, May 27.

would endorse the ticket thus to be presented.[26] Schurz
thought that the bulk of the Germans would "probably
flock to the Reunion and Reform Associations."[27] In
view of the increasing probability of a second Liberal ticket
with a candidate more likely to appeal to the Democratic
convention, Schurz hinted strongly to Greeley that it would
be the part of wisdom for the latter to withdraw from the
field.[28] But the practical-minded *Tribune* chief did not
intend to surrender the long-desired prize at the whim
of visionary reformers. The outlook all over the country,
he replied with some heat, was favorable. The Democratic
convention was "far more likely to adopt and ratify the
Cincinnati ticket" than Schurz was "to support it heartily,"
and he was determined to "accept unconditionally."[29]

So much dissatisfaction with the candidate, in a "party"
without traditions or organization, made inevitable the consideration of another nomination. The first definite move
in this direction came not from the middle western reform
associations but from the members of the Free-Trade
League in the East, acting evidently upon the suggestion
of the *Evening Post* that the selections this time should not
run the risk of the "dangerous machinery of a convention,"
but be left instead to an assembly of "notables."[30] Late
in May, a circular was issued "in behalf of the American
Free-Trade League, and friends of a Revenue Tariff who have
associated or coöperated with it." They deemed it their
duty "to protest in the most emphatic manner against the
betrayal of the Cause of Reform by the recent Convention
at Cincinnati." By the packing of the convention with

[26] Letters of Hoadly and Brinkerhoff to *Cincinnati Commercial*,
quoted in *N. Y. Tribune*, May 6; *Cincinnati Courier* and *Cincinnati
Volksfreund*, quoted in *ibid.*, May 8, 9.

[27] Schurz to Greeley, May 6. *Schurz's Writings*, II, 366.

[28] Schurz to Greeley, May 18, *ibid.*, 373–376.

[29] Greeley to Schurz, May 20, *ibid.*, 377.

[30] Schurz to Godkin, May 20, *ibid.*, 378.

those unfriendly to tariff reform—who had no right to be represented there—protection had triumphed, "and by the nomination of Horace Greeley on this platform they made the abandonment of principle too conspicuous to be mistaken." Free-traders were, therefore, absolved from any further support of the movement. But, although the cause of reform had been betrayed in the convention, there was still hope of accomplishing much by the election of tariff reformers to Congress. Accordingly, all similarly minded were exhorted to make tariff reform the chief issue, and to organize clubs for that end in every county, and thus defeat the politicians. To give a public expression to these views, a call was appended for a meeting at Steinway Hall on May 30, to be presided over by Bryant and addressed by such reformers as Wells and Atkinson.[31]

The Ohio reformers responded in a letter (dated May 27) expressing most hearty agreement with the step taken by the League, and urged that it be followed up by prompt and emphatic action to oppose the election of either Grant or Greeley. They suggested that the forthcoming meeting either nominate new candidates itself or call another meeting, to be held not later than June 27, for that purpose. The signers, headed by Cox, Hoadly, and Stallo, pledged themselves to support any candidate who would represent truly the Reunion and Reform platform.[32] The *Tribune* complained that the Ohioans had put an interpretation upon the meeting which had not yet been given it by its originators.[33]

The Steinway Hall meeting was well attended, whether from mere curiosity, as the *Tribune* unkindly suggested, or from more serious motives. The free-trade leaders from

[31] *N. Y. Tribune*, May 27. The circular was signed by Bryant, Sands, Minturn, Lloyd, Sterne and other prominent members of the League.

[32] *Ibid.*, May 30. This letter was read at the Steinway Hall meeting.

[33] *Idem.*

the City and New England did all the talking.[34] Bryant presided, and speeches were made by Professor Perry, of Williams College, Wells, Atkinson, Simon Sterne[35] and Lloyd. Both Adams and Greeley were applauded when their names were mentioned[36] but the sentiment of the participants was uncompromisingly hostile to the Cincinnati convention and all its works. Wells was the only speaker who did not openly declare his intention to bolt, and he said that he had "been in the woods" ever since the convention. The others denounced in strong and picturesque rhetoric the trickery of the politicians, and, rejecting both Grant and Greeley, held that the free-traders should seek a standard-bearer of their own. Atkinson suggested as a suitable candidate C. F. Adams of Massachusetts, Groesbeck or Cox of Ohio, and, probably out of courtesy to the venerable chairman, Bryant of New York.[37] Before adjourning the meeting adopted resolutions denouncing the work of the Cincinnati convention, ple dging themselves to continue the reform agitation, and empowering the chairman to appoint a committee to aid if possible in securing the nomination of acceptable reform candidates.[38] Such a committee composed of some of the most active free-

[34] Prominent representatives from both parties, like John A. Dix, Charles O'Conor, and John N. Griswold, were on the list of vice-presidents but none of them were present. *N. Y. Times*, May 31.

[35] Sterne claimed that he was the only regular Democrat taking part in the meeting.

[36] The *Tribune's* account of the meeting (May 31) made much of the demonstration for its candidate, but the *Evening Post* (June 4) claimed that Greeley claqueurs of a not very respectable sort were scattered through the audience, but that the real enthusiasm was for Adams. Atkinson wrote to Sumner (June 1) that the marked feature of the meeting was the enthusiasm shown for Adams at every mention of his name.` Sumner MSS.

[37] Bryant considered it necessary to issue a card (July 8) stating that the mention of his name as a presidential candidate was "absurd." Godwin, *Bryant*, II, 323 f.

[38] *N. Y. Tribune*, May 31; *Evening Post*, May 31, June 4.

traders of the City was at once named.[39] But definite action looking to a new ticket was delayed until the assurance of Grant's unanimous renomination by the Republicans removed the last hope of a more acceptable candidate from that party.

Though the regular Republicans ridiculed and belittled the Liberal defection,[40] there was much anxiety in administration circles as to the course of politics, preceding and after the Cincinnati convention. No efforts, financial, managerial, or oratorical were spared to elect the party ticket in the "Spring States."[41] As a counterstroke to the Liberal meeting in Cooper Institute,[42] Grant's supporters in the City, acting with his approval and assistance,[43] had taken the unprecedented step of calling a mass meeting, April 17, to endorse the administration. General Sickles appeared as the chief apologist, and letters of endorsement from Republican congressional delegations were presented.[44] In April when C. F. Adams was being discussed as the probable Liberal candidate, he was offered, through Senator Conkling, the Republican nomination for vice-president.[45] "Everything political, English and American," wrote Mrs. Blaine to her son on May 1, "seems to be in a sort of

[39] J. J. Cisco was chairman, Sands, Minturn, Pell and Lloyd were among the members. *N. Y. Tribune*, May 31.

[40] See typical editorials in the *Boston Advertiser*, Jan. 30, Apr. 1 and Blaine's reassuring letter to his son, Mar. 6, Hamilton, *Blaine* 298. Grant predicted in a letter to Washburne, May 26, that the Liberal ticket would not be kept in the field. He thought that Greeley's nomination had "apparently harmonized the [Republican] party by getting out of it the 'soreheads' and knaves who made all the trouble because they could not control." Grant, *Letters to a Friend*, 69.

[41] Lyford, *Rollins*, 266–270; Oberholtzer, *Cooke*, II, 352.

[42] See above, p. 59 f.

[43] Porter to Clews, Apr. 17, 19, Clews, *Twenty Eight Years in Wall Street*, 319 f.

[44] *N. Y. Times*, Apr. 18; *N. Y. Tribune*, Apr. 18; *Nation*, Apr. 25, p. 265.

[45] Adams, *Adams*, 392.

snarl. Things, I believe, will all come out right. Your father was so impressed with the fatal influence which any concession on the part of Mr. Fish would have on our political situation, that he went in to talk over matters with him Sunday evening. Was there till a very late hour."[46] And again, a fortnight later, she wrote: "And just now people are constantly coming to him [Speaker Blaine] to talk on the presidential question. What can be done with the situation, occupies all heads, and some few good people put their hearts over the bars."[47] Some of Sumner's Republican friends besought him, before and after the Liberal convention, not to abandon the party.[48] But, in spite of all fears for the outcome, there was no serious movement within the party to put up a new candidate. With the advantage of his position, as before noted,[49] Grant's renomination was inevitable[50] and after the Liberal convention probably none of the leading opponents of the administration, except Sumner, expected a different result.

Up to the time of the assembling of the Republican convention, Sumner's course in the campaign had remained in doubt. He was known to be friendly to the Liberal movement, and it was reported in March that he was to preside over its convention.[51] In an interview he spoke highly of the aims and personnel of the approaching gathering,[52] and even went so far, in private, as to draft resolutions for its

[46] Hamilton, *Blaine*, 300.

[47] *Mrs. Blaine's Letters*, I, 126.

[48] Bowen to Sumner, Feb., Sumner MSS.; Wilson to Sumner, Mar. 17, *ibid*. (regretting the "terrible fact" that they are to take different sides in the campaign); Forney to Sumner, May 13, *ibid*. Other appeals of this sort mentioned in Pierce, *Sumner*, IV, 520.

[49] See above, p. 40.

[50] See editorial in the *Boston Advertiser*, Mar. 29, on the general lack of opposition to the selection of Grant delegates.

[51] *Chicago Tribune*, Mar. 16; *Nation*, Mar. 21, p. 177.

[52] *Chicago Tribune*, Mar. 23.

platform.[53] But the most urgent entreaties from close
personal friends who were going into the movement failed
to bring him out openly for the Liberal cause.[54] After the
convention, he pointed out Greeley's strong qualities but
otherwise remained non-committal.[55] He seems still to
have had a fatuous hope of defeating Grant's renomination.[56]

In a speech in the Senate on May 31, just before the Republican convention, while some of the delegates thereto were
in the galleries, he made a last desperate effort to overthrow
the President by a rhetorical onslaught. This "philippic
of the classic type" was a passionate arraignment of Grant
on well-nigh all the charges of public and private misdoings
that had ever been brought against him. A wide range of
history, not to mention the Bible, Virgil, Juvenal, and
Shakespeare, was traversed to illustrate and substantiate
his case, and Stanton's dying condemnation of the General
was dramatically invoked.[57] The speech was answered three

[53] Those concerning equality before the law and the finality of the
war amendments. The resolutions were brought to the convention by
F. W. Bird. Pierce, IV, 519. Liberal leaders hoped to win Sumner by
an emphatic pronouncement on these matters. Wells to Trumbull,
Apr. 22, Trumbull MSS.; Wells to Sumner, Apr. 14, Sumner MSS.;
Atkinson to Sumner, Apr. 11, *ibid.* Sumner evidently wrote a letter in
March to a radical friend in Louisiana to influence Republicans of that
state to go for the Liberals. Greeley obtained this letter and desired
to make it public. T. W. Conway to Sumner, Apr. 2, Sumner MSS.

[54] See letters to Sumner from the following in the Sumner MSS.:
Bowles, Mar. 9, 30, Apr. 14; Scovel, Mar. 22; Reid, Mar. 28; Wilkes,
Apr. 5; Barney, Apr. 6; Robinson, Apr. 9; Bird, Apr. 11; White,
Apr. 13; Atkinson, Apr. 8, 11, 13; Wells, Apr. 14. See summary of
these letters in Pierce, IV, 516.

[55] Pierce, IV, 519.

[56] *Ibid.*, 515, 519. A telegram, dated May 22, from Arkansas Republicans asking if the report was true that Sumner had come out for
Greeley, is endorsed on the back in Sumner's handwriting and was
evidently his reply: "I wait action of Philadelphia Convention hoping
for nominati (sic) that will unite Republican party which Grant
cannot, Charles Sumner." Sumner MSS.

[57] *Sumner's Works,* XV, 83–171; Pierce, IV, 523–526; *Cong. Globe,*
42 Cong., 2 Sess., 4110 ff; *Nation,* June 6, p. 366.

days later, in language equally vigorous and personal, if less classical, by such able advocates as Logan and Carpenter, who fully reassured the friends of the administration.[58] Sumner's "philippic" was generally looked upon as a special plea against Grant's renomination by a man nursing a personal grievance,[59] and while it furnished abundant campaign material of a sort it was utterly futile at so late a day against the solid administration ranks at Philadelphia.[60]

The convention there being wholly controlled by the "machine",[61] a unanimous and enthusiastic support of the President was abundantly manifested. In the opening session eulogistic speeches of the good campaign sort were made by Logan, Gerrit Smith, Morton, Oglesby, and others who all took for granted General Grant's unanimous renomination.[62] The nomination itself was staged with all the proper effects.[63] The substitution of Senator Henry Wilson for Colfax, after a considerable contest, was made at the wish of the President.[64] Colfax had been

[58] *Cong. Globe*, 42 Cong., 2 Sess., Appendix, 522–530, 548–563; Flower, *Carpenter*, 395-401.

[59] Cf. Storey, *Sumner*, 415; *N. Y. Herald*, June 3; *Milwaukee Weekly Sentinel*, June 11; Curtis to Sumner, June 5, Sumner MSS.; Robinson to Sumner, June 24, Robinson, "*Warrington*," 354 f.; *Lippincotts Magazine*, Sept., pp. 352–355. Curtis wrote Norton (June 30) that the speech was "unpardonable." Cary, *Curtis*, 230.

[60] The *Springfield Republican* (weekly, June 21) said that Sumner had made a serious mistake in not making his speech before the Cincinnati convention. See to the same effect, *Atlantic Monthly*, Aug., pp. 253 f.; *Nation*, June 13, p. 381; Pierce, IV, 527.

[61] The *Nation's* correspondent wrote that the convention's work was "so thoroughly cut and dried that it was impossible to be in any way excited over its progress to completion." *Nation*, June 13, p. 388.

[62] *Proceedings of the Phila. Con.*, 10 ff.

[63] Cullom, *Recollections*, 174. The *Nation* (June 13, p. 381) said that the nomination was made "with much elaborate 'enthusiasm.' "

[64] White, 393; Austen, *Tyler*, 74. Bowles wrote to Colfax, Apr. 5: "I find a growing conviction that the people who are running the 'machine' mean to slaughter you at Philadelphia." Hollister, *Colfax*, 371.

opposed by Cameron and had aroused the enmity of Washington newspaper men,[65] while the nomination of the popular Massachusetts leader was considered an appropriate offset in his state to Sumner's defection and a good bid for the labor vote.[66] From the standpoint of the good of the party organization,[67] as well as from that of personal fitness, as it later proved,[68] the change was wise. Colfax apparently took his defeat in good part.[69] The organization, relieved of the disturbing independents, was well united for the campaign. Bowles, with his usual fairness, wrote from the convention: "The republican national convention is claimed by its friends and conceded by its foes, to have proved a great success. Its close to-day was on the whole as brilliant as its opening yesterday."[70] And the *Republican* in its editorial comment admitted that "At present the omens are certainly with Philadelphia."[71]

The renomination of Grant on a platform clearly endorsing protection,[72] afforded the tariff reformers no comfort.[73] If they were to have a ticket to their liking they must act at once. Some of the more zealous and less reasonable among them had still hoped for a new ticket after the Steinway Hall conference.[74] But the more practical members of the élite, like Schurz, Bowles, and White, had now

[65] Hollister, 373; *Nation*, June 13, p. 387.

[66] Hollister, 373; *Nation*, June 13, p. 381.

[67] Cf. *Nation*, June 13, p. 381; "Warrington's" letter in *Springfield Weekly Republican*, June 21.

[68] Cf. Cullom, 175.

[69] Hollister, 375.

[70] *Springfield Weekly Republican*, June 14.

[71] *Idem.*

[72] Stanwood, *Hist. of the Presidency*, 347.

[73] Cf. editorial in *Springfield Weekly Republican*, June 14.

[74] See, for instance, Atkinson to Sumner, June 1, Sumner MSS. Wells wrote to Trumbull (June 15) that the coming conference might have an "important influence" though he did not explain in just what way. Trumbull MSS.

come to the conclusion that the nomination by the free-traders of a new candidate like Adams would simply split up the opposition. They favored Greeley's election in preference to Grant's, and realized that the only hope of such an outcome was in the union of all of the opposition. This they knew would be impossible so long as there was any chance of a new ticket; and the best plan seemed to be the calling of a conference in which all elements of the opposition should be represented to ascertain the relative strength of the Greeley and the anti-Greeley forces.) By this means, they thought, some of the extreme free-traders even might be led to support Greeley as the only available opposition candidate.[75] Schurz, having received assurances of Greeley's good intentions and of his deep respect for the great Liberal mentor,[76] was gradually adapting himself to the idea of supporting the leader whom fate and the politicians had given the cause at Cincinnati.[77] Now he wanted, instead of his "assembly of notables," this all-opposition conference of Democrats and Greeley Liberals as well as of pronounced reformers.[78]

The invitations were to be issued by the leading free-traders in pursuance of the action of the Steinway Hall meeting.[79] On June 6, the day of Grant's renomination, letters were sent out from New York City, signed by Schurz, Cox, Bryant, Ottendorfer, and Jacob Brinkerhoff, to

[75] Schurz to Grosvenor, June 5, *Schurz's Writings*, II, 379–381; White to Trumbull, June 13, Trumbull MSS.

[76] White to Schurz, June 9, 15, *Schurz's Writings*, II, 382 f.

[77] In his letter to Greeley of May 11 he was giving advice about the letter of acceptance. *Ibid.*, 372. In his letter of June 5 to Grosvenor he said that if he tried to accept the ticket then "the words would stick in my throat." But he would do his best "when the issues are finally made up." *Ibid.*, 381.

[78] *Nation* editorial, June 27, p. 416. See also Governor Randolph's speech in the New Jersey Democratic state convention on the origin of the Fifth Avenue gathering. *N. Y. Tribune*, June 27.

[79] *Nation*, June 13, p. 381; see above, p. 113.

about two hundred Liberals and Democrats in all parts of
the country, inviting them to meet in conference at the
Fifth Avenue Hotel on June 20 "for the purpose of consultation, and to take such action as the situation of things
may require." The committee professed to deem it necessary that all the elements of opposition be united for a
common effort in the presidential election.[80] Youthful
members of the Free Trade League, especially the Lloyd
brothers, were most active in making the arrangements.[81]
Nevertheless the *New York Tribune*, assuming that the
aim of the conference would be to consider the best means
of uniting the opposition, and that it could reach but one
conclusion—the necessity of supporting Greeley to defeat
Grant—showed an entirely friendly attitude.[82]

About one hundred persons from twenty states attended
the Fifth Avenue meeting.[83] The *Tribune* analyzed the
gathering as thirty Greeley men, fifteen "violent anti-
Greeley men" and the rest "open to conviction."[84] The
leading independents from New England, New York, and
the Middle West were all on hand.[85] Among the prominent Democrats in attendance were ex-Governor Pillsbury of Maine, ex-Governor English of Connecticut, ex-
Governor Randolph and Senator Stockton of New Jersey,
ex-Secretary Stuart of Virginia, ex-Governor Graham of

[80] *Annual Cyclopedia*, 1872, p. 779.   Copies of this letter are in both
the Sumner and the Trumbull MSS.   The notice was given a conspicuous place in the New York dailies.

[81] Lloyd, *Lloyd*, I, 33, 37.

[82] *N. Y. Tribune* editorials, June 15, 18, 20; Reid's comment on Watterson's article in *Century Magazine*, LXXXV, 44.

[83] *N. Y. Tribune*, June 21.   Seven southern states were represented.

[84] *Ibid.*, June 22.

[85] The *Tribune* claimed (June 22) that a large number of young men
from the City were brought in to applaud the speakers of the Free Trade
League.   Cox was chairman, Bryant vice-president and H. D. Lloyd
secretary.

North Carolina, B. H. Hill and H. W. Hillard of Georgia.[86]
Probably the most pronounced Greeley men present were
William Dorsheimer of New York and J. B. Grinnell of
Iowa.[87] Senator Fenton was stopping at the hotel and his
rooms were filled with politicians to whom reports were
brought from time to time of what was going forward in the
convention, although the proceedings were supposed to be
entirely secret.[88]

It was soon apparent that the conferees were overwhelmingly opposed to the launching of a new ticket. Senator
Trumbull opened the formal discussion with a strong plea
for a union on Greeley as the only hopeful means of defeating Grant.[89] To get more directly the sentiment of the
different sections represented, the states were called upon in
alphabetical order. The responses indicated clearly the
general situation: the southern Liberals and Democrats
were solidly and enthusiastically for Greeley; the promoters
of the Liberal movement in the Middle West, with the exception of certain prominent German leaders and ultra-
free-traders, would support the Cincinnati ticket; of the
eastern representatives, all but one or two Democrats and
all of the Liberals not connected with the League advocated
union under the Greeley banner. But the pronounced
free-traders of New England, New York, and Ohio were as
hostile as ever to the proposed mis-alliance.[90]

Schurz made the last and most notable speech of the conference. He showed conclusively that it was now too late
to think of a more acceptable ticket. Such a ticket would
not be endorsed by the Democratic convention, and their
only hope of defeating Grant was in uniting on the candi-

[86] See list in *ibid.*, June 21.

[87] The *Tribune* said (June 18) that so far as it knew none of the "prom-
nent friends" of Greeley had been invited.

[88] *Ibid.*, June 22.

[89] *Ibid.*, June 21; White, 391.

[90] *N. Y. Tribune*, June 21, 22; *Evening Post*, June 25.

dates that they had in the field. Personally, he confessed frankly, he would have favored a "more conservative ticket," but he "felt at this time with such public interests at stake, men must seek, not personal ideas, but practical good, and the nearest practical good they could accomplish." The foremost of the "public considerations" which determined his course at this time, he said, was the situation at the South. The people of that section were manifesting a desire for a thorough reconciliation through this movement. They felt that the Liberal movement meant for them enfranchisement and freedom from further oppressions. Under no circumstances could he take a step which would aid in continuing the present oppressive administration and in repelling the sincere advance toward a reconciliation of the sections.[91] To his reform friends, who were inclined to carp at him for supporting a man like Greeley, he gave the same explanation of his course—the exigencies of the South.[92] He was entirely correct in holding that the only hope of defeating the Republicans and of hastening full home rule at the South was in uniting the opposition solidly upon the Liberal ticket. No one was more disappointed at the outcome of the Cincinnati convention, but, with his convictions regarding the tendencies of the present administration, his most honorable course was to play the game to the finish. At any rate, it was not for the visionary, inefficient doctrinaries to upbraid him for

[91] Summary of speech in *N. Y. Tribune*, June 21. For a critical and not altogether fair review of it, see *Nation*, June 27, pp. 413, 416.

[92] Schurz to Godkin, June 23, *Schurz's Writings*, II, 384. Schurz, years later, made this statement regarding his policy in this conference: "I realized that it was a fine chance to make a protest and a declaration of principles, but loyalty to the bolting South forced me to support Greeley." Lloyd, I, 35. For a reflective estimate by a contemporary of the influence of Schurz's speech, see Brinkerhoff, *Recollections*, 220.

inconsistency. If, as Schurz cuttingly told them,[93] they had gone to Cincinnati and expended only a portion of the energy there that they were now devoting to protesting against the convention's action, they might have saved the day.

The resolutions submitted to the conference by Parke Godwin, a reformer of the type to which Schurz referred, furnish an excellent example of the advanced reforms demanded by this group and of their wholly unworkable plans. The chief of Godwin's demands were: a reorganization of the finances with a revenue tariff and a return to specie payments; a thorough reform of the civil service; a substitution for the corrupt and oligarchical national convention of "spontaneous nominations," and the direct election of president and vice-president; the abolition of the franking privilege; that since the Liberal candidates lacked the requisite qualifications to deal with the great problems that would confront the next administration, there be substituted for them Charles Francis Adams and William S. Groesbeck; and finally, that the persons present should pledge themselves to labor with all their might for the success of this new ticket. To give unity to their efforts and to distinguish them from other political organizations, they were to "assume the name of the American Democratic-Republican party."[94]

No action was taken on Godwin's resolutions, but after the conference the radical free-traders made a demonstration hardly less quixotic. Following Schurz's speech, Cox sought to restore good feeling among the reformers by urging them, since it was likely that they would act together either in the present campaign or in future ones, not to indulge in extreme criticisms that must tend to

[93] See his opening remarks in his speech at the conference, *N. Y. Tribune*, June 21.
[94] *Ibid.*, June 22.

embarrass their hearty and harmonious coöperation.[95]
A resolution was then adopted to adjourn the conference
sine die, "without any further expression of opinion than
those had from the individual members."[96]   But as the
delegates were leaving, Judge Stallo announced a meeting
next day of those opposed to the present action.[97]   This
rump convention was attended by only about twenty-five,
more than half of whom were from New York or Ohio.[98]
With all inharmonious elements excluded, their unanimity
was perfect; they could denounce protectionists to their
hearts' content.   Resolutions were adopted containing an
emphatic statement of the reforms called for in the Missouri
Liberal platform, and strongly condemning both Grant and
Greeley.   As an especial shot at politicians and existing
parties, one of their resolutions declared "That undue devotion to party has already greatly damaged the republic,
and we now engage ourselves to discountenance, in every
possible way, the despotism of party organization, and the
abject submission of voters to the dictates of party politicians."   Not satisfied with the declaration of their principles, they proceeded to nominate a ticket of their own with
William S. Groesbeck, of Ohio, a prominent independent
Democrat, for president, and Frederick Law Olmsted, the

[95] *N. Y. Tribune* June 21.

[96] *Idem.*

[97] *Idem.*

[98] The *N. Y. Tribune* (June 22) gives a list of twenty-two of the
"most prominent."   The best known names were Ottendorfer, Lloyd,
Seamon, Sterne, and Bacon of New York; Atkinson of Massachusetts;
Dexter, Oliver, Stallo, and Collins of Ohio.   Cox left after a vain attempt to dissuade the meeting from taking any action that would further
disorganize the opposition.   The *Springfield Weekly Republican* (June
28) said that these men were the least influential of those participating
in the Fifth Avenue conference.   The *Chicago Tribune* (June 25) said
that the second conference was composed of six Democrats and eight
Republicans, the latter being "respectable gentlemen, indeed, but too
transcendental for this age of the world."

noted New York artist, for vice-president.[99]   The administration press spoke with great respect of the new ticket,[100]
welcoming any movement that promised a further division
of the opposition, while the Bourbon *Chicago Times* warmly
advocated Groesbeck's endorsement by the Democrats.[101]
But the reformers' ticket had but a brief existence.   The
next day Olmsted issued a card declining the honor,[102]
and about a month later, Groesbeck came out for Greeley.[103]

Thus, in spite of its failure to conciliate all of the reformers,[104] the Fifth Avenue conference had most favorable
results for Greeley.   The Liberals were united in his
support so far as that could be brought about.[105]   The conference had afforded the opportunity for the great Liberal
leader, Schurz, to come out squarely for the Cincinnati

[99] *N. Y. Tribune*, June 22; Lloyd, I, 36. For an appreciative estimate of the work of this gathering, see *Nation*, June 27, p. 413.

[100] See editorials in the *N. Y. Times*, June 22, and the *Albany Evening
Journal*, June 22.

[101] *Chicago Times*, June 24.

[102] *N. Y. Tribune*, June 24.

[103] *Ibid.*, July 30; *Nation*, Aug. 1, p. 65. Greeley wrote to Glancy
Jones, June 27: "I would not crowd Groesbeck. He will be all right."
Jones, *Jones*, II, 154.

[104] The *Evening Post* (June 25) deplored the lack of enthusiasm for
reform shown by the southerners and thought that "the meeting furnished a rather disheartening illustration of the partisan condition of
politics, and of the profound want of respect even among those calling
themselves reformers, for the animating spirit of reform, in other words,
principle." The *Nation* strongly criticized Schurz for going over to
Greeley. See editorial, June 27, p. 416. Henry D. Lloyd wrote, June
24, that the reformers made a great mistake in following Schurz and not
striking out for themselves. "We tried once more to unite fire and gun-
powder without an explosion and succeeded as well as we deserved."
Lloyd, I, 37.

[105] Cf. *Springfield Weekly Republican*, June 28; *Atlantic Monthly*,
Aug., p. 255.

ticket.[106]   Greeley's paper could see nothing but good to the cause of its candidate from the independent demonstration. It considered very lightly the defection of the Free Trade Leaguers "who went to Cincinnati thoroughly convinced that the salvation of the country depended upon the immediate abolition of the duty on pig iron, a mere economic question, a question of detail for a ways and means committee."[107]   But the *Tribune* was greatly rejoiced at the overwhelming sentiment expressed for the Liberal candidates and particularly the pledges of support, which the occasion had called forth, from Schurz and Trumbull. "The meeting has harmonized the discordant element and largely conquered the discontent. To-day the Liberal movement is united and confident with Lyman Trumbull and Carl Schurz at its head."[108]

The sentiments expressed in the Fifth Avenue conference foreshadowed the action of the reform group of the Liberals. The editorial "quadrilateral" supported Greeley faithfully throughout the campaign.[109] The *Springfield Republican*, the most discriminating of their journals, declared at the outset that it was not a "Greeley organ" and that "while celebrating his many and great virtues, it will not conceal his few and conspicuous vices. It will strive to present him as he is, and to contrast him with Gen. Grant as he is, and not to paint either as he is not."[110]   Bowles, in the main, seems to have lived up to this ideal of campaign

---

[106] The *Christian Union* (June 26, p. 10) observed: "Indeed, it looks to us . . . as if the conference had come together—like the famous German dwarfs of the fairy story, to hump their backs to form a bridge upon which their countryman, good Carl Schurz, could walk over to Mr. Greeley. He is safe over!" Cf. Watterson, "Humor and Tragedy of the Greeley Campaign," 41.

[107] *N. Y. Tribune*, June 26.

[108] *Ibid.*, June 21.

[109] See editorial on "The Independent Press" in *Golden Age*, Nov. 9.

[110] *Springfield Weekly Republican*, June 14.

journalism remarkably well.[111]   Schurz[112] and Trumbull[113] both entered actively into the campaign, and made a number of effective speeches.   Those of the former were, as his biographers put it, "naturally against Grant rather than for Greeley."[114]   But he rendered good service to the cause where it was sorely needed—among the German element— and won the deep gratitude of the Liberal candidate.[115] Other prominent independents, like Grosvenor in Missouri,[116] Koerner in Illinois,[117] Brinkerhoff in Ohio,[118] Judge Selden in New York,[119] and Bird in Massachusetts,[120] were among the active Liberal campaigners.   Judge Chase throughout the campaign expressed his preference for Greeley whenever he had opportunity.[121]   Sumner, as will be noted,[122] came out for Greeley rather late in the campaign.

On the other side, the *Nation*,[123] the *Evening Post*[124] and the *Atlantic Monthly*[125] supported Grant, frankly as a choice

[111] Cf. Merriam, II, 193.

[112] See his St. Louis speech of July 22, in his *Writings*, II, 392 ff. Greeley wrote to Glancy Jones soon after the Fifth Avenue conference (June 24): "Do not distrust Schurz.   He is all right."   Jones, *Jones*, II, 154.

[113] White, 394–399.

[114] Bancroft-Dunning, *Schurz's Political Career*, 352.

[115] Greeley to Schurz, Nov. 10.   *Schurz's Writings*, II, 443.

[116] See his speech at the Fifth Avenue conference in *N. Y. Tribune*, June 21.

[117] Koerner, *Memoirs*, II, 560 ff.

[118] Brinkerhoff, 222.

[119] Campaign speeches in *N. Y. Tribune*, Aug. 19, Oct. 21.

[120] *Nation*, Aug. 29, p. 129; Oct. 24, p. 258.

[121] Schuckers, *Chase*, 593; Warden, *Chase*, 734; Hooper to Sumner, July 2, Sumner MSS.   Galusha A. Grow's biographers say that Grow "gave Greeley his moral but not his active support."   DuBois and Mathews, *Grow*, 274.

[122] See below, p. 155.

[123] *Nation*, June 27, pp. 414, 416; July 11, p. 20; Aug. 15, p. 100; Aug. 22, p. 116; Oct. 17, p. 244.

[124] *Evening Post* editorial, Oct. 25.

[125] *Atlantic Monthly*, July, p. 127 f.; Aug., p. 256.

of evils. The German press was, for the most part, never reconciled to Greeley.[126] Matthews [127] and Hoadly[128] went back to the Republicans. Stallo refused to vote for either candidate,[129] and Cox would take no part in the canvass, as he considered that there must be a complete reorganization of parties before the needed reforms could be secured.[130] The bulk of the New England independents,[131] especially the "Adams men," and practically all of the leading members of the Free Trade League[132] in New York finally opposed the Liberal ticket.

[126] Statements of German editors in the Fifth Avenue conference, *N. Y. Tribune*, June 21; *Staats Zeitung*, quoted in *ibid.*, Sept. 7, 20; *Evening Post*, Oct. 1.

[127] Warden, 732; *N. Y. Times*, Aug. 3.

[128] Campaign speech, quoted in *N. Y. Tribune*, Aug. 26.

[129] St. Louis speech, quoted in *Milwaukee Weekly Sentinel*, Sept. 24.

[130] Cox to Sumner, Aug. 3, Sumner MSS.

[131] See editorials criticizing the attitude of the independents in the *Springfield Weekly Republican*, June 28, Oct. 18; Robinson, "*Warrington*," 136, 354, 355, 357; Adams, *Adams*, 392. An excellent statement of the point of view and ideas of the New England independents is given in the speech of C. F. Adams, Jr., at Quincy, Sept. 30, and printed in the *Springfield Weekly Republican*, Oct. 4.

[132] Mahlon Sands, the secretary of the League, in a letter to the *World*, Nov. 8, wrote: "I do not know of a single free-trade delegate to Cincinnati from this State, with the exceptions above stated [Selden and Dorsheimer] who voted for Mr. Greeley or even said a word in his favor." N. Y. *World*, Nov. 11.

CHAPTER V

THE DEMOCRATIC-LIBERAL COALITION

From the more or less definite assurance of Democratic leaders,[1] the Liberals, when they went into their national convention, were relying on the support of that party. Had they named a relatively unobjectionable candidate there could have been little doubt of a harmonious coalition, but the outcome at Cincinnati unsettled the situation. Greeley, while on most issues as much on common ground with the Democrats as any pronounced Republican would have been, had by his peculiar style of journalism tended to give an exaggerated emphasis to his opposition.[2] But the party had made too great calculations on the movement and done too much to promote it to withdraw easily at this late day. Their main reliance of carrying the election had

[1] John Van Buren, Governor Hoffman's secretary, assured Wells in a letter, April 20: "One thing rely upon—you need do nothing at Cincinnati except with reference to drawing Republicans into the movement. Disregard the Democrats. The movement of that side will take care of itself. There will be no cheating nor holding back on their side. They will go over in bulk and with a will." Quoted by Wells to Trumbull, Apr. 22, Trumbull MSS., and by Trumbull to White, Apr. 24, White, *Trumbull*, 379. See also letters of Marble and Belmont to Schurz, Apr. 23, White, 373.

[2] Cf. Blaine, *Twenty Years of Cong.*, II, 524; Rhodes, VI, 430 f. R. B. Hayes wrote in his diary, May 6, that if the Democrats adopted Greeley they might win by a large majority, but he thought that an attempt to secure his endorsement would cause a dissent in the party that would make possible Grant's reëlection. Williams, *Hayes*, I, 367. Grant wrote to Washburne, May 26: "I predict that Greeley will not even be a candidate when the election comes off. The Democrats are not going to take him, and his following in the Republican ranks is not sufficient to make up an electoral ticket, nor is it composed of respectability enough to put on such a ticket." Grant, *Letters to a Friend*, 69.

been in uniting with the discontented Republicans, and they were well assured that this element would support Grant rather than a straight Democratic candidate.[3] Under these circumstances, the party's leaders would not act precipitately. A. K. McClure, after the Liberal nominations had been made, "was surprised to find before midnight that a number of the Democratic leaders there sent out instructions to their States to hold themselves in readiness to accept the Liberal Republican ticket."[4] The Democratic national committee met in New York a few days later and fixed the time and place for their national convention, but took no further action.[5]

The most prompt and unanimous endorsement of Greeley came from the South. The abuses of radical rule were felt, of course, most grievously in this section, and there now seems to have been little confidence in the Democratic party, acting alone, as an agent of deliverance. Greeley's sympathetic and conciliatory attitude toward the South since the close of the war had done much to counteract the resentment at his course in the past and to create a kindly feeling for him in that section.[6] And certain southern leaders, who had no enthusiasm or respect for Greeley himself, accepted his candidacy as a possible opportunity for the South to extricate herself from her discredited position.[7] Prominent Democratic leaders all over the South early declared for coalition[8] and by far the greater number of influential south-

[3] Blaine, II, 525.

[4] McClure, *Old Time Notes*, II, 336.

[5] Some of the members, in newspaper interviews, commented on the political outlook in their states. *Chicago Tribune*, May 9.

[6] Cf. Blaine, II, 525; Watterson, "Humor and Tragedy of the Greeley Campaign," 40; Ross, "Horace Greeley and the South, 1865–1872."

[7] Lamar to Rumelin, May 6, July 15, Mayes, *Lamar*, 170 f.

[8] See letters in *Greenville Enterprise*, May 29; Harrell, *Brooks and Baxter War*, 119; Harrell's letter in N. Y. *World*, May 14; B. H. Hill's speech at Atlanta in June, Hill, *Hill*, 350 ff. See also Ingersoll, *Greeley*, 547 and an editorial in the *Springfield Weekly Republican*, May 10.

ern papers advocated that policy.[9] Roger Pryor, returning from a southern trip a couple of weeks after the Liberal convention, reported that the southern delegates would come to the Democratic convention solidly for Greeley.[10] The only marked opposition from this section developed in Georgia, where the Stephens brothers and Robert Toombs bitterly opposed an endorsement of Greeley, but even here the coalition sentiment prevailed.[11]

In the West, with the exception of the German element of the party, the Liberal nominations were, on the whole, apparently well received. Henry Watterson, the Democratic member of the "quadrilateral" of editors, in his report of the convention to his *Courier-Journal*, made a strong plea for Democratic endorsement. Greeley's exceptional 'running qualities' were set forth at length, and the impotence of the Democrats acting by themselves was warningly emphasized. "No man in himself," Watterson had the audacity to assert, "could possess fewer objectionable traits to the Democrats, who will take him, if they take the movement which put him in the field, with real enthusiasm." It would have required no little effort, he was convinced, to overcome the Democratic prejudice for a candidate like Adams or Trumbull, but despite all the politicians, the masses of the Democrats would "go it with a whoop" for Greeley. In spite of this assurance, however,

[9] See editorials in the *Southern Recorder*, May 7, 21; *Greenville Enterprise*, May 8, 15; *Charleston Courier*, quoted in the *Greenville Enterprise*, May 22; *Richmond Whig and Advertiser*, May 10, quoting a dozen Virginia papers all conditionally for Greeley; lists of southern papers supporting the Liberal ticket in *N. Y. Tribune*, May 10, 11, 18, and in the *Springfield Weekly Republican*, May 10. The N. Y. *World*, with its strong anti-Greeley bias, thus analyzed the southern press (May 14): S. C., Tenn., and Mo. enthusiastically and almost unanimously for Greeley; Ga., N. C., La., Md., Del. for a straight Democratic ticket; Va., Ala., Ky. divided.

[10] Quoted in San Francisco *Evening Bulletin*, May 22.

[11] Avery, *Ga.*, 501; Hill, 65, 350 ff.; Phillips, *Toombs*, 267.

Watterson made his final appeal to expediency. "On the whole, the Democracy cannot do better than to prepare to support them [Greeley and Brown], for it requires but little foresight to see that it is that or four more years of Grant and Grantism, misrule at the North and bayonet rule at the South, with no end of dangerous possibilities."[12] William Allen, of Ohio, the old Jacksonian war-horse, was no less enamored of the editor of the *Tribune*. "From the beginning of the movement," he told a reporter, "I considered Greeley of all candidates named, the one around whom the masses of the Democratic party could most easily rally, and they would with rare exceptions rally around him, and elect him, if the leaders pursued the part of wisdom by avoiding a nomination at Baltimore."[13]   Certain leading party organs of the Middle West hoisted the Liberal ticket immediately, subject to the action of their national convention,[14] and only two influential sheets stood out up to the last against a coalition.[15]   The way in which Democratic sentiment rapidly came around to the Liberal candidates is well shown in Wisconsin. The foremost Democratic paper in that state (the *Milwaukee News*) was at first strongly inclined to think that the Democrats would make separate nominations,[16] but it requested to be informed of the party sentiment in all sections of the state.[17]   The result of its canvass, reported a week later, was that all but four of the Democratic papers in the state were favor-

[12] Watterson's letter printed in *Chicago Tribune*, May 9.

[13] Interview in *Cincinnati Enquirer*, quoted in *N. Y. Tribune*, May 14.

[14] Besides the *Courier-Journal*, the *Missouri Republican*, May 4, and the *Cincinnati Enquirer*, *St. Louis Times*, and *Indianapolis Sentinel*, quoted in the *N. Y. Tribune*, May 10 and in the *N. Y. Herald*, May 11. The *Madison Democrat* (May 4) put Greeley and Brown at the head of its column under the caption, "Reform Candidates."

[15] *Chicago Times* and Detroit *Free Press*, quoted in *N. Y. Tribune*, May 18.

[16] *Milwaukee News*, May 4.

[17] *Ibid.*, May 5.

able to coalition, and of the members of the central committee expressing an opinion, four were for Greeley, two
opposed. The letters received were about five to one for
the Liberal candidates, and in nearly every case a willingness was expressed to abide by the action of the national
convention.[18] In Michigan a meeting of the Democratic
association at Detroit, May 21, declared in favor of "harmonizing the action of the Liberal Republican and Democratic parties in the coming election."[19] Some time before
the Baltimore convention, the predominant sentiment of
the western Democratic leaders was for united action.[20]
A few recalcitrants, like Daniel Voorhees,[21] of Indiana, were
not sufficient to counteract this tendency.

But the real Democratic opposition to Greeley came
from the states of New York, New Jersey, Pennsylvania,
and especially Delaware in which the spirit of Bourbon Democracy seems at this time to have been most pronounced.
The Washington *Patriot*, which claimed to be the official
party organ, complained bitterly at first that Greeley's
administration would be certain to be radical, and that
there would be no advantage in changing from one set of
Republican managers to another, but it refrained from advising the party as to the course it should follow.[22] The
next month it left the matter to the national convention
whose decision would be "obligatory."[23] The New York
World was by far the strongest and most persistent oppo-

[18] *Milwaukee News*, May 12. In less than a fortnight (May 24) this
paper was strongly advocating the acceptance of the Liberal candidates
and platform.

[19] Dilla, *Politics of Mich.*, 138; *N. Y. Tribune*, May 25.

[20] Kerr to Trumbull, June 16, Trumbull MSS.; *Nation*, June 20, p.
397.

[21] See account of his opposition speech in Congress in N. Y. *World*
May 14 and his speech at Terre Haute, reported in *N. Y. Tribune*, May
27.

[22] Washington *Patriot*, May 8, 9.

[23] *Ibid.*, June 19.

nent of coalition. For a decade past the *World* had been contending with its Republican rival with all the bitter personalities that characterized the journalism of the period and had never failed to denounce the ideas and hold up to ridicule the political aspirations of the editor of the *Tribune*. It seemed, therefore, like carrying the plea of party expediency too far to ask this organ of conservative Democracy to champion the candidacy of Horace Greeley. Marble, in the South at the time of the nomination, wired his paper to oppose Greeley,[24] and this it proceeded to do in the most thorough manner. His nomination was greeted as that of "the most conspicuous and heated opponent of the Democratic party that could be found in the whole country."[25] The paper promised to be bound by the action of the Democratic national convention, but in the meantime pledged itself to do everything that it could to prevent Greeley's endorsement.[26] The *World* thus became the centre of the anti-coalition sentiment, collecting and displaying expressions of Democratic opposition to the Liberal ticket from all over the country.[27] But its own contributions to this end surpassed them all. The epithets of abuse that Greeley had so freely hurled against the Democrats in times past were reprinted from old *Tribune* files,[28] while his present overtures to the party were contemptuously ridiculed.[29] The *Tribune's* support of certain radical southern measures and its opposition to the Missouri Liberal movement

[24] So stated in *World* editorial, May 25.

[25] *Ibid.*, May 4.

[26] *Ibid.*, May 7.

[27] For examples, see *ibid.*, May 11, 27, June 5.

[28] *Ibid.*, June 6. The *World* declared (June 7) that by the time of the Baltimore convention not much of Greeley's record would remain to be canvassed by the Republican papers, and that Democrats should not be moved by anything Republicans could say against him in the remainder of the canvass, if the convention accepted him.

[29] *Ibid.*, May 23, 28.

of 1870 were used to alienate conservative northern support.[30]
A still less exalted line of argument was that in the distribution of offices by Greeley the Democrats would fare but
slimly.[31] Greeley's availability was challenged; he had
always proved a weak candidate, and his election for president was utterly unthinkable.[32] He was not the sort of
candidate that a discriminating voter—least of all a discriminating Democrat—could support. "Wherever in any city
of the State you find a ring organ, you find a supporter of
Mr. Greeley, a candidate for whom the honest, thinking
mass of Democrats could no more vote than a Jew could be
persuaded to eat pork, or the Union League Club to hang
upon its walls a portrait of Jefferson Davis."[33]

The *World's* recalcitrant attitude was roundly denounced
by Democratic papers eager for coalition, a considerable
number of them charging it with working deliberately in
the interest of Grant.[34] In the New York Democratic state
convention, May 15, which attracted wide attention,[35] the
influence of the pro-Greeley, machine element prevailed.
The Cincinnati platform was heartily endorsed, and, while
a resolution to instruct for Greeley and Brown was tabled,
it was understood that the delegation would vote as a unit

[30] *World*, May 27, 30, June 12.

[31] The *World* said editorially (June 15) that if there was any possibility of Greeley's election he ought to give assurances that he would
appoint a full Democratic cabinet, no more than the interior department,
at most, should be conceded to the Liberals. But (it said) it was
generally understood that Greeley desired Adams for the state department, Fenton for the treasury, Trumbull for attorney general, possibly
Montgomery Blair for postmaster general, and John Cochrane for collector of the port of New York.

[32] *Ibid.*, May 15, 24, 29.

[33] *Ibid.*, May 18. Cf. *Ibid.*, May 20, 29.

[34] *Ibid.*, May 22, 25, 29 (quoting charges of this sort); *Richmond Whig
and Advertiser*, May 14; *Mo. Republican*, June 6; *St. Louis Times*,
quoted in *People's Tribune*, May 29.

[35] See *Chicago Tribune*, May 17.

for the Liberal candidates.[36]   The more eminent representatives of the party in the state were left off the delegation,
which was composed largely of the ring element.[37]   Even
Belmont, though the national chairman, was not given a
vote, by reason, as he claimed, of his supposed connection
with the *World*.[38]   The *World* charged that the convention's
action was in accordance with a bargain between the Tam-
many-Fenton Republicans and the ring Democrats, by
which, after Greeley's nomination was secured at Cincinnati,
he was to be endorsed by the Democrats of the state, and
in return the Republican legislature was to stifle reform
measures in order to give Governor Hoffman the opportunity
to gain sufficient prestige by his vetoes to win the senator-
ship.[39]   The true party sentiment in the state was held to be
strongly antagonistic to Greeley.[40]

But the leading Democrats in New York, however much
chagrin they might feel at the miscarriage of their plans,
considered that the best policy now was to go on with the
coalition program.   August Belmont, who had served faithfully for the past dozen years as the national chairman,
wrote that while Greeley was to him "the most objectionable person whom the Liberals could select," he was of the
opinion that the best policy now was to endorse the Liberal
candidates and platform.   He thought, too, that this was
the general sentiment of the party in the state.[41]   Samuel
J. Tilden thought that the movement had been so long encouraged by Democratic leaders and that the party had

[36] *N. Y. Tribune*, May 16; Albany *Argus*, May 16.

[37] Cf. Alexander, *Political Hist. of N. Y.*, III, 287–289.

[38] Belmont to Woolley, May 21, reprinted in N. Y. *World*, June 8,
from *Cincinnati Enquirer*.

[39] *Ibid.*, May 17.   The *Nation* (May 30, p. 345) thought that, while
Greeley could not be a party to such a scheme, the character of his supporters and of the managers of the Democratic state convention, as well
as the course of events thus far, lent color to such a story.

[40] N. Y. *World*, May 18, 25.

[41] Belmont to Woolley, May 21, N. Y. *World*, June 8.

come so to count upon it that it was too late for them to
back out.[42] Veteran Democrats like Horatio Seymour[43]
and Fernando Wood[44] also came over to Greeley before the
Baltimore convention. But there were some old-time leaders who found it hard or impossible to support their erst-
while vilifier. Thus John J. Taylor, a dominant leader of
the party in his section of the state, whose congressional
career had been cut short by his support of the Kansas-
Nebraska bill,[45] protested strongly, in a letter to Tilden,
against the proposed action. Greeley's endorsement, he
was certain, would so divide the Democrats as to cause
defeat when success was within their reach "by a judicious
nomination either wholly Democratic or partly and princi-
pally Liberal Republican." He thought that the party
might well unite on Trumbull, Adams, Davis, Cox, and
even, in last resort, Sumner; but he feared that he could
not maintain his self-respect and vote for Greeley. Taylor
suggested as a most acceptable combination, in case a
straight Democratic ticket seemed inadvisable, Trumbull
with a reform Democrat, like Tilden himself, as running
mate. He was not too much of a "Bourbon" to support
"with pleasure" a ticket of that sort. "I care nothing for
the issues that are passed," he concluded earnestly, if not
altogether ingenuously, "but Mr. Greeley is directly against

[42] Tilden to Casserly, July 3, Tilden, *Letters*, I, 310. In declining to
act as a vice-president of the Steinway Hall meeting Tilden had stated
that he preferred Greeley to Grant. Tilden to Sands, May 29, *ibid.*,
304.

[43] *N. Y. Tribune*, May 21. Greeley wrote to Glancy Jones, June 24:
"Tilden is heartily with us and at work. So is Hancock. So is Seymour." Jones, *Jones*, II, 154.

[44] Wood to Sumner, June 29, Sumner MSS.

[45] Alexander, II, 250. In 1858 when Taylor was the Democratic
candidate for lieutenant governor, the *Tribune* said editorially (Sept.
17, 1858) that, after the discredit that Taylor had gained by his support
of the Nebraska bill, it would be disappointed if he did not run behind
his ticket.

us upon the great living issues, those issues which began with our government and must last as long as it lasts. He has not besides the qualities that fit for the presidency, but others which would make him the prey of the designing and corrupt."[46] All the persuasions of life-long political friends could not bring Charles O'Conor, at this time or later, to support a former political foe whom he regarded as a "tenderhearted Moloch, whose life-long mission of hate has filled the land with fratricidal slaughter of the white race," and whose "chief passion" was a "love of éclat."[47] But such protesting voices,[48] like that of the *World*, were drowned amid the general cry of the politicians for success at any price.

In the Pennsylvania state convention, May 30–31, there was considerable sentiment shown, especially by the delegates representing Democratic strongholds, for a straight party nomination at Baltimore,[49] and their resolutions contained the steadfast party declaration that "the Democracy of Pennsylvania can find no better platform upon which to stand than the great leading principles enunciated in the inaugural address of President Jefferson and the farewell address of the immortal Jackson; upon these two great state papers we plant ourselves and enter the contest of 1872."[50] But a considerable majority of the delegates present were for Greeley and a majority of those selected for the national convention were known to favor coalition.[51]

---

[46] Taylor to Tilden, July 13. Tilden, *Letters*, I, 306 f. For similar sentiments, see J. W. Harper to Marble, Aug. 12, Harper, *House of Harper*, 305; Wheeler, *Sixty Years of American Life*, 96.

[47] O'Conor to Tilden, Aug. 24, Bigelow, *Tilden*, I, 218.

[48] In Massachusetts Robert C. Winthrop, who had never before supported a Republican ticket, declared for Grant in preference to Greeley. See Winthrop to Clifford, Aug. 8, Winthrop, *Winthrop*, 278.

[49] *N. Y. Tribune*, May 31.

[50] *Annual Cyclopedia*, 1872, p. 664.

[51] *N. Y. Tribune*, June 1. See also Jones to Chase, June 20, Chase MSS.

The Bourbons were greatly in evidence in the New Jersey convention, June 26, and tried, amid much excitement, to put through a resolution declaring against the nomination at Baltimore of any but a Democratic candidate. But after a conciliatory speech from ex-Governor Randolph, who explained the utter failure of the attempts since the Liberal convention to secure a more acceptable coalition candidate and urged the support of Greeley as the certain and only means of overthrowing Grant, resolutions of qualified approval for the Cincinnati platform were adopted without dissent, and the state committee was instructed to unite with any other organization opposed to the present administration.[52] Still the Bourbon spirit found some expression; the state's delegation was divided.[53]

In Delaware, however, appeared the most pronounced exhibition of Bourbonism. In that state there had been no Liberal organization, and the Democrats had no sympathy with the movement. Senator T. F. Bayard, one of the foremost leaders of the national as of the state Democracy, was decidedly opposed to the party's supporting a candidate from outside its own ranks.[54] The state convention, June 11, would commit itself to no platform beyond "the Declaration of Independence and the Constitution of the United States, desiring alone to regulate its action thereby." The war amendments were declared to be illegally adopted, "and the state of Delaware having rejected them, as a sovereign state, is not morally bound by them." To remove all doubt as to their attitude regarding the national ticket, they pledged themselves "to leave no honorable means un-

[52] *N. Y. Tribune*, June 27; *N. Y. Times*, June 27.

[53] The *N. Y. Times* said (June 27) that Greeley would probably have the full support of the state's delegation, though he would not begin to poll the full party vote in the state, but in the Baltimore convention only a half of the delegation proved to be in favor of the Liberal candidate. *Proceedings of the Dem. Nat. Con. at Baltimore*, 66.

[54] Spencer, *Bayard*, 58.

tried to elevate to the chief magistracy of the republic a true exponent of Democratic principles."[55]

But Delaware was alone in her hopeless insensibility to the appeal of party expediency. Some time before the Baltimore convention it was apparent that the Liberal ticket would be taken over with practical unanimity. Of the thirty Democratic state conventions held during May and June, twenty-six instructed for a coalition or by their resolutions favored such a policy.[56] The Washington *Patriot*, shortly before the national convention, bowing to the inevitable, urged a union on the Liberal ticket as a choice of evils.[57] Toward the end of June even the *World* was "reluctantly constrained to believe that the endorsement of Greeley at Baltimore is one of the absurd possibilities of American politics." Such action, it was confident, "would not represent the Democratic party but only its trading politicians."[58]

In the Baltimore convention, which was by no means representative of the best and strongest elements of the party,[59] the machinery was all prepared for putting through the Liberal platform and candidates with the greatest show of unanimity and enthusiasm. Belmont's opening speech was an apology for the step that the party was about to

[55] *Annual Cyclopedia*, 1872, p. 235; *N. Y. Tribune*, June 12.

[56] The four not committing themselves in this way were La., Md., and Pa., not taking definite action, and Del., openly hostile. See reports of the conventions under the respective states in *Annual Cyclopedia*, 1872.

[57] Washington *Patriot*, July 1, 3, 8.

[58] N. Y. *World*, June 25.

[59] The correspondent of the *Nation* wrote (July 18, p. 40): "A higher general average of intelligence and character was, I think, discernible at Philadelphia than here; and, indeed, there was no very successful representation of that intellectually able class which may be called the legal-minded constitutional Democracy, as distinguished from the negro-hating and office-seeking Democracy."

take,[60] and ex-Senator Doolittle as permanent chairman was well fitted to put on the humiliating program with the least embarrassment and friction.[61] The resolutions committee reported the Cincinnati platform verbatim, the chairman urging that it had already been adopted by all but four state conventions.[62] The opposition to the report was ably presented by Senator Bayard. The Liberal platform, he argued, contained many things that the Democrats respected and adhered to, but likewise much that they desired to modify and correct. The party should go before the country with its own statement of the issues of the day, and not slavishly follow the sentiments of another organization. In this position, he asserted, he was voicing the unanimous conviction of the party in Delaware.[63] In reply, M. P. O'Connor,[64] of South Carolina, and Judge Reagan,[65] of Texas, feelingly urged a full acceptance of the Liberal platform as the only salvation for their section. The report was adopted by a vote of 670 to 62.[66] The Liberal nominees were endorsed with like facility, Greeley receiving on the first ballot 686 votes to 38 for other candidates and 8 blank,[67] and Brown meeting with still less opposition.[68]

[60] *Proceedings Baltimore Convention*, 3–5.

[61] Cf. *Nation*, July 18, pp. 38 f. For Doolittle's speech, see *Proceedings*, 16–20.

[62] *Proceedings*, 41.

[63] *Ibid.*, 45–48.

[64] *Ibid.*, 48–50; O'Connor, *O'Connor*, 56–60.

[65] *Proceedings*, 51.

[66] *Ibid.*, 53. The opposition came from N. J., Pa., Del., W. Va., Ga., Fla., Miss., Mo., and Ore. Delaware's vote in the negative was greeted with hisses. *Ibid.*, 54. Greeley wrote to a friend, July 16, that, while the endorsement of the Liberal ticket had been a foregone conclusion, he was astonished that the Democrats should accept the platform. Benton, *Greeley on Lincoln, etc.*, 226 f.

[67] *Proceedings*, 66. The votes for other candidates were James A. Bayard, 15 (Del., 6; N. J., 9); Jeremiah S. Black, 21 (Pa.); William S. Groesbeck, 2 (W. Va.). The blanks were: Fla., 2; Ga., 4; W. Va., 2.

[68] *Ibid.*, 67. John W. Stevenson, of Kentucky, received 6 votes from Delaware, and 13 were blank (Fla., 2; N. J., 9; W. Va., 2). Both nominations were confirmed unanimously. *Ibid.*, 67, 71.

State coalitions were effected with equal success. In the states electing their officials this year, separate conventions were usually called by the allied organizations to meet at the same time and in the same city, and the negotiations between them were conducted by a conference committee, the proceedings in some cases being closed with a joint ratification meeting.[69] In most cases the candidates were apportioned between the two parties without any serious friction.[70] It was noticeable, however, that in states where the Democrats were relatively strong they appropriated the lion's share of the offices, while in Republican strongholds the Liberals were allowed the first places on the tickets.[71] The list of gubernatorial nominees that the coalitionists put in the field was truly imposing. Of the Liberals, Francis W. Bird in Massachusetts (after the withdrawal of Sumner, the first choice), Gustave Koerner in Illinois, and Austin Blair in Michigan; and of the Democrats, Francis Kernan in New York, Charles R. Buckalew in

[69] For accounts of such joint conventions, see *Springfield Weekly Republican*, Sept. 13; *N. Y. Tribune*, Sept. 5, 6; Koerner, *Memoirs*, II, 560–562; Dilla, 140 f.; Wilder, *Annals of Kansas*, 583–585; Gue, *History of Iowa*, III, 50.

[70] In Louisiana and Arkansas there was considerable disagreement over the fusion tickets, but the matter was later adjusted in each case. *Annual Cyclopedia*, 1872, pp. 28, 477–481; Harrell, 145. The Georgia Liberals asked to have a representative of their faction placed on the electoral ticket, but the Democrats refused. Avery, 502. The *Mo. Republican* (Sept. 2) deprecated the illiberal policy of the Democrats in certain counties in the composition of their local tickets, but later (Oct. 5) declared that cases of this sort were fewer than might have been expected. A circular sent out from Connecticut Democratic headquarters to party workers gave this advice: "Be liberal in the distribution of offices to the Liberal Republicans; give them their full share with a view to bind them for future operations." Quoted in San Francisco *Evening Bulletin*, Oct. 8.

[71] Thus in N. Y., Pa., Ind., and Mo. old-line Democrats headed the fusion tickets, while in Mass., Vt., Ill., Mich., and Kan. the honor was accorded to a Liberal.

Pennsylvania, and Thomas A. Hendricks in Indiana, were all notable figures in the political annals of the period. The state forces of the coalition were thus harmoniously organized for the activities of the campaign.

The formal preliminaries of coöperation with the Liberals had now been arranged by the active leaders of the Democracy. It remained to be seen whether the rank and file of the party would carry out the bargain at the polls. From the outset, the attitude that the Democratic voters would assume towards their life-long enemy, now become their regular candidate, had been recognized on all sides as the decisive factor in the campaign. The Republicans accordingly did their best in the press and on the stump to excite the traditional Democratic prejudice against Greeley. Their congressional campaign committee busied a corps of workers in culling from the files of the *Tribune* the choicest specimens of editorial abuse.[72] Of the ammunition thus supplied the administration organs made copious use against the coalition forces.[73] Considerations of this sort rendered it impossible for a few leading Democrats to give Greeley a hearty support, even as the regular party candidate. Manton Marble relinquished his editorship of the *World* during the campaign in order that this leading party organ, after a preliminary expression of protest,[74] might give a fairly cordial support to the coalition. The Sage of Deerfield with difficulty brought himself to speak for a candidate

[72] Detroit Post and Tribune, *Chandler*, 315; *Chicago Tribune*, June 30.

[73] For examples of the use of such material, see *N. Y. Times*, July 19; *Harper's Weekly*, Aug. 3; Boston *Commonwealth*, July 13; *Cincinnati Semi-Weekly Gazette*, May 31; *Milwaukee Weekly Sentinel*, June 18; *Kan. Commonwealth*, July 10, 12. See also on Greeley and the Democrats from a Republican viewpoint, Blaine, *Political Discussions*, 110; Booth, *Speeches*, 147 ff.; Conkling's campaign speech, printed in *N. Y. Times*, July 24. For the attempt of New York Republicans to draw off Democratic votes by naming an old-time leader of that party for governor, see below, p. 179.

[74] See its editorial of July 11.

whose abuse of the party had been "so gross,"[75] and many
humbler Democrats must have shared his repugnance.   But
even Bourbons, like Voorhees[76] and Bayard,[77] recognizing
their obligations to the regular party ticket, finally took
the stump; and heroic efforts were made to give the best
appearance to a humiliating situation.   The Democratic
voter was assured that Greeley's past denunciations of
their party were merely the sounding utterances of a
partisan editor in the heat of a forgotten conflict, ex-
ploded shells to be disregarded.[78]   Bayard, using a more
congenial argument, reminded the Delaware irreconcilables of the coöperation of the Liberals with the Democrats in the past Congress, and urged that only by coalition
in the present canvass could the Democrats hope to end
federal tyranny at the South.[79]   Against the fear that
coalition might mean an abandonment of principles, the
faithful were assured that no Democratic principle could
suffer through Greeley's success since the chief places in
the cabinet and other important offices would go to true
representatives of their party.[80]   Indeed the prospect that
the Democrats would gain greatly by the anticipated reorganization of parties was much emphasized.   The Democratic

[75] Seymour to Tilden, Oct. 3.   "But for you and Kernan," he wrote,
"I should not move this fall, as it is, I will do what I can."   Tilden,
Letters, I, 311.

[76] Ingersoll, 566 f.

[77] Spencer, 58.

[78] Cox, *Three Decades of Federal Legislation*, 627; Julian, *Later
Speeches*, 16.

[79] Spencer, 164–166.   For a similar argument, see an editorial in the
People's Tribune, Oct. 16.   Seymour, in private correspondence, justified Democratic support of Greeley on the ground that he could "be
made use of in drawing negroes out of office."   Seymour to Tilden, Oct.
3, Tilden, *Letters*, I, 311.

[80] See, for instance, editorials in N. Y. *World*, July 17, Oct. 30.   There
was much discussion over the composition of Greeley's cabinet.   It was
widely reported that Seymour was to be secretary of state.   See New
York correspondent in the *Cincinnati Semi-Weekly Gazette*, May 31.

party, it was conceded, had been greatly weakened, but the impending break-up of the Republican organization would enable it to become one of the great parties of the future.[81] Such arguments for coalition, predicated upon the prospect of its success, might hold reluctant Democrats so long as the prospect remained bright. But in October, when the tide was clearly against the coalition,[82] the Democratic voters seemed not unlikely to drift with it, and most fervent appeals were addressed to them from both Democratic and Liberal quarters to rally to their candidates and still save the day.[83]

The N. Y. *Sun* (quoted in *Springfield Weekly Republican*, Aug. 2) suggested this combination: state, Charles Francis Adams, Mass.; treasury, Sanford E. Church, N. Y.; war, John M. Palmer, Ill.; navy, Austin Blair, Mich.; interior, James B. Beck, Ky.; postmaster-general, Richard Taylor, La.; attorney-general, William S. Groesbeck, Ohio. J. R. Doolittle predicted in a letter to Sumner (July 24) that Greeley would select for his secretary of state a man like Buckalew, Hendricks, or Sumner himself. Sumner MSS. In his speech at Portland, Maine, in August, Greeley said distinctly that in case of his election he would not confine his appointments to Republicans. *N. Y. Tribune*, Aug. 16; Ingersoll, 649.

[81] The California Liberal national committeeman issued a circular in which he argued that the Democrats would not absorb the Liberals, but that the election of Greeley would lead to the breaking up of the Republican party, and that the Liberals and Democrats would constitute the two great parties of the future. A copy of this circular is in the Sumner MSS.

[82] See below p. 182.

[83] See editorials in N. Y. *World*, Oct. 30, 31, Nov. 1, 4; Washington *Patriot*, Oct. 24; *Milwaukee News*, Oct. 20; *Chicago Tribune*, Oct. 22; *Springfield Weekly Republican*, Oct. 25; *Leslie's Newspaper*, Nov. 2; *Spirit of the Times*, Oct. 12; *Mo. Republican*, Oct. 28. The *N. Y. Tribune* (editorial Oct. 26) declared that if the liberal ticket got the full Democratic vote there was no doubt of its success, but that if ten per cent stayed away from the polls defeat was equally certain. It vividly pictured the present low state of the party and its hopeless future, and solemnly warned Democratic voters: "Opportunities neglected are opportunities no more. Democrats who vote their party of no account in 1872 will hardly find it to vote for or against in 1876."

The common opinion that the Democratic leaders in the main were faithful to their obligations under the party compact,[84] finds support in an examination of the character and personnel of the organized opposition that arose within the party. Some time before the Democratic national convention, an agitation was started for a representation of "true Democrats" at Baltimore who in case the regular convention endorsed the Liberal candidates should put a genuine Democratic ticket in the field.[85] Such a rival gathering, with a small attendance and not very creditable leadership, was held at Baltimore. Resolutions were adopted denouncing the action of the national convention, and declaring for states' rights and strict construction. Provision was made for the formation of a national organization and the calling of a convention on September 3 at Louisville.[86] In the meantime, the candidates of the Labor Reform party having withdrawn, negotiations were entered into by certain of their leaders with the "straight-out" Democrats.[87] At a convention of one wing of the labor party, in August, it was decided to recommend Charles O'Conor of New York and Senator Saulsbury of Delaware to the Louisville convention as suitable candidates, and a committee was appointed to confer with the "straight-out" convention on the best measures to be taken for a successful campaign.[88]

The Louisville convention assembled on the appointed day with a good attendance. A platform was adopted declaring for states' rights and strict construction and a recognition of the interests of labor, and denouncing protection and monopoly. Charles O'Conor, who had written

[84] See Rhodes, VI, 433; Ingersoll, 562.
[85] Circular, quoted in the N. Y. *World*, July 3.
[86] Proceedings reported in the *N. Y. Tribune*, July 9–11.
[87] *N. Y. Herald*, July 27, 30.
[88] N. Y. *World*, Aug. 23.

a letter to the convention setting forth his ideas of government and politics in general, was named for president with John Quincy Adams of Massachusetts for vice-president.[89] Both candidates promptly declined, but their "party" refused to recognize such an action and placed itself in the ridiculous position of supporting candidates against their expressed wishes.[90] The "straight-outs" made pretenses of carrying on an active canvass in a number of states, and their doings were given an exaggerated prominence by the Republican press. In twenty-three states they had electoral tickets[91] and in three[92] state tickets as well. Conventions, mass meetings, and campaign organizations of this faction were reported from time to time from various sections.[93]

The character of the "straight-out" leaders, with a few exceptions, was not such as to make the movement a protest worthy of respect. The chief promoter of the Louisville convention was Colonel Blanton Duncan of Kentucky who after discrediting himself with the Confederacy had become a turn-coat.[94] In the campaign of 1876 he was an ardent

[89] McKee, *Conventions and Platforms*, 147 f.; Stanwood, *Hist. of the Presidency*, 349–351; *N. Y. Herald*, Sept. 4–6; *Chicago Times*, Sept. 4–6.

[90] *Chicago Times*, Sept. 14, Oct. 10; *Pomeroy's Democrat*, Oct. 5, 12, 26. O'Conor wrote to Tilden, Aug. 24: "To hold an office charged with the dispensation of extensive patronage, not the world's mass of vanity would tempt me. Of course I will not be a candidate." Bigelow, *Tilden*, I, 218.

[91] Stanwood, *Hist. of Presidency*, 352.

[92] Illinois, Indiana, and Michigan. See *Annual Cyclopedia*, 1872, pp. 391, 397, 538; Dilla, 142. In New York a state ticket was not named out of deference to Apollo Hall which favored Kernan, the Democratic-Liberal candidate for governor. *Pomeroy's Democrat*, Aug. 6.

[93] *Albany Evening Journal*, Aug. 12; *Chicago Times*, Aug. 17, 19, 21, 23, 30, Sept. 16, 20, 23, 27, Oct. 19; *N. Y. Times*, Sept. 21; *Cincinnati Semi-Weekly Gazette*, Nov. 1, 5; *Milwaukee Weekly Sentinel*, Sept. 24; San Francisco *Evening Bulletin*, Oct. 23; Wilder, 580, 586; Davis, *Political Conventions of Cal.*, 320; Avery, 502.

[94] *Chicago Tribune*, Aug. 9; *N. Y. Tribune*, Aug. 13.

green-backer.[95] The leading organs in the North were
Storey's *Chicago Times*, "Brick" Pomeroy's *Democrat*, and
other notorious copperhead papers about New York City.[96]
The main support of the faction in the East was James
O'Brien's Apollo Hall organization in New York.[97] In the
South the leading adherents, while in many cases eminently
respectable, were of the extreme irreconcilables who had
been doing so much to injure their party ever since the war,
men like Alexander Stephens, Hershel V. Johnson, and
Henry A. Wise.[98] It was repeatedly charged by the coalitionists that the whole "straight-out" movement was but
an administration decoy for discontented, unwary Democratic voters, and there seem to have been some grounds
for such a charge. The statement was widely made, without convincing contradiction, that the faction's literature
was sent out under the franks of Republican congressmen
and distributed by Republican office holders acting under
the direction of the Republican congressional campaign
committee,[99] and, in one state at least, the Republican leaders went still further in securing support for a movement
whose whole tendency was to divide and weaken the opposition.[100] The open affiliation of prominent "straight-outs"

[95] *Industrial Age*, Sept. 16, 1876.

[96] See a partial list of these papers in *N. Y. Times*, Aug. 2.

[97] N. Y. *World*, Aug. 28; *Pomeroy's Democrat*, Oct. 6.

[98] Avery, 502; *Wis. Weekly State Journal*, Aug. 27. Stephens had
a high opinion of Grant and his policies. See Crawford, "What the
Vice-President of the Confederacy thought of General Grant." *Independent*, LIX, 679 ff.

[99] *N. Y. Herald*, Aug. 22; *Chicago Tribune*, Aug. 20, 21; *N. Y. Tribune*, Aug. 13.

[100] Hamilton, "The Election of 1872 in North Carolina" in *South
Atlantic Quarterly*, XI, 151. See also the *Elmira Gazette's* statement
regarding the movement in southern New York, quoted in the N. Y.
World, Sept. 3. Senator Morton was charged with being in consultation with the managers of the Louisville convention, but he denied any
knowledge of their doings. Foulke, *Morton*, II, 265.

with the Republicans the next year and the appointment of some of them to federal offices seemed to Democratic papers to be conclusive evidence of the truth of their charges.[101]

[101] For references to such cases, see N. Y. *World*, Jan. 3, 1873; *Milwaukee News*, May 24, 1873; *Madison Democrat*, Jan. 3, 1873; *Milwaukee Sentinel*, Jan. 28, 1873.

CHAPTER VI

THE POLITICAL CAMPAIGN OF 1872

The campaign of 1872 was primarily one of personalities. Probably no previous national campaign had been conducted so largely on the basis of personal abuse and misrepresentation.[1] The efforts of the Liberals to break up the old party made the Republicans most bitter toward that element of the opposition, and the politicians who largely controlled the Liberal movement after Greeley's nomination found their readiest and most congenial arguments in the abuse of the President and his advisers. All impartial, or in any degree fair-minded, observers admitted the disgraceful perversions of the canvass. "We designed it to be a campaign of ideas, and it became a campaign of personalities," Schurz wailed shortly after the election.[2] "The amount of lying done in the present Presidential canvass," the *New York Observer* thought, "is fearful to contemplate. And the persistence in it, after its exposure and refutation, is more fearful still. We have watched eight successive campaigns, and we are quite sure for total depravity, this beats them all."[3] Similarly the *Nation*, in prefacing a long list of picturesque campaign epithets, expressed the opinion that "The campaign work is a shower of mud to a far greater extent than that of

[1] Professor Jesse Macy says ("The Scientific Spirit in Politics," *Am. Pol. Sc. Rev.* XI, 3) that "The campaign of 1872 seemed to exemplify the new [scientific] spirit." But such a spirit in this canvass, as the following account should show, was altogether more seeming than real.

[2] Schurz to White, about Nov. 15, *Schurz's Writings*, II, 444.

[3] *N. Y. Observer*, Sept. 26. The *Christian Advocate* the same week (Sept. 26) commented: "The pending political canvass is distinguished for its personalities which in violence, recklessness of the truth and impertinent intermeddling with the private affairs of the parties assailed, are unprecedented and simply scandalous."

any other campaign within our remembrance."[4]   In accepting a renomination to Congress, on the last day of July,
James A. Garfield declared: "The battle has already begun in
a spirit of unusual violence, and bids fair to be as fierce and
disreputable in the spirit in which it is carried on as any we
have ever witnessed."[5]   Bayard Taylor wrote from Switzer-
land in September: "How glad I am to be away from home
this summer! I can even smell the stench and feel the
venom of the campaign at this distance, and there are few
features of it which do not create disgust."[6] The characterization of a presidential campaign by a political writer in the
preceding March seems most prophetic and aptly descrip-
tive of the ensuing contest: "A presidential campaign is a
discussion with sticks; nobody reasons, everybody lies as
hard as ever he can, and the forces are in the nature of clubs.
When the war opens, it is presumed that recruiting is over
for this time, that the facts of the case and the rhetoric of
the statesmen have adjusted voters to their places in opposing ranks, nothing remains but to see who can make the
most noise and demolish the most character."[7]

The press contributed greatly to this work of calumny
and misrepresentation. Political journalism with such
editors as Wilbur Story, Donn Piatt and "Brick" Pomeroy
was not likely to be over-scrupulous, and the editors of the
leading party organs fell about as low as these pariahs of
the press. Whitelaw Reid, who assumed the management
of the *Tribune* upon Greeley's nomination, wrote that the
policy of this paper in the campaign was to be "aggressive,"[8]
and he followed out this aim most consistently, regardless

---

[4] *Nation*, Aug. 8, p. 83.

[5] *Garfield's Works* (Hinsdale ed.), II, 34.

[6] Taylor and Scudder, *Taylor*, II, 595.   R. C. Winthrop wrote, Aug.
16, "The canvass thus far strikes me as the most disgusting one in
American history." Winthrop, *Winthrop*, 279.

[7] Wheeler, "President-Making" in *Lakeside Monthly*, March, p. 242.

[8] Reid to Sumner, May 16, Sumner MSS.

of other considerations.[9]   The *New York Times*, the leading administration organ in the East, under the editorship of Louis Jennings, then as always a British citizen, resorted to personal abuse and a perversion of facts to a degree that with fair-minded readers should have tended in great measure to destroy the reputation for probity which it had gained the previous year in the crusade against the ring.[10] Nothing better can be said for the tactics of the leading Democratic journals like the New York *World* and the Washington *Patriot*. The minor organs all over the country, while not so skillfully libelous and vituperative, tried hard to make up for it by greater violence of expression.[11] The *New York Herald*, which in its exclusive rôle of sensational journalism could afford to keep aloof from strict party allegiance, declared that the abusive journalism of 1872 closely resembled that of thirty years earlier, caricatured by Dickens in Martin Chuzzlewit.[12] A considerable number of religious papers took an active part in the canvass, usually in support of the Republican ticket, often with as great zeal and as blind partisanship as the regular organs.[13] There

[9] For a criticism of the *Tribune's* policy, see *Nation*, July 25, p. 50.

[10] See editorial, "A Crime in Journalism," in *Springfield Weekly Republican*, Aug. 2.

[11] This is borne out by an examination of a considerable number of such papers. The *Maryland Union's* reference to the President (July 18) as "that ambitious and utterly depraved horse-jockey who now oscillates between the White House and Long Branch" would be hard to beat in abusive political journalism.

[12] *N. Y. Herald*, Sept. 20.

[13] For a good summary of the position of the religious press in the campaign, see *Central Presbyterian*, Oct. 9. For examples of such support of Grant, see editorials in *Christian Union*, May 15, June 12, July 10; *Independent*, passim; *Advance*, Oct. 31; *Christian Advocate*, Aug. 1, 8, Nov. 14; *Zion's Herald*, quoted in *Madison Democrat*, May 13. Certain regular Republican organs made much of the support of Grant by the religious press, see *Milwaukee Sentinel*, May 28, Oct. 22; *Kan. Commonwealth*, June 30. Tilton's *Golden Age* was the leading religious paper

was a large output of campaign pamphlets attacking candidates with more or less humorous burlesque, or with still
more humorous pretensions at historical discussion.[14]

The pencil of the cartoonist was employed as never before
in a national campaign to supplement the pen of the political
writer. The celebrated Thomas Nast in *Harper's Weekly*,
in his zeal to please flattering administration leaders,[15] dis-
torted the physiques and morals of the prominent Liberals
and Democrats with an indiscrimination that called forth
earnest but vain protests from the editor.[16] Matt Morgan,
late of the *Tomahawk*, whom Leslie brought from England to
rival Nast,[17] while less artistic and pointed, was even more
brutal and malignant in his caricatures of the President and
his advisers.[18]

Campaign oratory as usual was supplied in great abun-
dance. The administration rallied all of its forces for the
contest. The senatorial clique were constantly in the front
rank and members of the cabinet saw much active service.[19]
Speaker Blaine, after securing his own state in September,
moved on to the western battle-field.[20] Henry Wilson as
vice-presidential candidate, with his long political experience
and qualities of popular appeal, was a most active and effect-

supporting Greeley. The *N. Y. Herald* (Aug. 18) said of its attitude in
the campaign: "The *Golden Age* is mild in religion, but balances it by
being fiercely political."

[14] See, for instance, Chamberlain, *Issues of 1872;* Welch, *That Convention;* Budlong, *President Greeley, etc.;* Cross, *Modern Ulysses.*

[15] Paine, *Nast,* 221–227.

[16] *Ibid.,* 216–218, 243, 244.

[17] *Ibid.,* 227.

[18] *Idem.* See examples of Morgan cartoons in *Leslie's Newspaper,*
May 4, July 13, Aug. 3, 17, Sept. 7, 14, 28. For contemporary criticism
of Nast and Morgan, see "Greeley Among the Artists," in *Nation,* Nov.
14, p. 310; *Atlantic Monthly,* May, 642 f; *Christian Union,* May 15.

[19] Conkling, *Conkling,* 435–448; Foulke, *Morton,* II, 255–268; Detroit Post and Tribune, *Chandler,* 312–316; Flower, *Carpenter,* 271 ff.;
Ingersoll, *Greeley,* 563.

[20] Hamilton, *Blaine,* 274–276, 302; Ingersoll, 563.

ive campaigner, lending strength to the party at some of its weakest points.[21] A great host of congressmen, state officials, and lesser federal office-holders were at the command of the national committee.

Colfax's attitude in the campaign was a matter of considerable interest and concern. The coalition press represented that he was cherishing a grievance against the administration, and his failure to give any aid to the cause during the early canvass occasioned considerable anxiety among the Republican managers. Finally, in August, in response to urgent appeals from Senator Chandler, who represented that the Vice-President's silence was being used to injure the ticket, he made a number of speeches in his state, but, in marked contrast to the usual personalities of this campaign, at all times refraining from attacks on his old friend Greeley.[22]

In accordance with the prevailing custom, the President took no active part in the canvass. "*My judgment is*," he wrote Conkling, "*that it will be better that I should not attend any convention or political meeting during the campaign.* It has been done, so far as I remember, by but two Presidential candidates heretofore, and both of them were public speakers, and both were beaten. I am no speaker, and don't want to be beaten."[23] The President's estimate of his weakness as a public speaker was not exaggerated, and the party lost nothing by his abstention. His brief attempts at speeches, made at non-political gatherings during the summer, as reported,[24] hardly made good sense, to say nothing of being effective. Most of the time was passed quietly at his summer house in Long Branch. In a newspaper interview he asserted most characteristically that he had consented to

---

[21] Nason, *Wilson*, 410–413; *Atlantic Monthly*, Aug., p. 255. On Wilson's skill as a politician, Hoar, *Autobiography*, I, 218.

[22] Hollister, *Colfax*, 377, 378, 381.

[23] Grant to Conkling, July 15, Conkling, 435.

[24] See N. Y. *World*, Aug. 7; *Chicago Tribune*, Sept. 22.

run for a second time with reluctance, but that he had been so abused that he desired to see if the majority of the people were still with him, or if they credited his detractors and slanderers.[25]

The Liberal cause did not lack for able and distinguished defenders. Though many of the independents had left the Liberals after the Cincinnati convention, the coalition had the support of some of the best campaigners of the Republican party in years past, as well as practically all of the leading Democrats. Prominent senators like Schurz, Trumbull, and Tipton, and old-time campaigners like Banks, Julian, Doolittle, and McClure were certain of a large and attentive hearing.[26]

Sumner was slow in giving public support to the coalition, though after his outburst against Grant there was no possibility of his acting with the Republicans. He went so far in private as to send Greeley suggestions concerning his letter of acceptance,[27] but failed for some time to pronounce himself openly.[28] Finally, on July 29, in response to a letter of inquiry from colored voters, he came out fully in support of Greeley.[29] Sumner's open defection, being that of one who had so personified the radical cause, was bitterly denounced by the Republicans[30] and received with corresponding satisfaction by the coalitionists.[31] "Mr. Sumner," wrote Greeley, "you know that I thank you for your

[25] *N. Y. Herald*, Aug. 6.

[26] Cf. Ingersoll, 562.

[27] Ashley to Sumner, July 15, Sumner MSS.

[28] Early in July Sumner was strongly urged by coalition leaders to declare for Greeley. See Doolittle to Sumner, July 13, Sumner MSS. and C. A. Henland to Sumner, July 13, *ibid.* His colored friend, Frederick Douglass, in a letter on July 5, suggested that Sumner take no part in the campaign, *ibid.*

[29] *Sumner's Works*, XV, 175–195.

[30] *Ibid.*, 196–201; *N. Y. Times*, Aug. 3; Sumner to Smith, Aug. 6, 7; Frothingham, *Smith*, 327; *Harper's Weekly*, Aug. 17.

[31] Pierce, *Sumner*, IV, 531; *N. Y. Tribune*, Aug. 2, 5.

noble letter."[32]   Sumner was now urgently besought both
by Democratic and Liberal leaders to make at least a few
speeches especially in the Maine canvass.[33]   But owing to
his enfeebled health and his impending departure for Europe,
he confined his further efforts to an address which was given
to the press late in August.[34]

The vice-presidential candidate of the coalitionists, in
contrast to the administration's candidate, proved to be no
help as a campaigner, but quite the opposite.   Gratz Brown
had made much trouble for the Liberals in the convention.
In the campaign, in spite of his good union record and his
prestige as an original Liberal governor, he proved a heavy
drag on the ticket.   Coming East in August to attend a
class banquet at Yale, he made a speech in extremely bad
taste in criticism of things eastern and ended up by getting
intoxicated.[35]   Brown's former intemperate habits were a
matter of common knowledge and had been urged against
his candidacy at Cincinnati.[36]   The *Springfield Republican*
now demanded that Brown be withdrawn from the ticket
and a man like Groesbeck, Cox, Trumbull, or Hancock substituted.[37]   Brown promptly secured a testimonial from
Missouri officials and other prominent citizens as to his good
habits while governor,[38] but the mischief was done, from
this time on his candidacy was never treated seriously by
the administration press, and his supporters were placed
constantly on the defensive.   The stories of Grant's public
intoxication, at once set afloat by the coalitionists,[39] appar-

---

[32] Greeley to Sumner, July 31, Sumner MSS.

[33] See letters from Allen, July 30; Doolittle, Aug. 2, 6; Sinclair, Aug.
10; Schell, Aug. 10; White, Aug. 12; Lang, Aug. 20 in Sumner MSS.

[34] *Sumner's Works*, XV, 208–254; Pierce, IV, 534.

[35] *Nation*, Aug. 8, 22, pp. 82, 114.

[36] *Springfield Weekly Republican*, May 10, Aug. 2.

[37] *Ibid.*, Aug. 2, 9.

[38] *Ibid.*, Aug. 23.

[39] *Ibid.*, Aug. 2; Winthrop, *Winthrop*, 280.

ently did not help matters for them, as charges had been made too indiscriminately against the President to give additional ones, whether well founded or not, any weight with the public.

Greeley met the demands of a most trying presidential candidacy surprisingly well. As has been seen, he acted in harmony with the most influential Democratic leaders, and, after a transient fit of impatience, with independents like Schurz. His overtrustfulness of political advisers,[40] which would not unlikely have weakened his administration had he been elected, tended to prevent discord in ᾽the coalition organization. He was tireless in consultations and in attention to campaign details, maintaining a hopeful spirit which he seems to have been able to impart to those about him.[41] Greeley was not troubled by the conventional restraints imposed at this time upon presidential candidates. In August he made some non-political speeches in Rhode Island and in his native state of New Hampshire, followed by real political speeches in the Maine canvass.[42] The following month, when it was all too evident that the tide was setting against the Liberals, their candidate made a remarkable tour of the "October States," speaking in New Jersey, Pennsylvania, Ohio, Kentucky, and Indiana, everywhere to large crowds.[43] On the whole, Greeley was a great success as a campaigner. His co-workers seem to have been highly elated at the powers he developed on the stump,[44] and the Liberal organs expressed unfeigned admiration.[45] More

[40] McClure, *Old Time Notes*, II, 338; White to Schurz, June 9, *Schurz's Writings*, II, 382.

[41] Grinnell, *Reminiscences*, 225; Barnum, *Recollections*, 768.

[42] *N. Y. Tribune*, Aug. 13, 14, 16; Ingersoll, 564, 645–650.

[43] *N. Y. Tribune*, Sept. 19–30; Ingersoll, 565–571, 650–664.

[44] Zabriski, *Greeley*, 292; Grinnell, 225; Watterson, "Humor and Tragedy of the Greeley Campaign," 42; Halstead, "Horace Greeley" in *Cosmopolitan*, VIII, 465.

[45] *Springfield Weekly Republican*, Sept. 27; *Chicago Tribune*, Sept. 27.

impartial observers also paid tribute to Greeley's campaign oratory.[46] The administration press was, of course, greatly concerned at the impropriety of a presidential candidate's traveling about the country speaking in his own behalf, and likened Greeley's tour to Johnson's "swing around the circle."[47] The ultra-conservative New Englander, Robert C. Winthrop, thus voiced his disgust: "Greeley travels about in his white coat like the *Candidate* in the worst of old Roman days, soliciting votes for himself and playing humble to the multitude, in a style never before exhibited by a Presidential aspirant. It is loathsome beyond expression to any one who respects or loves his country."[48] But improper or not, there was no question of the eagerness of the people to see and hear the famous editor of the *Tribune*. The demonstrations with which the Liberal candidate was received all along his route were so pronounced as to create some uneasiness at Republican headquarters, even at a time when Grant's reëlection had seemed assured.[49]

A novel feature introduced into the campaign speaking was that of women campaigners. The woman's movement was decidedly aggressive this year, representatives of the Equal Rights Association attending the different national conventions with the purpose of getting their cause endorsed. The Cincinnati and Baltimore conventions refused to recognize the issue, but the Republicans expressed their sympathy in a rather non-committal plank. For this action, and because Grant had appointed postmistresses and Wilson was an avowed sympathizer with the cause, the

[46] *N. Y. Herald*, Sept. 23, 29; Joseph Choate quoted by Reid, in *Century*, LXXXV, 44.

[47] *Cincinnati Semi-Weekly Gazette*, Sept. 24; *Atlantic Monthly*, Nov., p. 639.

[48] Winthrop to ———, Aug. 16, Winthrop, 279.

[49] Blaine, *Twenty Years of Congress*, II, 534.

Association gave its support to the Republican ticket.[50] The leaders of the Association received a small subsidy from the Republican national committee, and they held a number of mass meetings, addressed by their most persuasive speakers.[51] To offset this unusual campaign attraction, women orators were also secured for the Liberal cause.[52]

In the work of all these various classes of campaigners there was little appeal to reason and intelligence; the campaign was in no sense one of "education." Constant efforts were made to arouse passion and prejudice and both sides resorted to about all the tricks known to American politics for misleading and confusing the average voter.

The writings and speeches of the campaign abounded in "charges,"—"libellous accusations brought against the candidates of the opposite party."[53] The extended list of Grant's short-comings in Sumner's "Philippic" furnished a convenient summary which was freely augmented and embellished by the coalitionist editors and speakers; and Greeley's erratic policies and personal eccentricities furnished an easy mark for the denunciation and ridicule of his opponents. It is profitless to perpetuate the reckless criminations and recriminations that were exchanged between the rival camps, but suffice it to say that the President was a corrupt, debauched tyrant,[54] and that Greeley was everything discreditable from a near traitor to a complete fool.[55] The lesser

[50] Harper, *Anthony*, I, 415–419; Stanton and others, *Hist. of Woman Suffrage*, II, 517–520.

[51] Harper, I, 420–422; *Golden Age*, Oct. 12; Stanton, *History of Woman Suffrage*, 520.

[52] See, for instance, *N. Y. Tribune*, Oct. 26.

[53] Ostrogorski, *Democracy and the Organization of Political Parties*, II, 337.

[54] N. Y. *World* editorials, July 18, Aug. 7, 19; *Chicago Tribune*, July 29; Cross, *Modern Ulysses*; Garland, *Grant*, 417; *Spirit of the Times*, June 1.

[55] *N. Y. Times* in nearly every issue through the campaign; *Kan. Commonwealth*, Aug. 18; Chamberlain, *Issues of 1872;* Budlong, *Pres-*

candidates were disposed of indiscriminately, when no more
specific personal accusations were at hand, as respectively
"feeders at the public crib" and "soreheads." A favorite
form of personal argument was that furnished by a contrast
of the characters and careers of the rival candidates for president. Viewed from the one side, Greeley was "the man
of the pen . . . the genius of peace," the champion of
reform and the reconciler of the North and South, while
Grant was "the man of the sword . . . the genius of
war," the instigator of a military rule and of administrative
corruption and the oppressor of the South.[56] From the other
side appeared Grant, the man of action, the savior of the
union, and the steady and efficient administrator towering
above Greeley, the mere theorist with all sorts of imprac-
ticable and revolutionary ideas, unstable in a crisis, and
subject to the influence of unscrupulous, designing friends.[57]
From the long-standing factional fights that had given
rise to the Liberal bolt in many of the states, the inter-
changes of personal abuse in the local canvasses seem to have
been, if anything, still more numerous and bitter than in the
national.[58]

ident Greeley, etc.; Conkling's New York speech, *N. Y. Tribune*, July 24.
See a summary of some of the most extreme "charges" against Greeley
in the editorial "Does Calumny Pay?" in *N. Y. Tribune*, Nov. 22.
Everett P. Wheeler says that he and many other Democrats finally
voted for Greeley as a protest against the abuse with which he was
assailed. *Sixty Years of American Life*, 97.

[56] Ward, *Ward*, 289 f.; *Schurz's Writings*, II, 429–435; *Sumner,
Works*, XV, 211–213; *Nat. Quart. Rev.*, June, pp. 105 ff.; *Chicago
Tribune*, June 6, July 18. N. Y. *World*, Oct. 28; B. F. Perry's article
in *Greenville Enterprise*, July 10; *Spirit of the Times*, Aug. 24; N. Y. *Sun*,
quoted in *People's Tribune*, May 29.

[57] *Old and New*, Sept., pp. 257 ff.; *North Am. Rev.*, Oct., pp. 416 ff.;
Booth, *Speeches*, 153; Adams, *Storrs*, 259–278; Conkling's New York
speech, July 23. *N. Y. Times*, July 24 and in Conkling, *Conkling*, 436
ff.; *Harper's Weekly*, Aug. 24; *Mo. Democrat*, July 3.

[58] See Julian, *Pol. Recollections*, 342 f.; Dilla, *Politics of Mich.*, 144;
Foulke, II, 257–264; Watkins, *Neb.*, III, 127; Callahan, *W. Va.*, 241;
Herrick, *Phelps*, 39; Clay, *Memoirs*, I, 275 f.

To attract the unreasoning voter there was a resort to "hoopla" campaigning. The coalitionists sought to take advantage of the personal emphasis in the campaign and carry their candidate safely through on a wave of popular excitement. It was freely predicted that the campaign would be another one of song and laughter, in which Greeley's white hat and coat would take the place of the log cabin.[59]   The paraphernalia for such a demonstration was abundantly provided and the Republicans responded with counter demonstrations.   Lampooning campaign songs were furnished by both sides in unlimited number.[60]   Greeley hats and other distinctive campaign insignia were much in evidence.[61] Hilarious mass-meetings with parades in which strongly-phrased transparencies bore a conspicuous part were made to appeal to the voter's emotions and prejudices.[62]   Campaign clubs were especially numerous, the formation of such organizations being constantly reported by both parties as

[59] *N. Y. Herald*, May 5, 6; *Chicago Tribune*, May 12; *Cincinnati Commercial*, quoted in *N. Y. Tribune*, May 7.

[60] "A Singing Campaign" in *Nation*, Oct. 10, pp. 231 ff.; *N. Y. Herald*, July 29, Aug. 2; *Chicago Tribune*, July 9, Platt, *Autobiography*, 64 f.; *Mo. Democrat*, Aug. 7, 9, 25, 28, Sept. 11

[61] Andrews, *Own Time*, 74. Enthusiastic Greeley supporters donned white hats at Cincinnati immediately after the nomination. *N. Y. Tribune*, May 6.

[62] The following were some of the legends appearing on the transparencies at a mass meeting in Richmond: "The Farmer of Chappaqua in Nov. next will ditch our lands and drain off the carpet-baggers." "Dr. Greeley our over-seer for the next four years—hog and hominy plenty then."   .   .   .   "We go for a wood chopper in preference to a horse jockey." "The country wants grubbing. Farmer Greeley slings a healthy axe,"—and the never-failing slogan—"The pen is mightier than the sword." *Richmond Whig and Advertiser*, June 28. See also the account of a Democratic-Liberal mass meeting at Jefferson City, Mo. in *People's Tribune*, Oct. 9.

a convincing proof of healthy activity.[63] "Chappaqua Farmers," "Wood-Choppers," "Liberal Guards," and "Greeley Veterans" were opposed by "Tanners Clubs" and "Grant Invincibles," and "Ida Greeley Grays" vied with "Nelly Grant Blues." In a campaign turning mainly on the picturesque qualities of the rival candidates, the Liberals would unquestionably have had a great advantage, but, as some of the un-excitable journals pointed out, the day of hard-cider campaigns was long passed.[64]

The attempts of both parties to set off a "bomb shell" during the campaign were equally ineffective. In July, a small Republican paper in southern New York brought forward the so-called Carmichael letters to prove that Greeley had been a party to some sort of bargain with the Democratic leaders prior to his nomination.[65] The story, with all sorts of exaggerated interpretations, was copied by administration papers from one end of the country to the other,[66] while it was characterized by the coalition press as merely another "Roorback." For a time the story seems to have made some impression, but failure to back it up with documentary proof soon caused it to fall flat.[67] In the Credit Mobilier affair the coalitionists might have exploited a real live scandal if they could have fully laid bare the facts.

[63] *Chicago Tribune*, July 8, 9, 15, 18; passim; *N. Y. Tribune*, May 20; *N. Y. Times*, Aug. 8, 15; *Richmond Whig and Advertiser*, June 14, Sept. 23; *Kan. Commonwealth*, July 21, Aug. 18; San Francisco *Evening Bulletin*, July 24, 25, 26; Oct. 24, 25. For an account of the formation of a club in this campaign which had a permanent existence, see Wight, *Payne*, 24.

[64] *Nation*, May 30, p. 345; *Evening Post*, June 7.

[65] See summary of the charges in *Evening Post*, July 19. The paper making the "exposure" was the *Binghamton Republican*.

[66] See Albany *Evening Journal*, July 10–29; *Boston Advertiser*, July 18, 24; *Cincinnati Semi-Weekly Gazette*, July 26; *Wis. Weekly State Journal*, July 30; *St. Paul Weekly Press*, Aug. 1; *Kan. Commonwealth*, July 9; Minneapolis *Evening News*, July 17, 25.

[67] *Springfield Weekly Republican*, Aug. 2.

Letters appearing to implicate prominent Republicans in bribery were published in the *New York Sun* early in September,[68] and considerable prominence was given to the charges by the Democratic-Liberal press during the remainder of the campaign.[69] But too many groundless charges were afloat and the *Sun* in particular had "cried wolf" too often to have the public very deeply impressed by a new exposure from that source.[70] Leading Liberal papers even expressed doubt at first as to the authenticity of the letters.[71] The accused persons denied promptly and emphatically all connection with the enterprise, in a way which served very nicely the purposes of the campaign, but occasioned some of them no little embarrassment in the subsequent congressional investigation.[72] But the charges as made by the coalition press were far from exact. Prominent Democrats as well as Republicans later proved to be implicated.

Racial interests and prejudices were appealed to in this campaign to a most unfortunate extent. The negro voter, as a new and uncertain element in national politics, was the subject of unusual solicitude, getting more recognition than he has ever had since. Both parties made direct and earnest appeals for the race's support. Speakers for the radical cause reminded them of their great debt to the Republican party for freedom and political and civil rights, and warned them that the triumph of Greeley and the Dem-

[68] Reprinted in *N. Y. World*, Sept. 6; *N. Y. Tribune*, Sept. 7.

[69] N. Y. *World*, and *N. Y. Tribune*, Sept.–Oct. passim; Washington *Patriot*, Sept. 17, 23; *Chicago Tribune*, Sept. 7, 9, 12, 14. See on the efforts of Liberal papers to get the facts of this case, Townsend, *Washington, Outside and Inside*, 401 ff. See Greeley's discussion of the exposure in his Indianapolis speech, Sept. 23, *N. Y. Tribune*, Sept. 24.

[70] Cf. *Nation*, Sept. 26, p. 194.

[71] *Springfield Weekly Republican*, Sept. 6. The *N. Y. Tribune* in reprinting the charges from the *Sun* (Sept. 7) said editorially that they published them "with all possible reserve."

[72] Crawford, *Credit Mobilier*, 111 f.; Hollister, 384; Hamilton, *Blaine*, 276–287.

ocrats would mean the overthrow of the war amendments
and the inauguration of a racial conflict in which the negroes
would be at the mercy of the Ku Klux.[73]   This augument
was summed up by Douglass in the striking figure: "The
Republican party is the ship and all else is the sea."[74]
Shortly before the election, the Republican congressional
campaign committee issued a circular to the southern negroes, urging them to go to the polls and offer their votes
and, if they were interfered with in any way, to take the
names of their assailants and justice would be meted out
later by the Republican Congress and administration.[75]
The coalitionists, on their side, appealed to the negro voter
to support their cause out of gratitude for the great services
of Greeley and Sumner to their race.[76]   Grant was accused
of slighting their people at home and insulting them abroad
in his dealings with Hayti.[77]

The race, as such, took a prominent part in the campaign.
In April a colored national convention for the purpose of
considering the best interests of the negroes had met at New
Orleans with representatives from fourteen states.   There
was a considerable sentiment in this gathering for following
Sumner and Greeley into the Liberal organization, but,
largely through the influence of their chairman, Frederick
Douglass, they endorsed the administration and pledged
support to the nominees of the Philadelphia convention.[78]
The Cincinnati convention had a considerable number of

[73] *N. Y. Herald*, Aug. 16; *N. Y. Tribune*, July 18, 23, 25, Aug. 1 (reports of campaign speeches in N. C. and Va.).

[74] Washington, *Douglass*, 286; *Harper's Weekly* (editorial), June 22.

[75] *N. Y. Herald*, Oct. 29.

[76] *Richmond Whig and Advertiser*, Sept. 3; *Greenville Enterprise*, July 10;
N. Y. Herald, July 28 (report of N. C. campaign); Harrell, *Brooks and
Baxter War*, 133; *Sumner's Works*, XV, 177.

[77] *Sumner's Works*, XV, 178; *N. Y. Herald*, Aug. 16 (report of Cooper
Institute negro debate).

[78] *Annual Cyclopedia*, 1872, p. 775; *New Orleans Republican*, Apr.
11-13; Douglass, *Life and Times*, 507 f.

colored delegates from the South.[79]   The Republican convention boasted nearly one hundred negro members, who
were shown all respect and accorded a patient hearing when
they desired to express their sentiments.[80]   A colored national Liberal convention was held at Louisville in September
and the coalition candidates and platform were formally endorsed and a national executive committee appointed.[81]
Both parties had colored speakers and the activities of negro
state and city organizations and the position of negro papers
were reported from various parts of the country.[82]   No less
than fifteen colored candidates were put in nomination for
state offices in the South, in all cases but one by the Republicans.[83] Frederick Douglass, the most conspicuous representative of his race, was accorded the high honor of heading
the Republican electoral ticket in New York, and subsequently of acting as messenger to carry his state's vote to
Washington.[84]   After the election, it was reported that a
serious effort was being made to secure a cabinet position for
a colored leader.[85]   All in all, as the *Springfield Republican*
put it, "Sambo" was "trumps in politics this year."[86]

[79] *N. Y. Tribune,* Apr. 26, 30, May 3.

[80] *Springfield Weekly Republican,* June 14; *Nation,* June 13, p. 387.

[81] *N. Y. Herald,* Sept. 27. The *N. Y. Herald* said of a joint debate
between colored orators at Cooper Institute in August: "Throughout
the proceedings there was a display of ignorance, bigotry, and ruffianism
revolting to those who have been taught to believe that the ballot is the
palladium of our liberties." *N. Y. Herald,* Aug. 17. See the issue of
Aug. 16 for a full account of this meeting, and also the comment by the
Liberal participant in Saunders to Sumner, Aug. 20, Sumner MSS.

[82] *Annual Cyclopedia,* 1872, pp. 497, 783; *N. Y. Tribune,* Aug. 29;
San Francisco *Evening Bulletin,* Aug. 12, 13; Hamilton, "The Election
of 1872 in North Carolina," in *South Atlantic Quart.,* XI, 151; Saunders
to Sumner, Aug. 20, 1872, Sumner MSS.

[83] The negro candidates were in Ark., La., and S. C. *Annual Cyclopedia,*
1872, pp. 25, 481, 736, 737; Harrell, *Brooks and Baxter War,* 140. A
negro was nominated as a Republican elector in Maryland, but later
withdrew to support Greeley. *Maryland Union,* May 9, July 18.

[84] Douglass, 508 f.

[85] *Springfield Weekly Republican,* Nov. 15.

[86] *Ibid.,* June 14.

Shamelessly open bids were made for the support of other
racial elements. The coalitionists represented that Henry
Wilson's former Know Nothing connection was clear evidence of his hostility to all foreign-born citizens.[87]   Greeley's
life-long friendliness to the Irish was counted upon to give
the bulk of that vote to the Liberal candidate.[88]   But the
Germans were the race most appealed to by both sides.
This element, as previously noted, had in large numbers
been alienated from the administration and had regarded
with much favor the new independent reform movement.
Greeley, however, with his views on sumptuary legislation
and on the tariff, was most objectionable to many Germans,
who found Grant, with all his short-comings, a preferable
candidate.[89]   An unfortunately large emphasis in the canvass was given by both sides to the attitude of the Germans
as a distinct element in the population.[90]

[87] *N. Y. Tribune*, Aug. 21, 22, 26, 31, Sept. 2; *Chicago Tribune*, July
20. For Wilson's reply, see Nason, 413. An army order issued by
Grant excluding Jewish traders was used to prejudice that race against
the President.   N. Y. *World*, Aug. 7; Washington *Patriot*, Aug. 24;
Leslie's Newspaper, Oct. 19.

[88] *Leslie's Newspaper*, Aug. 24.

[89] See above, p. 108. Greeley wrote to Schurz, May 8: "Of course
the most of the Germans dislike me, not so much that I am a Protectionist as that I am a Total Abstinence man. They will not vote for
me so generally as they would have voted for Adams or Trumbull."
Bancroft-Dunning, *Schurz's Political Career*, 350.

[90] In the Baltimore convention Governor Hoffman dramatically
presented what purported to be the "manifesto" of 15,000 New York
Germans calling for Greeley's endorsement, *N. Y. Tribune*, July 11;
Proceedings Balt. Con., 56. A "German National Convention," representing twenty-four states and under the auspices of certain German-
American Associations was held in New York City, Oct. 24, at which
resolutions were adopted condemning the coalition and pledging their
best efforts to elect Grant and Wilson. *N. Y. Herald*, Oct. 25. Schurz
addressed large German mass meetings in Chicago and New York, *N. Y.
Tribune*, Aug. 12, Oct. 2. See also references to the German vote in
Illinois in Hay's letters to Reid, Aug. 1, 4, Thayer, *Hay*, I, 344 f.

Still more reprehensible than the racial appeals were those made to sectarian prejudice. The most marked appeal of this sort was in the state canvass in New York where the Catholic connection of the coalition candidate for governor raised a storm of bigoted opposition from administration organs, both secular and religious.[91] The anti-Catholic argument was later used to some extent against the national Liberal ticket in different parts of the country.[92] Of all the travesties on reasonable and honorable political deliberations which this campaign presented, this was the most disgraceful.

In the presentation of the more definite and formal campaign arguments, it was inevitable, after the over-running of the Liberal ranks by the politicians and the consequent personal trend of the canvass, that reforms which had been foremost considerations with the organizers of the Liberal movement should be largely subordinated. Thus in the cases of two of the chief reforms, those of the tariff and the civil service, the non-committal plank and the nomination of the leading champion of protection had largely destroyed the one and Greeley's political associations rendered him a most inappropriate exponent of the other.[93] But there was some pretense that the movement was still continuing in the direction of these reforms. Soon after the convention, Greeley pledged himself, in accordance with his theory of con-

[91] See articles by Eugene Lawrence and Nast cartoons bearing on this issue in *Harper's Weekly*, Oct. 12, 26, Nov. 2; the (Chicago) *Standard*, Nov. 7; *Christian Advocate*, Sept. 19; N. Y. *World*, Sept. 9, 16, Nov. 4; *N. Y. Times*, Sept. 9; *N. Y. Tribune*, Sept. 30; Hay to Reid, Aug. 1, Thayer, I, 343.

[92] See, for instance, editorial referring to sectarian opposition to Greeley in *Madison Democrat*, Oct. 22.

[93] Cf. *Atlantic Monthly*, Oct., p. 510. The *Nation* said of the civil service issue (Aug. 15, p. 100): "Although the opposition to Grant has largely drawn its ammunition from the record of his shortcomings with regard to the civil service, civil-service reform is hardly mentioned in the Greeley canvass."

gressional determination, to sign a free-trade measure if one were passed,[94] and his supporters defended this disposal of the question as the best possible at the time.[95]   Even the free-trade *World* could find reasons for supporting Greeley in preference to Grant on this issue.[96]   But the contradictory position in which the coalition was placed on the tariff issue was humorously evinced by the appeal made to the manufacturers by a leading Democratic paper of the North West to support Greeley on the ground that he had faithfully championed their cause for forty years.[97]

An anti-monopoly argument in which the opposition could attack the administration more effectively was that regarding abuses in the public land grants.   The Republican policy in the matter was arraigned in a manner which should have appealed strongly to the western farmer in this period of discontent.[98]

Civil service auguments consisted largely of a denunciation of patronage abuses under Grant, which, bad enough at best, were magnified to the fullest extent and portrayed in the darkest colors.[99]   As an escape from such intolerable conditions competent sponsors, like Schurz, professed to have confidence in a real reform of the service under Greeley.[100] But the failure of the Liberal candidate to take any especial

[94] Interview in N. Y. *Sun*, quoted in *Memorial to Greeley*, 227.   See also Greeley's emphatic declaration to the same effect in his speech at Easton, Pa., Sept. 28.   Quoted in White, *Trumbull*, 401.

[95] See, for instance, *Milwaukee News*, Mar. 20 (commending Greeley's position before the convention); *Springfield Weekly Republican*, June 28; Ward, *Ward*, 259; Pelzer, *Dodge*, 251; *Schurz's Writings*, II, 433.

[96] N. Y. *World*, July 23.

[97] *Milwaukee News*, Sept. 15.

[98] Julian, *Later Speeches*, 24; Pelzer, 251.

[99] Spencer, *Bayard*, 167–173; White, 395–399.

[100] *Schurz's Writings*, II, 434 f.   Schurz had had correspondence with Greeley on this subject (a portion of which he read in the speech just cited) and had been otherwise assured of the Liberal candidate's good intentions toward the civil service.   See *ibid.*, 372, 382–383, 385–386,

interest in this reform in the past (although a specialist in promoting reforms which gained his interest) and his close association in party organization with some of the most discreditable spoilsmen of his day[101] lent strength to the contention of the President's defenders that Greeley's accession to the presidency would give free rein to a new wholesale spoils system.[102]

The administrationists took the offensive in pushing to the front the financial issue. Full credit was taken to their party in this field for the steady payment of the national debt, the maintenance of good credit, and the fall in the gold premium, with an honest, efficient and economical administration making possible a reduction of taxes.[103] The time-honored prosperity argument was much played upon. The country had never been more prosperous, it was claimed: there were few failures, credit was good, and everything was booming,—"the hum of prosperous industry rises from every section and mercantile confidence reigns supreme."[104] The Republican party was, of course, mainly responsible for all these blessings. "And I do say," declared John A. Logan, after a panegyric on the material greatness of the United States, "that you never saw such rapid progress and development until the Republican party came into power. . . . In voting for Grant you vote for prosperity, for peace, for civilization, for Christianity, for the grandest glory that ever shone around a republic in the history of the

391–392. George Wilkes, in his *Spirit of the Times*, gave chief emphasis to the "One-Term Principle" throughout the canvass, and blamed the coalition leaders for not giving more attention to this issue.

[101] In his correspondence with Schurz (letter of July 8) Greeley warmly defended his political associates. *Ibid.*, II, 390.

[102] *North Am. Rev.*, Oct., p. 419; *Nation*, Aug. 15, p. 100; *Harper's Weekly*, Sept. 7.

[103] Conkling's speech, July 23, *N. Y. Tribune*, July 24; *Garfield's Works*, II, 38; Williams, *Hayes*, I, 369 f.; *Old and New*, Oct. pp. 385 f.; Boutwell's speech, July 17, *Nation*, July 25, pp. 49 f.

[104] *North Am. Rev.*, Oct., p. 417.

world."[105]   With another four years of "Grant's steady
hand on the helm," an enthusiastic organ predicted, the
country would "reach a development unparalleled in modern times."[106]   But all of this unparalleled prosperity would
be threatened, argued the Republicans, if the Democratic-
Liberal combination secured control.[107]   Greeley's erratic
utterances on the conduct of the national finances were all
carefully analyzed, and the conclusion was reached that he
would seek to put them all in practice simultaneously.
There was also, they feared, a grave danger from Democratic
influence of a repudiation of the national debt.[108]   Business
interests were held to be alarmed at the mere possibility of
the success of such reckless financiers, and the attitude of
leading capitalists did show unmistakably that their sympa-
thies were with the administration.   Lest there should still
be any doubt as to the position of "the interests" in the
campaign, a circular was issued on October 16, in New York
City, signed by some of the most prominent capitalists and
business firms in the metropolis, calling attention to the ap-
preciable reduction of the public debt as well as in taxation
during the past four years and concluding with this strong
testimonial for the President: "A careful consideration of
these results of prudent and faithful administration of the
National Treasury induce the undersigned to express the
confident belief that the general welfare of the country, the
interests of its commerce and trade, and the consequent
stability of its public securities, would be best promoted by

[105] Dawson, *Logan*, 205 f.   Cf. for similar expressions, Foulke, II,
267 f.; Martyn, *Dodge*, 282.

[106] *Milwaukee Weekly Sentinel*, Sept. 3.

[107] A Republican campaign speaker at Easton, Pa. predicted that if
Greeley was elected all the furnace fires in the Lehigh Valley would soon
be extinguished.   Quoted in White, 401.

[108] Conkling's speech, *N. Y. Tribune*, July 24; Williams, I, 373; *North
Am. Rev.*, Oct., p. 419 f.; *Old and New*, Oct., p. 388; Minneapolis *Evening News*, June 24.

the reëlection of General Grant to the office of President of the United States."[109]

The coalitionists did their best to extricate themselves from their discredited position on this issue. Financial disturbances were denounced as tricks of Wall Street, aided by the Treasury Department, to deceive the unwary voter.[110] The *World* held that Greeley had always been such a pronounced friend of capitalist and monopoly interests that it could not support him now if it were not for his pledge to leave these policies to congressional determination.[111] In his speeches in September, Greeley devoted much effort to explaining away the charges concerning his financial vagaries. In his remarks before the Cincinnati chamber of commerce and the Indianapolis board of trade he discussed current financial problems with a soundness and conservatism suited to reassure the most careful financier.[112] Other Liberal speakers strongly defended their candidate's financial orthodoxy,[113] and in their turn attacked the administration's financial policies.[114] But however many weaknesses might be exposed in the existing system, it was hard to overcome the arguments of big crops and the "full dinner pail."

In appealing to the labor vote the Greeley men were on much safer ground. Their candidate had been a life-long friend of the labor interest, and a pioneer champion of labor

[109] *N. Y. Times*, Oct. 16; Clews, *Twenty Eight Years of Wall Street*, 325–326.

[110] *Milwaukee News*, Aug. 16.

[111] N. Y. *World*, Aug. 9.

[112] *N. Y. Tribune*, Sept. 23, 27. See editorial comments in N. Y. *World*, Sept. 23; *N. Y. Herald*, Sept. 23; *Nation*, Sept. 26, p. 194.

[113] See Banks' speech at Portland, Sept. 1, *N. Y. Tribune*, Sept. 2. It was reported that Banks was to address the capitalists of the city from the steps of the Exchange in New York about August 20, but there is no report in the newspapers of such a meeting. See *N. Y. Tribune*, Aug. 12; *Nation*, Aug. 15, p. 97.

[114] For instance, Senator Fenton's speech at Albany, July 18, *Argus*, July 19.

organization.[115]   The vote of this element, with the failure
of their party to put a separate ticket in the field, was considered most doubtful,[116] and many direct appeals were made
to it by both sides.   Greeley was presented as a self-made
man, always a hard worker himself and the true friend of
other workers.   The laborer must in gratitude, as well as
in self-interest, support such a fellow-laborer and steadfast
supporter.[117]   In San Francisco opposition to the Chinese
was utilized by the Liberal speakers as an argument for their
ticket.[118]   The Republicans, on their side, could boast no
less a representative of labor than Henry Wilson, the "Na-
tick Cobbler," who in Congress had been a leading promoter
of the eight-hour movement.[119]   The characteristic argument was made that in the critical conditions then existing
between capital and labor,[120] the only safe course was in
allowing the all-wise Republican party to investigate the
question and secure laws that would afford justice to both

[115] Ingersoll, 444; Beveridge, "Horace Greeley and the Cause of
Labor," at Greeley Anniversary of Typographical Union, No. 6; Commons, "Horace Greeley and the Working Class Origins of the Republican
Party," *Political Science Quarterly*, XXIV, 468 ff.; Parton, *Greeley*,
290–292, 301–312.

[116] Cf. *N. Y. Herald*, Aug. 9.

[117] *Chicago Tribune*, May 12, June 8; *Milwaukee News*, Nov. 5;
Springfield Weekly Republican, Aug. 16; *Cincinnati Commercial*, quoted
in *N. Y. Tribune*, May 11; San Francisco *Evening Bulletin* (reports of
speeches) Sept. 12; *Golden Age*, May 11; *New Orleans Republican*,
May 4, 17; *Mo. Republican*, Aug. 1; Ward, *Ward*, 267; O'Connor,
O'Connor, 344.   Henry George in his San Francisco *Evening Post* was
an ardent supporter of Greeley. George, *George*, 239–240.   For
Greeley's discussion of his attitude toward labor in his campaign tour,
see speech at Jeffersonville, Indiana, *N. Y. Tribune*, Sept. 24; *Memorial
to Greeley*, 212 f.

[118] San Francisco *Evening Bulletin*, Sept. 12.

[119] Julian and Banks of the Liberals were also leading champions of
this measure.   See McNeill, *Labor Movement*, 130.

[120] This was the summer of the big strikes in New York City, *ibid.*, 143.

sides.[121]   The Republicans in their state platforms in certain cases also made a direct bid for the labor vote.[122]

But, as in the other two national campaigns of the reconstruction period, the war and its results furnished the chief lines of argument.   Morton had declared in the Senate the year before that the great issue in '72 would be the maintenance of the results of the war,[123] and so moderate a partisan as George William Curtis wrote in June that Grant was pitted "against every kind of Democratic, rebellious, Ku Klux, discontented, hopeful, and unreasonable feeling."[124]   The Republican leaders, seeing their administration on the defensive at so many points, resorted to the "bloody shirt" issue with a vengeance.   Their speakers fought the war over at great length and in all its horrors.[125]   Their party's great accomplishments in suppressing the rebellion and the necessity of its continuance in power were constantly emphasized.   Greeley was now denounced as an original secessionist in theory, and his attitude during war and reconstruction was represented as decidedly favorable to the southern cause.[126]   His conciliatory appeals to the South in his campaign speeches were interpreted by his opponents in the same way.   He was seriously charged with a purpose to pension southern soldiers, to pay the confederate debt, and to

[121] See editorial in *Milwaukee Weekly Sentinel*, June 18.

[122] *Annual Cyclopedia*, 1872, pp. 656, 663; Dilla, 143.   The Mass. Liberals also adopted a resolution strongly endorsing the cause of labor. *Annual Cyclopedia*, 1872, p. 503.   In Pennsylvania Buckalew agreed to be the candidate of the Labor Party for governor in case he received the Democratic nomination but he was defeated in the Labor convention by nine votes. *Ibid.*, 665.

[123] Foulke, II, 193.

[124] Curtis to Norton, June 30, Cary, *Curtis*, 230.

[125] See editorial on the Maine canvass in *N. Y. Herald*, Sept. 23.   See also on this feature of the Republican canvass, *Lakeside Monthly*, Dec., p. 468.

[126] Foulke, II, 263; Flower, *Carpenter*, 271; Conkling's speech, *N. Y. Tribune*, July 24; *Cincinnati Semi-Weekly Gazette*, Oct. 8; *Kan. Commonwealth*, Aug. 18, Sept. 15; Dilla, 144.

appoint to his cabinet confederate leaders like Raphael
Semmes.[127]   Radical papers and speakers, North and South,
predicted, in the event of the election of the coalition ticket,
the restoration to power of the rebel leaders with probable
future attempts at secession and the certain undoing of much
of the beneficent work of reconstruction.[128]   The Republicans
sought also to utilize the war issue in a more positive manner.
A convention of soldiers and sailors organized by General
Burnside, more successful as a politician than as a soldier,
met at Pittsburgh in September and passed resolutions
endorsing the Republican platform and candidates.[129]   A
loyal eastern organ thought this gathering was "one of the
largest and most imposing of the presidential year."[130]
Though apparently so fearful of former secessionists, when
supporting Greeley, the Republicans welcomed to their own
side influential leaders of that element.   John A. Mosby,
whose part in the war was not the least objectionable, was a
leading worker for Grant in Virginia.[131]

In opposition to the Republican war argument, the coalitionists put forward as their chief issue a plea for the recon-

[127] *Springfield Weekly Republican*, Aug. 16; N. Y. *World*, Aug. 12,
Sept. 3 (replying to such charges); San Francisco *Evening Bulletin*,
Oct. 14; Conkling's speech, N. Y. *Tribune*, July 24; N. Y. *Times*, July
22, 25, 31, Aug. 12, 14, 30, 31.

[128] Flower, *Carpenter*, 273; Williams, I, 373; Mayes, *Lamar*, 172;
Adams, *Storrs*, 286; Orcutt, *Burrows*, 137–143; Forbes to Sumner, Aug.
10, Forbes, *Letters*, II, 178–183; *North Am. Rev.*, Oct., pp. 420 ff.; *Old
and New*, Sept., p. 373, Oct., pp. 381 ff.; *Milwaukee Weekly Sentinel*,
Aug. 27; *Wis. Weekly State Journal*, Aug. 13; San Francisco *Evening
Bulletin*, Oct. 15; *Harper's Weekly*, June 8, 29, July 20, Aug. 24, 31,
Oct. 12, 19 and passim; *Mo. Democrat*, June 28; Minneapolis *Evening
News*, June 10, 18, 25, July 20, Aug. 19.

[129] *Annual Cyclopedia*, 1872, p. 783; N. Y. *Tribune*, Sept. 18; N. Y.
Times, Sept. 18, 19. A meeting of the Republican veterans of New
York State was reported in October, *Albany Evening Journal*, Oct. 3.

[130] *Boston Advertiser*, Sept. 20.

[131] See Mosby, "Personal Recollections of General Grant," in *Mun-
sey's Magazine*, XLIV, 762; Mosby's letter in N. Y. *Times*, May 25.

ciliation of the North and the South by the complete removal
of disabilities and a union of both sections for common reforms under the Liberal banner.   The Liberal movement in
its inception in the border states had sought primarily to
oppose the radical reconstruction policy, and in his letter
accepting the Cincinnati nomination Greeley made the har-
monization of the sections the keynote of his candidacy:
"I accept your nomination, in the confident trust that the
masses of our countrymen North and South are eager to
clasp hands across the bloody chasm which has too long
divided them, forgetting that they have been enemies in the
joyous consciousness that they are and must henceforth remain brethren."[132]   As other reform issues proved to a great
extent inexpedient[133] and the Republicans emphasized the
disloyalty issue, the coalitionists adopted reconciliation as
their great watch-word.[134]   Greeley made this his central
theme during his western trip, presenting his pleas for the
burying of past differences with great effectiveness.[135]   Other
speakers for the Liberals forcefully contrasted the radical
reconstruction policy with that for which their candidate
stood.[136]   This line of argument was emphasized especially
in the South where the abuses of the carpet-bag rule, fos-

---

[132] *Annual Cyclopedia*, 1872, p. 778. Greeley wrote to Ignatius
Donnelly, Aug. 29, that he wished "the canvass to turn on present
rather than past issues."   Donnelly MSS.

[133] "This was the one doctrine upon which the parties to the Alliance
could most readily coalesce."   Blaine, II, 531.

[134] See on the predominance of this issue, N. Y. *World*, July 13, Sept.
26; Washington *Patriot*, July 13; *Springfield Weekly Republican*, Sept.
20; *Golden Age*, Oct. 12; *N. Y. Herald*, Sept. 30; *Mo. Republican*, Aug.
3. The Liberal campaign pamphlet, "Mr. Greeley's Record on the
Questions of Amnesty and Reconstruction from the Hour of Gen. Lee's
Surrender," gives extracts from Greeley's editorials and speeches bearing on amnesty and reconciliation.

[135] See selections from his speeches in Ingersoll, 650–663; and *N. Y.
Tribune*, Sept. 19–30.

[136] *Schurz's Writings*, II, 395–401, 437–439; O'Connor, *O'Connor*,
333–344; Spencer, *Bayard*, 202 ff.; Ward, *Ward*, 259 ff., 275 f.

tered by a radical administration, were set over against the
sympathetic and conciliatory attitude of the Liberal candidate, ever since the close of the war, and the avowed aims of
the Liberal party.[137]   Some of the arguments that the radical
campaigners in the North employed most frequently against
Greeley were strongly urged in his favor at the South.[138]
The amnesty bill of May 22, 1872, passed evidently under
pressure of the Liberal opposition,[139] leaving only a few hundred under disabilities,[140] considerably weakened the Liberals' favorite issue.   Their opponents held that the great
weapon of the coalition was but a "spiked gun"[141] and they
also charged that "reconciliation" was anyway but an acci-
dental issue suggested by Greeley's happy phrase and that
it had not been emphasized by the organizers of the movement.[142]   But, considering the limited range of the policies
upon which the coalitionists could unite heartily and the

[137] See *Richmond Whig and Advertiser*, June 28, Aug. 16, Sept. 3;
Greenville Enterprise, May 15, 29, July 10, 31; *Maryland Union*, July
25; *N. Y. Herald*, July 13, reporting speeches at mass meeting at
Welden, N. C., July 12.   During his speech at this meeting Senator
Tipton of Nebraska shook hands with Senator Ransom as a symbol of
the desire of the Liberals for reconciliation.

[138] See, for instance, quotations from old files of *Tribune* showing
Greeley's attitude toward peaceful secession in *Southern Recorder*, May
21.   A constant radical charge against Greeley was his signing of Davis'
bond.   In Richmond the bond was lithographed for distribution as a
Liberal campaign document, N. Y. *World*, May 23.

[139] Cf. editorial in *Chicago Tribune*, May 24; White, 359; *N. Y.
Herald* editorial, May 24.

[140] Rhodes (VI, 329) on the authority of the *N. Y. Tribune*, says
between three hundred and five hundred.   Blaine II, 513 says "not
exceeding seven hundred and fifty in all."   Conkling in his New York
speech, July 23, declared: "Every rebel votes, and every rebel may hold
office now, except Jefferson Davis and less than two hundred others who
still spurn forgiveness."   N. Y. *Times*, July 24.

[141] See editorial in *Kan. Commonwealth*, May 24.   Cf. Conkling's
speech cited above.

[142] See editorials in *Harper's Weekly*, Oct. 12, and *Cincinnati Semi-
Weekly Gazette*, Oct. 22.

growing dissatisfaction with the radical southern policy, the issue upon which Greeley and his supporters elected to rest their case was probably the strongest one available.

During the early part of the canvass, before the first trial of strength, the advantage seemed to be with the coalition-ists. The apparently successful union of the two organiza-tions after the Democratic convention greatly increased the confidence of the Greeleyites.[143] Sumner's letter, late in July, was expected to win over many negroes and prominent anti-slavery men.[144] The administration leaders were for a time most apprehensive of the result. In July the Repub-lican national chairman sent urgent telegrams to the leader of the woman's movement to meet him in Washington for a conference and later informed her that the committee at the time had been "panic-stricken" over the outlook.[145] About the same time, R. B. Hayes admitted in the privacy of his diary: "I must say that I have just now a feeling that Greeley will be elected."[146] M. R. Waite wrote from Switz-erland that he was beginning to feel "nervous about politics at home."[147] Another European sojourner, General Sher-man, thought that Grant would be reëlected, "though several shrewd judges insist that Greeley will be our next President,"[148] and his more politically-minded brother could give no better assurance than that the "whole canvass is so extraordinary, that no result can be anticipated."[149]

[143] Shortly before the convention Chase expressed the opinion that not ten per cent of the Democrats would oppose Greeley while many Republicans would support him. Hooper to Sumner, July 2, Sumner MSS. See also Doolittle's optimistic letter to Sumner, July 13, *ibid.*

[144] Banks to Sumner, Aug. 2, *ibid.*

[145] Harper, I, 421.

[146] Entry of July 17. Williams, I, 368.

[147] Waite to Washburne, July 18, Washburne MSS.

[148] W. T. Sherman to J. Sherman, July 16, *Sherman Letters*, 337.

[149] J. Sherman to W. T. Sherman, Aug. 4, *ibid.*, 339. See also on the supposed uncertainty of the result, Oberholtzer, *Cooke*, II, 353.

The North Carolina state election, coming on August 1, was considered a most significant trial of strength. Both sides put forth every effort to secure the moral advantage of a victory in this first contest.[150] The canvass was bitterly and vigorously carried on from start to finish. Both organizations sent their strongest campaigners to the state, and the meetings were reported with great detail all over the country.[151] The first returns from the state election favored the coalitionists and there was great jubilation in Democratic-Liberal circles. The election of their national ticket, they boasted, was now fully assured, the Republicans, by making such desperate efforts to carry the state, having shown that it was necessary for their success in November.[152] These rejoicings proved to be premature and unwarranted as the final returns gave the state to the Republicans by a close but safe majority.[153] This election, emphasized in the popular mind far beyond its real importance, was apparently the turning-point in the campaign. The fortunes of the coalition, steadily mounting up to this time, show a perceptible decline during the remainder of the canvass.[154] Republican confidence was greatly revived by their success in the first skirmish. Hayes now thought Grant's reëlection quite certain,[155] and the President him-

[150] *Nation*, Aug. 1, p. 65; Greeley to Trumbull, July 5, Trumbull MSS.
[151] Hamilton, "Campaign of 1872 in North Carolina" in *South Atlantic Quart.*, XI, 148.
[152] N. Y. *World*, Aug. 2; *N. Y. Tribune*, Aug. 2; *Mo. Republican*, Aug. 2. The *N. Y. Herald* of the same date stated that if the apparent success of the opposition in North Carolina proved correct it would be generally regarded as settling the presidential contest. See also Hay to Reid, Aug. 4, Thayer, I, 345 f.; Trumbull to Donnelly, Aug. 3, Donnelly MSS.
[153] *Nation*, Aug. 15, p. 97.
[154] Cf. Reid's comment on Watterson's article in *Century Magazine*, LXXXV, 44; *N. Y. Herald* editorial, Aug. 25; *Nation*, Aug. 29, p. 129; Hudson, *Random Recollections*, 43-45.
[155] Williams, I, 368.

self would concede no northern state to his opponent.[156]
The shrewd Doctor Holmes, writing to Motley late in August,
after protesting that his opinion was not "worth two cents,"
very accurately predicted that from this time on the movement for Greeley would be a "*diminuendo*" and that for
Grant a "*crescendo*."[157]

Nevertheless the result was still generally regarded as in
doubt. The *Atlantic Monthly* in its September issue said:
"The election is as doubtful as any that the present generation of voters can remember."[158] In the New York State
Republican convention, on August 21, the strength of the
coalition seemed so formidable[159] that a counterstroke was
deemed advisable. Through the management of Thurlow
Weed and Henry Clews, the venerable Democrat, General
John A. Dix, was nominated for governor.[160] Dix consented
to run only after the personal solicitation of the President.[161]

[156] Grant to Washburne, Aug. 26, Grant, *Letters to a Friend*, 72.

[157] Morse, *Holmes*, II, 195. See also for the growing assurance of
Grant's supporters, Rollins to Porter, Aug. 22, Lyford, *Rollins*, 289 f.;
Luckey to Washburne, Aug. 30, Washburne MSS.; Winthrop to ———,
Sept. 2, Winthrop, 280; Curtis to Norton, early Sept., Cary, 231;
Young to Pryor, Sept. 16, Pryor, *My Day*, 352.

[158] *Atlantic Monthly*, Sept., p. 383. J. R. Doolittle wrote to Donnelly,
August 23, "I look upon the Greeley election as a thing almost certain."
Donnelly MSS.

[159] E. D. Morgan, the Republican national chairman, wrote to Dix,
Aug. 1: "I have on all proper occasions told our friends to nominate
for Governor some one of the distinguished gentlemen known as Reform
Democrats. I have believed that we can do better with such a
nomination than with a Republican. . . . I am anxious for the
success of Grant and Wilson, and I am disposed to adopt such proper
measures as will make success reasonably sure." Dix, *Dix*, II, 174.

[160] Clews, *Twenty Eight Years of Wall Street*, 297–303; Dix, II, 175;
Barnes, *Weed*, 485; *Nation*, Aug. 29, p. 130. Dix had come out for
Grant in July and had evidently been in close touch with Republican
leaders for some time. See his letter in *N. Y. Times*, Aug. 4; Morgan
to Dix, Aug. 1, Dix, II, 174. After his nomination the *N. Y. Times*
referred to Dix as a "Democrat." See editorial, Aug. 22.

[161] Clews, 304 f.

There was considerable uncertainty regarding New England owing to factional differences and the regard for Greeley in that section.[162]   A report that Senator Wilson had conceded New Hampshire to the enemy was widely circulated.[163]

The next test,[164] however, in the "September States," Vermont and Maine, showed that the Republicans were at least maintaining their old strongholds.   After active canvasses, both their tickets secured decided majorities,[165] and the coalition organs in vain sought to explain away the real result.[166]

But the decisive struggle remained to be fought out in the "October States," Pennsylvania, Ohio, Indiana and Nebraska.   The conditions in local politics seemed to give the coalitionists an excellent chance to retrieve themselves in these pivotal states.   In Pennsylvania the Republican candidate for governor was accused of complicity in frauds and a portion of the party, led by Forney and his *Press*, refused to support the ticket.[167]   The defection of ex-Governor Curtin to the coalitionists in September,[168] after the administration had vainly endeavored to keep his support,[169] was another hard blow to the state organization.   Grant wrote

[162] Lyford, 280–292.

[163] Rollins to Porter, Aug. 22, *ibid.*, 289 f.

[164] In the West Virginia state election, on August 22, both candidates for governor were Democrats, one running independently. *Annual Cyclopedia*, 1872, p. 801.

[165] *Nation*, Aug. 22, Sept. 5, 12, pp. 114, 145, 161; Dingley, *Dingley*, 98.

[166] See N. Y. *World*, Sept. 10; *Golden Age*, Sept. 14; *Spirit of the Times*, Sept. 14.   In a letter to a friend, Sept. 10, Greeley confessed: "Just now the skies look dark; a month hence they may be brighter; but in any case I shall be what I am, and shall have less care out of than in office."   Benton, *Greeley on Lincoln, etc.*, 229.

[167] McClure, II, 341–346; *Chicago Tribune*, June 13; *Springfield Weekly Republican*, Sept. 13; *Nation*, Apr. 11, 18, pp. 234, 250, Oct. 3, pp. 209 f.   Philadelphia *Press*, quoted in Washington *Patriot*, July 4.

[168] *Nation*, Sept. 26, p. 193.

[169] Randall to Sumner, Aug. 8, Sumner MSS.; Grant to Washburne, Aug. 26, Grant, *Letters to a Friend*, 71; McClure, II, 328.

THE POLITICAL CAMPAIGN OF 1872

that Curtin's defection would probably lose them the state in October.[170]   In Ohio, an original Liberal stronghold, the state campaign was well organized and hard fought on both sides.[171]   Indiana was the scene of a desperate political duel between the long-time rivals Morton and Hendricks. As the political future of both of these veteran party leaders was thought to hinge on this contest there could be no question of its thoroughness and bitterness.[172]   Senator Tipton's leadership in Nebraska was counted on to swing that state for the Liberals.[173]

The leaders of both national organizations fully recognized the crucial character of the October elections.   Greeley in June had advised against the adoption of a free-trade plank by the Democratic national convention as likely to endanger the state ticket in Pennsylvania.[174]   A private report from Republican headquarters in September stated that, while results thus far had favored the party, reverses in the October elections might defeat the national ticket. "Defeat in one of those states would endanger Grant, defeat in two of them would probably elect Greeley."   An analysis of the situation in the different October states showed considerable cause for Republican anxiety.[175]   The coalition press also maintained that the success of their ticket in two of these states would settle the national election.[176]   Sec-

---

[170] Grant to Washburne, Aug. 26, Grant, *Letters to a Friend*, 71.

[171] Brinkerhoff, *Recollections*, 221; Smith, *Rep. Party in Ohio*, I, 305.

[172] Foulke, II, 257; Holcombe and Skinner, *Hendricks*, 305; *N. Y. Herald*, Aug. 16 (political correspondence from Indianapolis).   Morton wrote to Blaine, July 22: "The contest here will be hard fought and most bitter, and we shall require all the assistance possible."   Hamilton, *Blaine*, 302.

[173] *Nation*, Oct. 10, p. 225.

[174] Greeley to Jones, June 24, Jones, *Jones*, II, 154.

[175] Glidden to Washburne, Sept. 15, Washburne MSS.

[176] N. Y. *World*, Oct. 7; *N. Y. Tribune*, Oct. 4.   John Hay wrote to Reid Aug. 1 from Springfield, Ill.: "If we carry Pennsylvania and Indiana the prospects here will be vastly increased."   Thayer, I, 344.

retary Fish wrote on the eve of the election that he was "very hopeful," but "not without anxieties."[177]

The fears of the administrationists proved not to be well founded. The October elections, with slight exceptions, went for the Republicans in a most substantial manner. Slight opposition gains here and there[178] detracted in no way from the conclusiveness of the general result.[179] No reason now remained to doubt the final outcome.[180] Certain coalition papers continued to encourage the faithful by factitious arguments and their national and state committees issued hopeful bulletins exhorting the party to greater activity,[181] but the figures were not to be mistaken. Liberals were now exhorted by Republican papers to return to the party fold; their efforts to form a new party, they were assured, had been a complete failure, and all that they could expect to do now would be simply to aid the old Democratic party.[182]

[177] Fish to Washburne, Oct. 7, Washburne MSS.

[178] Such as Hendricks' election in Indiana.

[179] Cf. *Nation*, Oct. 17, p. 241.

[180] The N. Y. *World* (Oct. 10) and the *Springfield Republican* (Oct. 11) practically admitted that there was slight hope of Greeley's election. Colonel McClure wrote to the Philadelphia *Press* that he considered the doubtful states as hopelessly lost, quoted in the *Cincinnati Semi-Weekly Gazette*, Oct. 18. For private opinions on the finality of the result, see *Sherman Letters*, 339; Winthrop, 280; Motley, *Correspondence*, II, 355. Greeley was apparently well aware of the significance of the result in the October states. See Watterson, "Humor and Tragedy of the Greeley Campaign," 42. Greeley to a Lady Friend, Oct. 14, Benton, *Greeley on Lincoln, etc.*, 234. "Straw votes" in four eastern colleges, Yale, Amherst, Brown and Wesleyan, were overwhelmingly for Grant. See reports in *Wis. Weekly State Journal*, Oct. 29, and *Springfield Weekly Republican*, Oct. 25, Nov. 1.

[181] For addresses of the national and state committees, see *N. Y. Tribune*, Oct. 10, 15, 16, 17, 19. For hopeful editorials, see *ibid.*, Oct. 9, 10, 24, 28; *Chicago Tribune*, Oct. 11; *Madison Democrat*, Oct. 14; *Mo. Republican*, Oct. 10; editorials quoted in *Nation*, Oct. 17, p. 241.

[182] See editorials in *Albany Evening Journal*, Oct. 10; *Kan. Commonwealth*, Oct. 19; *Cincinnati Semi-Weekly Gazette*, Oct. 25.

There was thus nothing surprising in the final result, except in the magnitude of the coalition's defeat.[183]   Greeley carried no northern state and but six of the border and southern states.   Virginia, West Virginia, Arkansas and Alabama, all of which had been wrested from radical control in state elections, went for the Republican national ticket.   Maryland was kept in the Liberal column by less than a thousand while Delaware was lost to Grant by about the same majority.   New Jersey went Republican for the first time in a national election.   Greeley's native state of New Hampshire, which had seemed so enthusiastic over her son's candidacy at first, repudiated him in the end by nearly six thousand.   New York, claimed for the coalitionists up to the very last,[184] rolled up a majority against them of 53,000, and Pennsylvania, which seemed so doubtful in October, now topped the Republican column with a majority of 137,000.   There was the same relative result throughout the North.[185]

The analysis of all the factors entering into the determination of this, as of any other national campaign, is a hopeless task.   At best only some of the more important influences can be definitely established.   Such a search must, of course, go much farther into the conduct and influences of the campaign than a mere consideration of the issues presented by the participants and other statements furnished for the consumption of the contemporary public.   The campaign managers of the period left few records of

[183] The *Boston Advertiser* on the day of the election (Nov. 5) estimated the electoral vote thus: Grant, 209, Greeley, 93, doubtful, 64, including New York and New Jersey.

[184] Fenton to Trumbull, Oct. 21, Trumbull MSS.   A correspondent of the *N. Y. Herald* (Oct. 30), after what was claimed to be a careful canvass, estimated that Grant would have a majority of 14,600 in the state and Kernan, the coalition candidate for governor, 7,000.

[185] Stanwood, *Hist. of Presidency*, 352; McKee, *Nat. Conventions and Platforms*, 159.

their activities, but some observations of things behind the scenes may now be taken.

In the first place, the Republican ticket was backed by a powerful organization with a large army of zealous workers. Party machinery was more highly developed than it had ever been in the past,[186] and where local weaknesses appeared special efforts were made to strengthen the organization at these points.[187] The congressional campaign committee, organized by Senator Chandler and James M. Edmunds, proved now a most efficient auxiliary of the national committee.[188] In the federal office-holders all over the country the Republicans had a faithful band of workers who could be called on at any time and for any needed service. Many of these officials seem to have devoted a good portion of their time during the campaign to raising funds, organizing clubs, speaking on the stump, and writing for party newspapers.[189] A large number of government employees, it was charged, were kept busy at the Republican headquarters in Washington in sending out franked documents and doing other work for the congressional campaign committee.[190] In Maine federal officials were accused of "colonizing" voters in the navy yards.[191] But by far the most offensive partisanship among Republican office-holders occurred in the southern elections. In some cases federal officials in this section openly devoted their time to party activities which extended to making arrests under the Enforcement Act,

[186] Cf. Kleeberg, *Formation of the Rep. Party*, 205, 217–18, 227. The *Lakeside Monthly* said editorially (Dec., p. 471) that the result of the election was a triumph for party discipline and organization.

[187] See, for instance, Lyford, 289.

[188] Detroit Post and Tribune, *Chandler*, 314 f.

[189] Joyce, *Checkered Life*, 168 f.; McDonald, *Whiskey Ring*, 42, 51, 327; *N. Y. Herald*, Sept. 23 (on activity of federal officials in the Maine election); *N. Y. Tribune*, Oct. 25 (printing assessment letter sent to a revenue collector by the congressional committee).

[190] Washington *Patriot*, Aug. 7.

[191] N. Y. *World*, Sept. 10.

colonizing negroes, and interfering at the polls.[192] With a
capable organization to lay the campaign plans and such
willing workers to execute them the administration began
with a big advantage.

The coalitionists, on the contrary, lacked efficient organization. Their papers were constantly exhorting them to
organize more fully and systematically, and after the Liberal defeats in the fall elections their campaign methods
were criticized.[193] In the midst of the canvass one of their
speakers wrote: "Never knew so good a cause so badly
handled. His [Greeley's] chiefs of organization incompe-
tent, and the whole campaign left to fight its own way, without generals or captains."[194]

Another influence working for the Republicans and
against the coalition was that of the financial interests.
Grant and the Republican organization were most intimately
connected with the captains of Wall Street. The President
had an especial weakness for millionaires and had never been
slow to accept their favors.[195] It was due chiefly to the ex-
ertions of Henry Clews, William E. Dodge and other New
York capitalists that the mass meeting had been called in
April to endorse the administration.[196] Ex-Senator E. D.
Morgan, a prominent financier and a cousin of J. P. Morgan
of Drexel, Morgan & Co.,[197] was this year the national chairman and William E. Chandler, who had been most successful
in raising large campaign funds in the past, was the secretary
and chief collector.[198] Jay Cooke's company was by far the

[192] Hamilton, "The Election of 1872 in North Carolina" in *South
Atlantic Quart.*, XI, 148 f.; Fleming, *Reconstruc. in Ala.*, 755; Davis,
Reconstruc. in Fla., 640 f.

[193] *N. Y. Tribune*, Sept. 10; *N. Y. Herald*, Sept. 23; *Golden Age*,
Sept. 14; *People's Tribune*, Sept. 4.

[194] O'Connor, 71. Cf. editorial in *Lakeside Monthly*, Dec., p. 471.

[195] Rhodes, VI, 383 f.

[196] Clews, 315; Martyn, *Dodge*, 282.

[197] Hovey, *Morgan*, 65.

[198] Oberholtzer, *Cooke*, II, 69–71, 352.

largest contributor. Cooke, who was a close friend of the President,[199] had very practical and direct interests to serve. The previous year his syndicate had secured a government loan,[200] and during the campaign he was negotiating for another installment.[201] He was also in the midst of his Northern Pacific promotion, for which the aid of the administration and Congress was so essential.[202] The firm's contributions, beginning with $10,000 for the spring election in New Hampshire, evidently totaled over $40,000.[203] Secretary Robeson was allowed $10,000 for the New Jersey campaign, for the sake of his influence in securing the navy account for the firm.[204] Special contributions were made to secure doubtful congressional districts. A request of this sort from Speaker Blaine was acceded to by Cooke's brother for the reason that the firm was not yet through its fights in Congress and that the Speaker was a "formidable power for good or evil and he has a wide future before him."[205] When in September prices on Wall Street suddenly fell and a panic threatened, the firm greatly aided the treasury department in making a "flank movement on the bears."[206] Lesser financial interests were freely called upon for tribute. The chairman of the New York state committee in October sent out circulars to the national banks, stating that "this committee has determined not to make assessments on Federal or State officers as has been usual heretofore, and, therefore,

[199] Oberholtzer, *Cooke* II, 454 f., 471. Cooke was also a close friend of Vice-President Colfax, whom he had urged to resign and enter the employ of the Northern Pacific in 1871. *Ibid.*, 230.

[200] *Ibid.*, 265–283.

[201] *Ibid.*, 353. Boutwell divided this loan the next year between the Cooke-Rothschild syndicate and the Morton-Morgan syndicate, Hovey, 77.

[202] Oberholtzer, II, 165, 178–181, 354.

[203] *Ibid.*, 357.

[204] *Idem.*

[205] *Ibid.*, 354.

[206] *Ibid.*, 354–356.

we have to rely upon such contributions as they together with other friends of the cause may please to make."[207] Many business men undoubtedly had real apprehensions as to the evils which would follow the election of the coalition ticket. The "Greeley scare," in addition to the usual disturbing influences of a presidential year, was depressing bond sales and business interests in general. To many these conditions seemed but a foretaste of what was in store if a financier like Greeley should become head of the government.[208]

The coalition, recognizing their great financial handicap, in being out of favor with these sources of large campaign funds, made some efforts to conciliate "the interests." Whitelaw Reid wrote to Jay Cooke, in June, with such a purpose. The promoter was assured that the Liberals in the resolution in their platform regarding public land grants for railroads had said nothing "calculated to interfere with the franchise of the Northern Pacific, or public confidence in it. They simply protest against the further grants of land for such purposes and pledge themselves to oppose them. For this it seems to me you ought to be greatly obliged since it prevents your lands from being cheapened in the market by undue competition."[209] But this rather dubious interpretation of a reform declaration seems to have been unavailing. Certain wealthy individuals[210] with political

[207] Washington *Patriot*, Oct. 25; *Nation*, Oct. 24, p. 258.

[208] Oberholtzer, II, 389; J. M. S. Williams to Sumner, July 15, Sumner MSS.; Veteran Journalist, "Personal Reminiscences of Horace Greeley," *Bookman*, XIII, 130; Pierce, IV, 544.

[209] Oberholtzer, II, 353.

[210] The *N. Y. Times* in a feature article the day before the election (Nov. 4) published a list of contributions to the coalition campaign fund totaling $219,500, and estimated that the entire amount received would be about $300,000. Among the leading contributors in this list were Senator Sprague of Rhode Island and his brother with $15,000 and $33,000 respectively; John E. Williams and brother, New York bankers, $15,000; A. T. Stewart $10,000; M. O. Roberts $10,000; John Cochrane $8,000; and Greeley and the *Tribune* $12,000. George Wilkes

ambitions backed the Liberal cause, but, in the main, the
moneyed men were found on the other side.[210a]

Thus with both federal office-holders and the "interests"
to draw upon, the "sinews of war" were controlled by the
administrationists. Their funds were expended most liber-
ally. The congressional campaign committee spent $30,000
in procuring extracts from Greeley's speeches and writings
for the press.[211] In the preliminary state elections no expense
was allowed to stand in the way of a full vote of confidence.[212]
The coalitionists, on the contrary, were at times hard put
to it for the necessary funds.[213]

The impossibility of reconciling large numbers of Democratic voters to Greeley's candidacy was probably decisive
in bringing about the overwhelming defeat of the coalition
ticket. Most of the Democratic leaders carried out their
part of the compact faithfully, if not cheerfully, but the rank
and file of the party recognized no such obligation. In all
parts of the country, both contemporary observations and
recent critical studies reveal the same general situation in
the Democratic party, such an antipathy on the part of
many old-line members to their candidate as even the hope

claimed that he bet $20,000 on Greeley which he would not withdraw
for fear of hurting the cause. *Spirit of the Times*, Nov. 9. Stewart,
according to the *Times* article, contributed also to the Grant fund. It
was reported early in the canvass that he had given $25,000 to the
Liberals, but this he later denied, and represented that he was entirely
friendly to Grant. Boutwell, *Reminiscences*, II, 205 f.

[210a] Greeley wrote to a friend, Sept. 11, "The Grant folks are full of
money, and are using it with effect." Benton, *Greeley on Lincoln, etc.*,
231.

[211] Detroit Post and Tribune, *Chandler*, 315.

[212] Oberholtzer, II, 352, 353, 356; Hamilton, "Election of 1872 in
N. C." in *South Atlantic Quart.*, XI, 148; *N. Y. Herald*, Sept. 23.

[213] *N. Y. Herald*, Sept. 23. (Editorial comment on the Maine state
election.)

of the defeat of the Republicans could not remove.[214]   A comparison of the returns of this with previous elections shows conclusively that large numbers of Democrats stayed away from the polls or refrained from voting for the national ticket.   In the states voting both in 1868 and 1872,[215] the Republican vote in the latter year increased 343,000, while the coalition vote decreased from that of the Democrats by 90,000.[216]

[214] *N. Y. Herald*, Sept. 23, Nov. 25; *N. Y. World*, Oct. 28, Nov. 9; Washington *Patriot*, Nov. 7; *Milwaukee News*, Nov. 8; Clay, I, 510; Julian, 348; Hay to Reid, Aug. 1, commenting on Democratic bolts in Illinois, Thayer, I, 344. Johnston-Woodburn, *Pol. Hist.*, II, 587 f.; Powell, *Dem. Party of Ohio*, I, 201; Dilla, 146 f.; Hamilton, "The Election of 1872 in North Carolina," *South Atlantic Quart.*, XI, 148, 151; Fleming, *Reconstruc. in Ala.*, 754; Haynes, *Third Party Movements*, 28–29; Alexander, *Pol. Hist. of N. Y.*, III, 300, 302 f.; Conrad, *Hist. of Del.*, I, 225.

[215] That is excluding Virginia, Florida, Missississippi and Texas in both cases.

[216] Stanwood, *Hist. of the Presidency*, 328, 351. A comparison of the vote in this election in strong Democratic sections in states where the opposition to the coalition was especially pronounced with that of previous elections shows a considerable defection in the party vote:

In Delaware the vote for Greeley was 11.2 per cent less of the total vote than that for Seymour in 1868, and 7.7 per cent less of the total than the vote for governor in 1870.

In Maryland the coalition vote for president was 5.4 per cent less of the total than that for governor and 12.9 per cent less than the percentage of the vote cast for Seymour.

In three New Jersey counties (Hudson, Sussex and Warren) the foregoing basis of comparison gives a decrease of 5.2 per cent from the presidential election of '68 and 7.1 per cent from the gubernatorial of '71.

In four strongly Democratic counties in Pennsylvania (Berks, Monroe, Northampton and Pike) the decrease from the national election of '68 was 6.7 per cent and that from the state election in October '72, 7 per cent. The figures are taken in each case from the *Evening Journal Almanac* for 1873. In all the states electing governors in 1872, with the exception of New York, the Democratic or coalition candidate for that office ran better than Greeley. In New York the plurality of the Re-

The fundamental explanation of the "tidal wave" of 1872 simmers down to this,—that the country had confidence in Grant and his administration, and did not wish at this time of readjustment from the great war to risk a doubtful experiment. All the charges that could be brought against the General were with great masses of voters more than offset by his fame as the great military hero.[217] The freedman, the new element in the electorate, had been taught to look upon Grant and the Republican party as their only salvation.[218] The past administration, in spite of all abuses, had been in many respects fairly efficient.[219] Times were still good, and the average voter was not greatly concerned over reform projects that seemed largely theoretical.[220] There was, to be sure, a growing unrest with existing conditions, especially in the West, which was soon to assert itself in a manner most disastrous to the Republicans, but the Liberals had failed to unite this opposition sentiment. Greeley, in contrast to Grant, was a most uncertain quantity. During his many years in the public gaze, in spite of the wide influence which he exerted, he had gained the reputation, which could not now be overcome, of a man of erratic, unstable qualities. And the political conjunction by which he had become a candidate was regarded by many as particularly suspicious. The Democratic party was still thought to be unreconstructed, and with the passions of the war still so warm it took no great stretch of the imagination to see in the party's sudden acceptance of its old vilifier a plot to get into office and

publican candidate for governor was less than two thousand greater than that for Grant and the sectarian issue in the state canvass would more than account for that difference.

[217] Cf. editorial in *N. Y. Herald*, May 8; Garland, *Grant*, 419–421; Linn, *Greeley*, 252; Albert E. Pillsbury (a Mass. Liberal) in *Memorial to Greeley*, 74.

[218] Cf. *Old and New*, Sept., p. 373, Nov., p. 631; Wallace, *Carpet-Bag Rule in Fla.*, 216.

[219] Cf. *North Am. Rev.*, Oct., pp. 417–419; *Lippincott's*, Sept., p. 355.

[220] Cf. *Lippincott's* Sept., pp. 356 f.

subsequently to restore something of the ante-bellum conditions.[221]   But, on their side, many of the Democrats did not trust their candidate.   The party was nominally united, but the Bourbon element, North and South, could not be reconciled.[222]   The result, then, can only be accounted for as a vote of confidence in Grant, either as a first choice, or, as with many, a choice of evils.   As an ardent Democratic campaigner explained: "The majority was so astonishingly large, that it leaves no room for disconsolacy, that circumstances might have made it different.   It was a clear Grant victory."[223]

[221] For a recent justification of this attitude by a thoughtful contemporary, see Wilson, *Dana*, 429 f.   The *Missouri Republican* (Nov. 6) attributed the result to the failure of the Democrats to follow out fully the "passive policy.".   Edward Dicey thought that if the Liberals had not joined with the distrusted Democratic party and had named a more suitable candidate they might have formed a new party.   See his article in the *Fortnightly Review*, Dec. 1874, p. 629.

[222] By this statement of Greeley's weaknesses as a candidate there is no intention to imply that some other coalition candidate could have beaten Grant, as some contemporary observers have held (see Hoar, *Autobiography*, I, 284; White, *Trumbull*, 402).   The weak points of the other candidates for the Liberal nomination have already been noted and, under the circumstances, it does not seem likely that any of them could have succeeded.   There has probably been a tendency to exaggerate Greeley's unavailability as compared with other possible candidates.   In the South, for instance, he had some peculiar elements of strength.   See Ross, "'Horace Greeley and the South, 1865-1872."

[223] O'Connor, 74.

CHAPTER VII

THE LATER ACTIVITIES OF THE LIBERAL REPUBLICAN
FACTION

In most accounts of the politics of the seventies the Liberal Republicans, as a distinct group, drop out of the narrative after the disastrous "Greeley campaign."[1] It is true that during the next four years the Liberal national organization had only a nominal existence, and that in some sections the party ceased to have, or really never had, a distinct local organization; but in other regions it was able in this period to keep together a following which exerted a considerable, at times a decisive, influence in state and local elections. A knowledge of this later activity of the Liberals is necessary for a clear understanding of the different character of the movement in different sections, and of the influence which it exerted on political parties. In treating this period, the activities of the Liberals in Congress will be first considered, next the position of the faction in state politics, and finally its connection with the national campaign of 1876, which marked the extinction of the Liberals as a separately organized faction.

I. THE LIBERALS IN CONGRESS, 1873–1876

In the last session of the Forty Second Congress, beginning in December, 1872, the policy of the Liberal members[2]

[1] Since this was written Dr. Haynes in his *Third Party Movements since the Civil War* has treated briefly certain phases of this period of Liberal activity.

[2] The classification of members varies in different places but the following lists, gathered from the *World*, *Tribune*, and *Evening Journal Almanacs* for 1873 and McPherson's *Hand-Book of Politics* for 1874, seem to include all who were at any time during the Forty-Second Congress identified with the Liberal faction. The dates of the

was watched with much interest for an indication of the faction's future alignment. The administration leaders, in the presence of their great victory, were in no mood to deal leniently with the bolters. This unconciliatory attitude was shown in the Senate early in the session when Cameron, after moving for an adjournment, refused to allow Sumner and Fenton to deliver the eulogistic remarks which they had prepared in memory of their deceased candidate.[3] In selecting committees the Republican senators completely ignored the Liberals, excluding them by the wording of their call from participating in the caucus.[4] The Liberal senators, of course, lost their chairmanships, and it now rested with the Democrats whether they should have any committee representation. The chief vacancies at the disposal of the Democrats were in the foreign relations, finance and judiciary committees on which Schurz, Fenton and Trumbull had been serving. After inviting the Liberals to a consultation, the Democratic senators decided to keep their own men on the finance and the judiciary committees, but from foreign relations Senator Casserly insisted on withdrawing in favor of Schurz. The other Liberal senators were given places on minor committees.[5] The question of the relation of the Liberal senators to the Democratic party was thus raised. Tipton and Rice attended the Democratic caucus and expressed an intention of acting with that party in future.[6] But the other Liberal senators were emphatic in declaring their independence of

expiration of the senators' terms are indicated. Trumbull (Ill.), '73; Rice (Ark.), '73; Sumner (Mass.), '75; Sprague (R. I.), '75; Fenton (N. Y.), '75; Schurz (Mo.), '75; Tipton (Neb.), '75; West(La.), '77; Hamilton (Tex.), '77. Representatives—Banks (Mass.);Blair (Mich.); Dodds (Ohio); Farnsworth (Ill.); Goodrich (N. Y.); Morphis, (Miss.).

[3] *N. Y. Herald*, Dec. 4, 1872; *Cong. Globe*, 42Cong., 3 Sess., 14.

[4] *N. Y. Tribune*, Dec. 6, 1872; Pierce, *Sumner*, IV, 549.

[5] *N. Y. Tribune*, Dec. 6, 1872; N. Y. *World*, Dec. 6, 1872.

[6] N. Y. *World*, Dec. 6, 1872.

both the old parties.[7] Schurz, before accepting the committee assignment tendered by the Democratic caucus, wrote to Senator Thurman expressing an appreciation of the honor, but explaining clearly that he did not wish to commit himself to any party. During the last campaign he had constantly disavowed any intention to join the Democratic party and his position was still the same. He stood on the Missouri platform; and he would support or oppose the administration accordingly as its policies were likely to advance or retard those ends. Thurman replied at once that he was instructed by the Democratic senators to say that they had understood Schurz's position and did not consider the proposed arrangement a surrender of principle either by him or them. With this understanding Schurz accepted the assignment.[8]

In the House, where committee assignments were made at the beginning of a new term and could be changed only by a suspension of the rules, it would have been difficult to oust the Liberal chairmen. The majority of the members were disinclined to making changes of that sort in the last session. A test vote came early in the session—December 2—when General Banks offered his resignation as chairman of foreign affairs on the ground that the House should be represented by one more unreservedly committed to its policies. But by a vote of 76–59 the House refused to accept his resignation.[9] This vote seems to have been regarded as a final disposal of the question of the reorganization of committees.[10]

[7] N. Y. Tribune, Dec. 6, 1872.

[8] Ibid., Dec. 7; N. Y. World, Dec. 7, 1872.

[9] Cong. Globe, 42 Cong., 3 Sess., 10 f.

[10] Butler was reported as seeking to put through a resolution to have the Liberals removed as the heads of committees, but it was said that most of the Republicans thought that the vote on Banks settled the matter. N. Y. Tribune, Dec. 9, 10, 1872. The Cincinnati Semi-Weekly Gazette (Dec. 6, 1872) thought that Banks' retention was a mistake. So long as the Liberals opposed the administration, it held, they should be treated like opponents.

On the leading measures involving reform issues in this session the action of the majority of the Liberal members was not especially creditable. In the Credit Mobilier investigation Goodrich dissented from the opinion of the majority of the judiciary committee, that a member could not be expelled for an act committed before his term of office;[11] but Farnsworth made a strong plea in defence of the implicated members.[12] The connection of the Liberals with the "salary grab" was decidedly open to criticism. Four Liberal senators and one representative supported the act, and but three senators and none of the representatives returned their back pay.[13]

In the election of 1872 none of the Liberal members were returned to the Forty Third Congress,[14] but five new members were classified as Liberals.[15]

Alarmed by the results of the state elections in 1873, the administration leaders in the Senate were ready to make terms with the Liberals at the opening of the new Congress. In their caucus it was suggested that Schurz, Sumner and Fenton be restored to their old party standing, but Conkling argued that some guarantee of their action in the future should first be exacted.[16] Subsequently the Liberals, though

[11] *Cong. Globe*, 42 Cong., 3 Sess., 1655.

[12] *Ibid.*, Appendix, 127–131.

[13] McPherson, *Hand-Book of Politics* for 1874, pp. 18–20. The *N. Y. Tribune* (Aug. 5, 1873) gives a detailed table of the vote and of the disposal of the back pay, as does also the N. Y. *World*, Aug. 26, 1873. Farnsworth divided his share among the counties of his district—an action that was much criticized. See *N. Y. Tribune*, Sept. 2, 1873, mentioning resolutions of a farmers' meeting in Illinois.

[14] Banks and Goodrich were defeated for reëlection and Blair for governor. *World Almanac*, 1873, pp. 39, 41, 54.

[15] *World Almanac*, 1873, pp. 79–80. In addition a Liberal member was returned from the 9th Ind. district, but he lost on a contest. *Evening Journal Almanac*, 1873, pp. 45, 54; *ibid*, 1874, p. 37; *Cong. Record*, 43 Cong., 1 Sess., 97. The Liberal member from La. was not seated until the end of the session. McPherson, *Hand-Book* for 1876, p. 2 n.

[16] N. Y. *World*, Dec. 3, 4, 1873.

they did not enter the caucus, were continued by the Republicans in the places that had been given them by the Democrats.[17]   Schurz, during the remainder of his term, adhered strictly to his independent position;[18]   Sumner's career ended before he became committed on partisan issues; and the rest of the Liberal senators gradually drifted to one or the other of the old parties.[19]   The Liberal representatives elected in 1872 were, in the main, identified during their term with the Democrats.[20]   In 1874 two of the Liberal members were reëlected as regular Democrats.[21]   A dozen other members, classified as "Liberal," "Independent," or "Reform," in nearly every case secured their election through Democratic support. With two exceptions the Liberals and Independents in the Forty Fourth Congress acted with the Democrats.[22]

[17] N. Y. *World* Dec. 5. Tipton was now acting with the Democrats. The *Mass. Weekly Spy*, a strong administration paper, said (Dec. 12, 1873) that the action of the Republican caucus marked the complete healing of the Liberal breach. The Liberal senators, it explained, did not come back as penitents and no pledges were exacted from them, their past services being a sufficient security.

[18] See Bancroft-Dunning, *Schurz's Pol. Career*, 356–361; *Schurz's Writings*, II, 450–472, 473–534; III, 115–152.

[19] West and Sprague are classed as Republicans by the *World Almanac* of 1874, but Sprague is still designated "Liberal" by the *Evening Journal Almanac*. Hamilton is termed "Independent" by the *World Almanac* for 1875, "Liberal" by the *Evening Journal*. McPherson (in his *Hand-Book* for 1876) in the last session of the 43rd Congress classifies Hamilton, Schurz, Tipton and Fenton merely as "Independents." But, in the main, Schurz was independent of both organizations, Tipton favored the Democrats and the rest the Republicans.

[20] McPherson, *Hand-Book* for 1876.

[21] Whitehouse of N. Y. and Banning of Ohio.

[22] The *Cincinnati Commercial* said that fourteen Liberals and Independents in the present House, with the exception of Prof. Seelye and General Banks of Massachusetts, had voted systematically with, the Democrats. Editorial, Oct. 18, 1876. Banks was suggested by Liberal papers as a most suitable coalition candidate for speaker. See *Madison Democrat*, Nov. 7, 1874, quoting *Chicago Tribune*. But, as the *Cincin-*

2. THE SOUTH

In the South the Liberal Republicans, as a distinct organization, had never been very important, and after the national campaign they merged readily with the old parties.   Only here and there some sign of the organization is to be noted. In Mississippi the lieutenant-governor and state treasurer elected in 1872 were classed as Liberals.[23]   In Louisiana some sort of organization was kept up, and the Liberals were specially mentioned in the call for the Democratic state convention in 1874.   There were only a few Liberals in the convention who had not yet gone over to the Democrats, but to secure the full support of the element concessions were made to them in the platform.[24]   The Congressman-at-large elected from Arkansas in 1872—a carpetbagger recruit of Senator Rice[25]—was nominally a Liberal, but was soon identified with the Democrats in Congress.[26] Frederick G. Bromberg, a leading Alabama Liberal, was sent to Congress in 1873 by Democratic support.   For a time he acted independently but before the end of his term he was committed to the Democratic party.[27]   Governor Walker, of Virginia, who had led the pioneer Liberal movement in 1869, was elected to Congress by the Conservatives

nati Commercial pointed out (Nov. 9, 1874), the Liberals could not expect any such concession as the Democrats now had a sufficient majority without them.   The Democrats with their large majority not only did not elect a Liberal Speaker, but they were not very free in giving them committee assignments.   The *N. Y. Tribune's* Washington correspondent predicted (Dec. 22, 1875) that Speaker Kerr's policy in this regard would alienate the Liberals.   See also *Milwaukee Sentinel* (Dec. 27, 1875) predicting that the Liberal representatives would be driven back to the Republican party.

[23] *World Almanac* for 1873, p. 44.

[24] N. Y. *World*, Sept. 3, 1874.

[25] Harrell, *Brooks and Baxter War*, 142.

[26] *Evening Journal Almanac* for 1874 classes him as a Democrat.

[27] *Memorial Record of Ala.*, II, 515.   Bromberg signed the address of the Democratic congressmen in 1875.

in 1874 and reëlected by the Democrats.[28]   There was no
room in the South at this time for any organization but the
radicals and conservatives—the Republicans and the Democrats.   The Liberal movement so far as the South was concerned was but a phase in the consolidation of all the conservative elements in support of the Democratic party.
The campaign of 1872 was the culmination of the movement, begun about 1869, of dissatisfied Republicans over to
the conservative opposition.

3. THE WEST

Throughout the West the period of Grant's second administration was one of party disorganization.   One of
the manifestations of the heated agrarian and anti-monopoly agitations of these years was the formation of "independent" parties as a means for securing the desired reforms.[29]   Much the same reforms had been sought unsuc-
cessfully in the Liberal movement, and in many cases the
same men who had been most active in organizing the initial
bolt from the Republican party were the promoters of the
new reform party in their state.   The Liberal state and
local organizations, both by direct coalitions with the new
movements and by their influence in securing Democratic
coöperation, largely made possible the successes that these
independent parties achieved.   But the general result of
this pooling of the opposition interests in the West, to which
the Liberals—intentionally or otherwise—contributed decidedly, was to better the position of the Democracy.

The Ohio independent demonstration of 1873, largely an
outgrowth of the Liberal and the Reunion and Reform move-

[28] Smith, *Executives of Va.*, 388.

[29] For a general account of these parties, see Buck, "Independent
Parties in the Western States" in *Turner Essays in American History*
(reprinted in Buck, *Granger Movement*, 80–102); Haynes, *Third Party
Movements*, ch. VI.   Haynes thinks that these parties "grew up con-
temporaneously with" the Liberal Movement "but largely independent
of it."   *Third Party Movements*, 48.

ments of 1871-1872, was of unusual interest, attracting nation-
wide attention. Ohio had been an original centre of the
reform agitation leading up to the national Liberal movement, and in the region about Cincinnati, in particular, the
Liberals had shown decided strength.[30] Following the election of 1872, there was much sentiment among Ohio independents, of both Republican and Democratic antecedents, for
the formation of a new reform party. A conference of leading
Liberals and Democrats was held at Columbus, on November 15, to decide on the future policy of the opposition forces.
An address on the result of the late election signed by the
allied chairmen was presented by Senator Thurman and
the Democratic participants all seemed to desire a continuation of the alliance. But the recommendation of the
Liberal committee that the opposition unite in one organization to be called the "Liberal party" came to nought.
Ardent Liberals demanded that the Democrats abandon
their organization, while Senator Thurman made it clear
that the old-time leaders of his party would never consent
to such a step.[31] The coalition was therefore continued
for a time on the old basis.[32]

[30] Cf. Williams, *Hayes*, I, 369. That the Liberal gains in this section
were large is shown by a comparison of the vote for president in Hamilton County in 1872 with that for governor in 1871 and president in 1868.
See *Evening Journal Almanac* for 1873, p. 106. The *Cincinnati Commercial* in 1874 (editorial, May 22) said of the Liberal Republican party
in Hamilton Co. that it had been "more tenderly nurtured here than in
any other quarter of the globe."

[31] *Cincinnati Semi-Weekly Gazette*, Nov. 19, 1872. There was evi-
dently considerable opposition in the Democratic party in the state to
Thurman's stand. See editorial in *ibid.*, Nov. 26, and the *Cincinnati
Enquirer* and other Democratic papers, quoted in *ibid.*, Dec. 3.

[32] In the Cincinnati city election in the spring of 1873 the Democrats
and Liberals, after considerable negotiations and wranglings, agreed on a
coalition ticket which was subsequently elected. *Cincinnati Commercial*, Mar. 7, 29, Apr. 8, 1873. In the Ohio constitutional convention
of 1873 there were 7 Liberal Republican members in a body of 105.
N. Y. *World*, May 7, 1873.

At first it was the intention of the Liberals to act with the Democrats in the state election of 1873. The two committees met and decided to call their separate conventions at the same time and place.[33] But an independent Democratic movement in June gave the Liberals an opportunity to act independently of the regular parties. This was the so-called "Allen County Democracy" Aroused over the refusal of their congressman to return his back pay and over the many other evidences of corruption in the old parties, they decided at their county convention at Lima, June 16, to start a reform party of their own, and called a mass convention to meet at Columbus, July 30, for that purpose.[34] Brinkerhoff, as the Liberal chairman, now issued a call for his convention to meet with the Allen County reformers.[35] Favorable responses from prominent Liberal Republicans and from those who were now termed "Liberal Democrats" came from all parts of the state.[36] Democrats who had been in the Reunion and Reform Association naturally went into the movement,[37] and even some prominent Democrats of the Bourbon type, evidently despairing of the old party, hastened to become charter members.[38] Both of the regular organizations were bitterly

[33] *N. Y. Tribune*, May 24, 1873.

[34] *Cincinnati Commercial*, June 18, 1873.

[35] *Ibid.*, July 2.

[36] *Ibid.*, July 26, 29, 1873; *Cincinnati Semi-Weekly Gazette*, July 1, 25, 1873.

[37] William S. Groesbeck, while refusing to act as the independents' candidate for governor, expressed hearty sympathy with the movement and made public a letter to a New York friend in which he characterized the old Democratic party as "spoiled," and suggested the formation of a new party to be termed the "Liberal Democracy:" *Cincinnati Commercial*, July 26; *Cincinnati Semi-Weekly Gazette*, July 29. This letter was widely quoted. See criticism in N. Y. *World*, July 30, 1873.

[38] George E. Pugh, a leader in the Vallandigham campaign of 1863, and Thomas Ewing were the most prominent representatives of this class in the new movement. Powell, *Dem. Party of Ohio*, I, 218.

opposed to this unsettling element in state politics.[39]   The Liberals held a preliminary convention on the morning of the day set for the regular independent mass convention and formally decided to unite with the independent Democrats.[40]

The resolutions of the independent Democratic-Liberal gathering, while reflecting to a considerable extent the dissatisfaction and unrest of the period, show the tempering control of the conservative Democrats: the abuses in both the old parties, which had now outlived their usefulness, were denounced and the duty of independent voting asserted; the reduction of the functions of government to the minimum was advocated, as well as "home government in all local affairs"; all grants, subsidies and special favors to corporations were condemned and a tariff for revenue only demanded.   The nominations, headed by Judge Isaac Collins—a former pronounced Democrat but prominent in the Reunion and Reform movement—for governor, were divided equally between the Democrats and Liberals.[41]

[39] For the Republican attitude, see especially the editorials in the *Cincinnati Semi-Weekly Gazette*. It charged (July 8) that the Liberals were seeking simply to secure a balance in the legislature, so that they might sell out in the senatorial election, and it called the leaders of the People's party "the Pharisees" (Aug. 8). The *Kan. Commonwealth* (Aug. 7) said that the Allen County Liberal coalition was "the 'Missouri movement' over again, minus the enthusiasm and brains that characterized the latter." For the Democratic opposition, see *Cincinnati Enquirer*, quoted in *Cincinnati Semi-Weekly Gazette*, July 4, 8, 1873; N. Y. *World*, July 18, 29, 1873. See also denunciations of the Ohio Liberals in the *N. Y. Herald*, Aug. 1, 1873, and *Nation*, July 31, 1873, p. 65. A resolution was offered in the Democratic Cuyahoga County convention for "dissolution of the partnership heretofore existing with the Liberals," but it was not adopted. *Cincinnati Commercial*, Aug. 6, 1873.

[40] *Cincinnati Commercial*, July 31, 1873.

[41] *Annual Cyclopedia*, 1873, pp. 609 f; Brinkerhoff, *Recollections*, 223. The detailed proceedings of the convention are given in *Cincinnati Commercial*, July 31, 1873, and *Cincinnati Semi-Weekly Gazette*, Aug. 1, 1873.

The new organization, adopting the name of "People's Party," made a vigorous canvass,[42] though the leaders stated frankly that they did not expect to win in their first effort.[43] The Liberal press and organization bore the brunt of the battle.[44] A special appeal was made to the labor vote in the campaign. Labor organizations had issued calls for the convention,[45] and their leaders were active in that gathering[46] and in the local organizations of the new party.[47]

[42] See circular of state chairman in *Cincinnati Commercial*, Aug. 15, 1873, and accounts of mass meetings in *ibid.*, Aug. 5, 18, 22, 29, Sept. 29 and passim.

[43] See Judge Collins' statement to that effect, quoted in *ibid.*, Sept. 6, and editorial in *ibid.*, Oct. 11. But Liberal papers thought that the movement might be the beginning of a national reform party. *Cincinnati Commercial*, July 8, 29, Oct. 13, 1873; *Chicago Tribune*, Aug. 1, 1873.

[44] Brinkerhoff had established a paper, the *Ohio Liberal*, as an organ of his party, and had built up a good organization. Brinkerhoff, 222 f. The *Cincinnati Commercial* and the *Cincinnati Volksblatt* gave strong support to the movement. Liberals like Brinkerhoff and Hassaurek were leading campaign speakers. The *Commercial* throughout the campaign referred to the independent party as the "Liberals," though Hassaurek had declared in the Columbus convention: "The Liberal Republicans have pronounced their own funeral oration. They met this morning just for the purpose of saying that the Liberal Republicans as a party organization has passed away. We are Liberal Republicans no longer." *Cincinnati Commercial*, July 31, 1873. Cox, Stallo, and Jacob Brinkerhoff supported the movement. See letters in *ibid.*, Aug. 5, Sept. 14.

[45] So stated in Brinkerhoff's call. *Cincinnati Commercial*, July 2, 1873.

[46] The representatives of labor organizations in the convention by unanimous consent were given special representation on committees. *Cincinnati Commercial*, July 31. One plank of the platform declared "That it is the duty of government to repeal all laws that favor capital to the prejudice of labor." Ewing addressed the delegates as "Democrats, Liberals, Workingmen, and Independents."

[47] See notice of ratification of the ticket by a labor organization, *ibid.*, Aug. 3, and of the nomination of a labor leader for the legislature, *ibid.*, Aug. 26.

Democratic leaders in the independent convention had suggested that the regular convention of their party might
adopt the "reform" ticket.[48]   But that party was resolved
to have nothing to do with its unfaithful members and allies and named a straight Democratic ticket headed by the
old Jacksonian leader, William Allen.[49]   A proposal to
endorse one of the independent candidates was most indignantly spurned.[50]   The Republican organization was now
most anxious to win back its seceded members.   A former
Liberal was placed on the state ticket[51] and direct appeals
were made to that element in the campaign.[52]   The Liberals
were especially hostile to the old-time Democratic leaders
whose refusal to disband their organization was preventing
the formation of a united opposition party;[53] but the result
of the new movement was simply to strengthen the position
of this element.   The independent ticket drew enough
Republican votes to enable Allen to secure the governorship and his son-in-law, Senator Thurman, to retain his
seat.[54]

[48] See Ewing's speech in the convention.   *Ibid.*, Aug. 31.

[49] Powell, *Dem. Party of Ohio*, I, 221 f.

[50] *Cincinnati Semi-Weekly Gazette*, Aug. 8, 1873.

[51] *Cincinnati Commercial*, May 22, 1873.

[52] See Noyes' speech of acceptance in *ibid.*, May 22, 1873; editorial
in *Cincinnati Semi-Weekly Gazette*, Aug. 12, 1873; Noyes' campaign
speech in *ibid.*, Aug. 26, 1873.

[53] See editorials deprecating continuance of a Liberal coalition with
the Democrats and insisting that that party should disband.   *Cincinnati Commercial*, July 24, 27, 28, Aug. 6, 1873; *Chicago Tribune*,
Aug. 1, 7, 8, 1873.   The *Commercial* desired Thurman's defeat for the
Senate by reason of his "reactionary" attitude in refusing to give up the
old organization (editorial July 29, 1873), and the same paper (Oct. 12)
thought that while the success of the Republican state ticket would not
much change conditions, the election of Allen would cause false hopes of
a national party revival and retard the formation of a new opposition
party.

[54] The independent ticket polled a little over 10,000 votes, over 4,000
coming from Hamilton county.   *World Almanac*, 1874, p. 43.   In the

In Indiana in the spring of 1873 there was a movement for the formation of a new party by the union of all opposition elements. Leading Democrats expressed a willingness to give up their organization and to unite with Liberals and reformers in a new party.[55] There was no state election this year, and apparently no definite action was taken. The Michigan coalition was continued harmoniously.[56] A call for a state judicial convention was signed by the chairmen of both the Democratic and the Liberal committees. The convention acted with entire harmony nominating an independent Republican, Judge Christiancy, who was later endorsed by the regular Republicans.[57] In the Kansas legislative elections the "Independents" and "Farmers," who included the Liberals,[58] secured enough members to elect a reform candidate to the Senate.[59] The California Liberal Republican organization,[60] apparently

Legislature four members were classed as "Independents." At least one of these was a Liberal. *Chicago Tribune*, Oct. 18, 1873 (reporting election of a Liberal in Cuyahoga Co.). A number of influences entered into the Democratic victory, such as the exposures in Congress and the panic, but the independent vote seems to have enabled Allen to pull through.

[55] *Chicago Tribune*, Washington correspondence on Hendricks' attitude, Mar. 24, 1873, and editorial, *ibid.*, Mar. 25. Hendricks, in a card in the *Indianapolis Sentinel* (quoted *ibid.*, Apr. 16), said that he desired the common action of all elements of the opposition, but was not certain whether that could be best brought about by the existing organizations or by the formation of a new party. He thought that the action of the Democratic and Liberal organizations in the various states would suggest the best plan to be followed.

[56] Detroit *Free Press*, Mar. 6, 1873, quoted in Dilla, *Politics of Mich.*, 148.

[57] Dilla, 148 f.

[58] The *Kan. Commonwealth* (Nov. 13, 1873) classified the Farmers and Independents as Republicans and "Democrats and Liberals."

[59] The Liberals had one senator, five representatives and a clerk in the House. Wilder, *Annals of Kan.*, 635–637. Ex-Governor J. M. Harvey was elected senator. P. B. Plumb, a leading Greeley supporter, was Harvey's nearest rival. Wilder, 638 f.

[60] A meeting of Democrats and Liberals was held in San Francisco soon after the election of 1872 (November 14) in reponse to a call

never very strong, became the "Liberal Reform Party" in 1873.[61] This and other independent, anti-monopoly organizations acted with the Democrats in the main in the local elections[62] and the combination was able to organize the legislature,[63] and control the election of the United States senators, an independent and a Democrat.[64]

In the formation of the anti-monopoly parties in the "Granger States" the Liberal leaders took a prominent part. In Illinois the Liberal members of the legislature at first maintained a separate organization[65] but leading Liberals soon helped to organize the "Independent" farmers' and anti-monopoly party.[66] [³] In the fall local elections the independents carried a large majority of the counties.[67]

for a meeting "for the purpose of effecting a reorganization of the Democratic and Liberal Party upon a firm basis." Apparently no definite action was taken. . San Francisco *Evening Bulletin*, Nov. 15, 1872.

[61] *Ibid.*, July 15, 1873.

[62] *Ibid.*, Mar. 13, July 26, 29, Aug. 19, 20, Sept. 11, Oct. 10.

[63] *Ibid.*, Dec. 3, 4. A former Liberal was elected speaker of the house.

[64] *Ibid.*, Dec. 20, 23. Booth, the independent elected, had been a strong supporter of Grant in 1872. The *Bulletin* held (May 15, 1875) that the California "Independent" party of 1875 was in no sense a continuation of the Liberal Republican movement.

[65] See their protest against Oglesby's election to the Senate, *Chicago Tribune*, Jan. 22, 1873. The Liberals had six members in the Senate and fifteen in the House. *Idem.*

[66] The editors of the *Industrial Age* of Chicago, one of the leading organs of the Granger movement and of the Independent party in Illinois, were Liberals. The *Milwaukee Sentinel* remarked sarcastically (Apr. 9, 1873) that "The alacrity with which certain 'liberal' newspapers and 'liberal' demagogues in Illinois have jumped astride of the farmers' movement against monopolies is edifying to behold." Horace White wrote to Ignatius Donnelly (July 23) regarding the prospects for the formation of a general anti-monopoly party. Donnelly MSS.

[67] The *Chicago Tribune* (Nov. 19, 1873) thus summarized the result of the election:

Farmers and Anti-Monopoly...............52 counties
Republicans.............................. 16 "
Democrats................................20 "
Independent.............................. 13 "

In the Minnesota state campaign all of the opposition elements, Democrats, Liberals, and Anti-Monopolists were united on a single ticket. A farmers' anti-monopoly party was organized largely through the efforts of Ignatius Donnelly, a late Liberal, who now sought to utilize the Patrons of Husbandry for promoting a new political organization.[68] The anti-monopolists put up a ticket composed of Democrats, a regular Republican, and a Liberal (for lieutenant governor).[69] This combination was endorsed by the state convention called jointly by "the Democrats and Liberal Republicans."[70] Party lines among the opposition seem to have been pretty much effaced for the time being. County conventions were variously referred to as "Liberals and Anti-Monopolists" and "Democrats and Liberals."[71] The Democratic attitude toward their allies was most respectful and cordial. Their leading organ never lost an opportunity to compliment the Liberals and to point out the harmony of interests between the Liberals and Anti-Monopolists and the Democratic party.[72] The Minnesota coalitionists elected one of the candidates on their state ticket, and, considering their lack of adequate resources and their inefficient organization, they made surprising inroads on the usual Republican vote.[73]

[68] Saby, *Railroad Legislation in Minn.*, 122. For the divergent opinions of the Granger leaders regarding Donnelly's scheme for a new party see letters in *Farmer's Union*, Aug. 2, 23, 30, 1873. The Donnelly papers for 1873 contain a large number of letters responding favorably to Donnelly's inquiry regarding the sentiment in different parts of the state toward the movement. Among the correspondents are such prominent Liberals as W. W. Mayo, S. M. Wilson, Samuel Mayall, and Ara Barton.

[69] *St. Paul Weekly Press*, Sept. 11, 1873.

[70] *Annual Cyclopedia*, 1873, p. 511; *St. Paul Weekly Pioneer*, Oct. 3, 1873. Donnelly wrote the next year that he and "scores of other Liberal Republicans" were members of this convention. Donnelly to L. E. Fisher, Apr. 1, 1874, Donnelly MSS.

[71] See reports in *St. Paul Weekly Pioneer*, throughout the campaign.

[72] See especially, editorials in *ibid.*, Apr. 1, July 11, Aug. 8, Sept. 11.

[73] See editorial in *Industrial Age*, Nov. 15, 1873.

In Iowa the leading Liberals were active in the new
Anti-Monopoly party, which for the time being absorbed the
Democratic organization.[74] In this hidebound Republican state the new movement, in spite of most inadequate
resources, made a good showing, especially in the local
elections.[75]

But by far the most successful coalition of the Liberals
with the Democrats in the West took place in Wisconsin.
Here the Democrats sought deliberately and skilfully to
retain the Liberals. Upon the advice of Democratic
leaders, a Liberal was supported as the minority candidate
for United States senator.[76] The party's leading organ was
most zealous in seeking continued coöperation with the
Liberals. "The signs of the times," it urged early in the
year, "make it alike the interest and duty of democrats and
liberal republicans to thoroughly consolidate their organization and push forward with united effort and unflinching
faith in the future."[77] The utterances of Liberal leaders in

[74] J. B. Grinnell and other Liberals were prominent in the Des Moines
Anti-Monopoly Convention. *Chicago Tribune*, Aug. 14, 1873. It was
reported that a motion to determine whether Democrats or Liberals
predominated in the convention was lost. *Milwaukee Sentinel*, Aug. 14,
1873. The *Milwaukee Sentinel* said (Aug. 15, 1873) that the convention
"was begotten of a sort of incestuous connection between Democracy
and Liberalism." Republican papers of the state predicted that most
of the Liberals would be back with the old party this year. See *Cedar
Rapids Republican*, quoted in *Chicago Tribune*, Aug. 15, 1873. The
Chicago Tribune referred to the opposition party in the state throughout
the campaign as "the Liberals." See political reports from the state in
the issues of Oct. 14, 16, 17, 20, 1873.

[75] See editorial in *Industrial Age*, Nov. 15, 1873. In the lower house
of the legislature there were 51 Republicans to 49 "Democrats, Liberals,
independents, anti-monopolists." *Annual Cyclopedia*, 1873, p. 382.

[76] *Milwaukee News*, Jan. 23, 1873. The Liberals had four assemblymen and two senators. The Republicans refused to give the Liberal
senators committee assignments and they were given places by the
Democrats. All of the Liberals but one senator acted with the Democrats. *Ibid.*, Jan. 11, 14, 22.

[77] *Ibid.*, Mar. 20.

different parts of the country were quoted with great respect.[78]   The failure of the Democrats in Ohio and New York to continue the alliance was greatly deplored,[79] while the successful coalition in Connecticut was held up as an example for the western opposition to emulate.[80]   In the spring county and city elections the coalition was well maintained, the "Liberal-Democratic" and "Democratic-Liberal," tickets, in which the candidates were fairly apportioned between the allies, meeting with marked success.[81] Republican papers were certain that the Liberals were coming back to the old party,[82] but there was little evidence of such a tendency.   In the main the opposition in the state was united and well prepared to conduct a reform, anti-monopoly movement in the fall.[83]   In the state campaign, waged over the predominant anti-monopoly issue, the coalition policy met with a signal triumph.   The call for a convention of "all Democrats, Liberal Republicans, and other electors of Wisconsin, friendly to genuine reform through equal and impartial legislation, honesty in office, and rigid economy in the administration of affairs" was signed jointly by the members of both the Democratic and the Liberal state committees.[84]   In the convention[85] the Liberal element was very prominent and was accorded two places on the state ticket, the nominee for attorney general,

[78] *Milwaukee News*, Mar. 16, 28, Apr. 16.

[79] *Ibid.*, Nov. 26; *Madison Democrat*, July 31, Oct. 10, 1873.

[80] *Milwaukee News*, Apr. 9, 1873; May 11, 1875; *Madison Democrat*, Apr. 8, 1873.

[81] *Milwaukee News*, Mar. 29, Apr. 1, 2, 3, 5, 20, 23; *Madison Democrat*, Mar. 29, Apr. 2, 1873.

[82] See editorials in *Milwaukee Sentinel*, Apr. 2, June 5, 7, 1873.

[83] Cf. editorials in *Milwaukee News*, May 15, Aug. 21, 1873.

[84] *Ibid.*, Aug. 30, 31; *Annual Cyclopedia*, 1873, p. 775.

[85] The "Reform Convention," which met at Milwaukee under the leadership of Dr. O. W. Wight the day before the coalition convention, after a conference, united with the Democratic-Liberals in a "People's Reform Convention," *Milwaukee News*, Sept. 25, 1873.

A. Scott Sloan, being the Liberal state chairman.[86] The opposition was officially termed the "People's Party," but the candidates, especially for local offices, were still referred to by Democratic papers as "Liberal Democratic,"[87] and a mass meeting to be addressed by a prominent Liberal was announced as a "Liberal Republican Rally."[88] The election brought the coalition complete success. The state ticket was elected by about 15,000 and the combined opposition had a majority of twelve in the legislature.[89] The Democratic leaders and organs for the most part showed much tactful restraint, holding that the victory was not for their party alone but for all the elements of reform in the state, and a Bourbon member who hastened to rejoice over the revival of the old party was rebuked.[90] "This is no petty personal victory," one Democratic paper explained, "no small partisan triumph. The victors are not Democrats alone, nor Liberal Republicans, nor Germans, nor Grangers nor Farmers; they are all these combined."[91]

[86] For detailed proceedings of the convention, see *ibid.*, Sept. 25; *Milwaukee Sentinel*, Sept. 25, 1873. The other Liberal on the ticket was Prof. Searing, the candidate for superintendent of schools, "who had done good service for Greeley last fall." *Wis. Weekly State Journal*, Sept. 30, 1873.

[87] See, for instance, the list of assembly nominations so headed in *Madison Democrat*, Oct. 27, 1873.

[88] *Ibid.*, Oct. 29.

[89] The report of the election in the *Annual Cyclopedia* for 1873 (p. 776) states that it "resulted in the success of the Democratic and Liberal Republican ticket." According to this authority two senators and eight assemblymen were "Liberals."

[90] *Madison Democrat*, Nov. 10, 1873. The N. Y. *World* announced (Nov. 5, 1873): —"we have . . . carried Wisconsin."

[91] *Madison Democrat*, Nov. 10, 1873. Alexander Mitchell of Milwaukee wrote to Ignatius Donnelly (Nov. 8) that the result in Wisconsin must be as pleasing to Donnelly as to the "Democrats and Reformers" in Wisconsin. Donnelly MSS. S. S. Cox of New York wrote (Nov. 12), congratulating Donnelly on the outcome of the western elections, and attributing the result to the farmers' movement. *Ibid.*

15

Thus, throughout the West independent opposition parties developed in 1873, in all of which the Liberals constituted the leading or an influential element.[92]   And in every case except Ohio these organizations acted in union with the Democrats.   That party could afford to view the general situation with complacency.[93]

In the Democratic "land-slide" of 1874, by which the national House of Representatives and many state offices came again into the party's control, the Liberal influence, especially in the West, either in close alliance with the Democrats or in the independent movements, was an important factor.   In Ohio the former Liberal vote was largely absorbed by the Democrats, contributing greatly to the election of their local, state, and congressional tickets.[94]   Indiana Liberal leaders seem now to have been

[92] The *Chicago Tribune* (Aug. 8, 1874) said editorially that the Liberal movement "failed in the Presidential election, but under one name or another it has continued to achieve success, ever since. Here it has been called Liberal Republican, and there Reform; elsewhere Independent, and elsewhere by a still different name. But wherever the old orthodox, straight-jacketed Republican party has been defeated, it has been defeated by men advocating the principles enunciated by the Liberal Republican convention of 1872."

[93] The *Milwaukee News* (Oct. 19, 1873) summed up the situation thus: "We welcome the result in California, the result in Iowa, the result in Ohio, the result in Oregon as one. They all indicate the overthrow of the rascally corrupt administration faction of the Republican party. Names are nothing. When we get that party definitely beaten we will agree on new names, if they shall be desired, and on a platform, and measures of government. Until then let the opposition fight under such various banners as they may adopt, according to their locality and prospects of success. . . . We call it People's Reform in Wisconsin. They call it Democratic in Ohio. They call it Anti-Monopoly in Iowa. They call it Independent in California. The movement is one. The victory is one—Let us all rejoice."

[94] See editorials in *Cincinnati Commercial*, Apr. 7, 1874; *Cincinnati Semi-Weekly Gazette*, Oct. 16, 27, 1874; N. Y. *World*, Sept. 24, 1874 (report of the political situation in Northern Ohio). These statements as to the support of the Democratic ticket by the Liberals seem to be

identified with the Democrats,[95] though a few of the more radical were in the Independent party.[96] The Michigan Liberal leaders organized a "National Reform Party" this year.[97] The new organization failed to coalesce fully with the Democrats, but a number of candidates were endorsed by the two organizations, acting separately, and the combined opposition made remarkable gains.[98] In Illinois the more radical of the Liberal element went into the Independent party,[99] but the most influential leaders who had been concerned in the movement joined the old parties, the more eminent going with the Democrats.[100] In the campaign special appeals were made to the Liberal vote.[101]

well borne out by the vote in Hamilton Co. *Tribune Almanac*, 1875, p. 76. Banning, the Liberal congressman from the Cincinnati district, was renominated by the Democrats and declared his firm adherence to that party. *Cincinnati Semi-Weekly Gazette*, Sept. 11, 1874. J. M. Ashley was defeated for the Democratic nomination in the Toledo district. *Milwaukee Sentinel*, Aug. 20, 1874.

[95] See correspondence from Indianapolis on the political situation in the state in *Chicago Tribune*, July 13, 1874. The activities of a "Democratic-Liberal" county convention in the state were noted. *Ibid.*, Aug. 3. John E. Neff, the Democratic candidate for secretary of state, had been a Liberal candidate for Congress in 1872.

[96] See, for instance, references to Frank C. Johnson, a former Liberal, as a member of the Independent party in Indiana. *Industrial Age*, June 20, 27, Oct. 24, 1874.

[97] Dilla, 155 f.

[98] *Ibid.*, 156–172; *Annual Cyclopedia*, 1874, pp. 557–559. The opposition secured three congressmen, all gains, and reduced the Republican majority in the legislature to ten.

[99] Bennett (*Politics and Politicians of Chicago*, 185) says that "Out of the scattered remnant of the Liberal movement was formed the Anti-Monopoly party." Cf. to the same effect, Lusk, *Eighty Years of Illinois*, 242. A considerable number of Liberals took an active part in the Independent conventions of this year. *Industrial Age*, May 6, 16, June 13, 1874; Moses, *Ill.*, II, 824.

[100] Koerner, *Memoirs*, II, 591; Bennett, 185.

[101] See statement of C. H. McCormick, the Democratic state chairman, that an invitation had been given to the Liberals to consult with the Democratic committee. *Industrial Age*, July 25, 1874. The call

The candidate for superintendent of public instruction supported by both the Democrats and Independents was elected,[102] and a coalition of these organizations was able to organize the new legislature.[103]   The "Democratic-Liberal" organization was continued in Minnesota with large gains in the legislature, though no congressman was secured.[104]   The Wisconsin coalition was continued under the designation of "Reform."   To maintain cordial feeling and to prevent defection, the congressional candidates were divided equally between the Democrats and the Liberals.[105]   But there was a considerable falling off in the opposition vote and the coalition lost the legislature.[106] Kansas Liberals were leading spirits in the opposition "Independent Reform Party," which secured a member of Congress.[107]   Even in Iowa, the "Vermont of the West," the Democrats and Liberals under the name "Anti-Monop-

for the Democratic state convention, addressed "To the Democracy, Liberals, and other opponents of the Republican party," was specially endorsed by a large number of leading Liberals. *Chicago Tribune,* Aug. 19, 1874.   The Liberal element was prominent in the convention over which Governor Palmer presided. *Ibid.,* Aug. 27; Koerner, II, 591. Farnsworth and Le Moyne (former Liberals) were Democratic-Independent candidates for Congress.

[102] *Annual Cyclopedia,* 1874, p. 404.

[103] *Chicago Tribune,* Jan. 5, 8, 9, 1875.   E. M. Haines, a former Liberal, now an Independent, was elected speaker of the house.

[104] The state convention was termed Democratic-Liberal. *St. Paul Weekly Press,* Oct. 1, 1874; *Chicago Tribune,* Sept. 24, 1874.   The Republicans secured a majority in the legislature of only three. *Annual Cyclopedia,* 1874, p. 565.   There was some dissension between the leaders of the two elements of the coalition, but the representatives of both in the legislature favored a union of the opposition.   Donnelly to Fisher, Apr. 1, 1874; Fisher to Donnelly, Apr. 22, 1874, Donnelly MSS.

[105] *Milwaukee News,* Sept. 18, Oct. 3, Dec. 30, 1874.

[106] *Annual Cyclopedia,* 1874, p. 811.

[107] Wilder, 646, 648, 655, 656; *Kan. Commonwealth,* Aug. 6, 7, 1874. There were two Liberals on the state ticket and M. J. Parrott, the Liberal state chairman, was an unsuccessful candidate for Congress.

oly" were able to elect a congressman.[108] Missouri was
the only state where the independents acted with the Republicans.[109] The Liberals and Democrats had continued
to act together in local elections in 1873,[110] but the reactionary and extreme partisan attitude of the Democratic leaders, with the state safely in their control, tended to alienate
their allies.[111] In 1874 the reform "People's Party" was
supported by the Republicans and Liberals.[112] Schurz
supported the movement vigorously, and it was generally
understood that success would mean his reëlection to the
Senate.[113] The Democrats, however, were triumphant by
a large majority.[114]

The defeat of four regular Republican candidates for the
United States Senate, including two of the President's
closest advisers, early in 1875, was accomplished by the
combined opposition of the Democrats and Liberals in the
legislatures. In Michigan a small group of discontented
Republicans united with the Democrats and Liberals
for the defeat of that valiant leader of the senatorial clique,
Zach Chandler, electing Judge Christiancy, a conservative

[108] *Annual Cyclopedia*, 1874, pp. 418f. A correspondent to the
Chicago Tribune (Aug. 18, 1874) from Dubuque said of the situation in
one of the congressional districts that the Democrats and Liberals were
well united, and that one of the leading candidates for the coalition
nomination was "a thoroughgoing Liberal-Republican."

[109] The success of the Democratic state ticket in Oregon was due to
the votes taken from the Republicans by the Independent party.
Chicago Tribune, July 8, 1874.

[110] See report of the election of the ticket of the "Democrats and
Liberals" in the St. Louis city election. *Madison Democrat*, Apr. 3,
1873.

[111] See Schurz to Grosvenor, Dec. 25, 1872, *Schurz's Writings*, II, 449.

[112] Editorial in *St. Paul Weekly Press*, Oct. 1, 1874.

[113] *Idem; Chicago Tribune*, Sept. 12, 22, 1874; *Madison Democrat*,
Sept. 24, 1874.

[114] *Annual Cyclopedia*, 1874, p. 579.

in high favor with the coalitionists.[115]   The election of 1874, culminating in Chandler's defeat, "marks the high-tide of Democratic . . . or at least of anti-Republican success" in Michigan during the Reconstruction period.[116] A bitter contest between rival Republican candidates in Wisconsin gave the opposition an opportunity for a similar move in that state. The Democratic organ urged a union of "Democrats, Liberals, and Reformers in the Legislature" with the bolting Republicans, if a candidate of satisfactory views could be agreed upon.[117]   Such a candidate was found in Angus Cameron, an independent Republican and a former Democrat, and Senator Matt Carpenter, another member of the President's inner circle, was retired.[118] The Republicans regarded Cameron's election as a real party defeat.[119]   In Minnesota the tactics of the coalitionists forced the Republicans to abandon the regular organization candidate and to elect as a compromise Judge McMillan, a conservative Republican, long out of active politics.[120]   The Democrats and Liberals had at first sup-

[115] Dilla, 174–179. Stocking, *Rep. Party in Mich.*, 124; Detroit Post and Tribune, *Chandler*, 338. The *Madison Democrat* (Jan. 23, 1875) said of the result: "The Liberal Democrats of Michigan deserve high praise for rising in this instance above mere party considerations and uniting with the handful of anti-Chandler Republicans in the election of such a man as Judge Christiancy."

[116] Dilla, 179.

[117] *Milwaukee News*, Jan. 23, 1875.

[118] The *News* said of Cameron's election (Feb. 4, 1875): "There is immense jubilation among all Democrats and Liberals." All of the Liberal members supported Cameron. *Ibid.*, Feb. 6. See also on this coalition victory, editorials in *Madison Democrat*, Feb. 4, 1875; *St. Paul Weekly Pioneer*, Feb. 12, 1875.

[119] The *Milwaukee Sentinel* declared (Feb. 4, 1875): "The Democrats have hit the Republican party of Wisconsin a hard blow in defeating Senator Carpenter. . . . We believe we crowed over the result of the election in Wisconsin in the fall. We take it all back—it was a Democratic victory."

[120] Holmes, *Minn.*, IV, 70 f.

ported the Liberal leader, Donnelly,[121] but later united upon an independent Democrat, planning to hold out until they could make an arrangement with bolting Republicans.[122] Upon overtures by the Liberal ex-Senator Wilkinson, the Republicans hastened to abandon their caucus nominee.[123] In Nebraska, Senator Tipton was succeeded by another Liberal, A. S. Paddock, who had the support of the Democrats and independents.[124]

The coöperation of the Liberals and independents with the Democrats was somewhat disturbed in 1875 by the injection of the greenback issue. The opposition in the West especially was divided over this issue. The reform People's party in Ohio in 1873 was not agreed on the subject and decided not to pronounce definitely on it, much to the dissatisfaction of the leading Liberal and the conservative Democratic elements.[125] The Independent parties in Indiana and Illinois in 1874 were committed to inflation,[126] and the Democratic organizations of Indiana and Ohio strongly leaned in the same direction.[127] The Illinois Democrats were saved from following in this course, it was claimed, by the influential Liberals who had joined with them.[128] The inflationist issue was squarely presented in the Ohio state campaign of 1875, when the Democratic

[121] *St. Paul Weekly Pioneer*, Feb. 12, 1875.

[122] The *St. Paul Weekly Pioneer* (Democratic) said (Feb. 19, 1875): "The Liberal-Democrats propose to stick to Lochren (the independent Democratic candidate) until an acceptable candidate can be found who can draw ten or twelve votes from the Republican side."

[123] Holmes, IV, 70.

[124] Watkins, *Neb.* III, 147 f. Paddock at first maintained an independent attitude on certain matters, as the southern question and the tariff, but joined the Republican caucus. *Ibid.*, 149 f.

[125] See the expressions of opinion on this issue at the Cincinnati mass meeting, in *Cincinnati Commercial*, Aug. 5, 1873.

[126] *Annual Cyclopedia*, 1874, pp. 403, 413.

[127] *Ibid.*, pp. 415, 667.

[128] See editorial in *Chicago Tribune*, Aug. 28, 1874.

Governor Allen on an inflationist platform was opposed by ex-Governor Hayes.[129]   The action of the Democrats on the currency question drove the great mass of the Liberal element of the state to the Republicans.   The Liberal organs and leaders, almost without exception, supported Hayes.[130]   Schurz was prevailed upon to return from Europe to take part in this campaign which was regarded as a most critical test of the currency question.[131]   He and Grosvenor, as representatives of the original Liberal reformers, made a vigorous and effective series of speeches.[132]   Schurz maintained that he was not speaking in the interest of the Republican party, but simply in that of an honest currency.[133]   The Liberal influence seems to have been decisive in defeating the Democratic candidate and his "rag-money" propaganda.[134]   But farther west the more radical Liberals

[129] *Annual Cyclopedia*, 1875, pp. 606 f.

[130] N. Y. *World*, July 15, 1875; *Boston Weekly Advertiser*, July 15, 1875; *Milwaukee Sentinel*, Sept. 28, 1875; *Cincinnati Commercial* throughout the campaign.   Halstead's *Commercial*, Hassaurek's *Volksblatt* and Brinkerhoff's *Ohio Liberal*, all supported Hayes.   The *Commercial* estimated (July 17, 1875) that two thirds of those voting the independent ticket in 1873 would now support Hayes.

[131] *Schurz's Writings*, III, 157–160; Bancroft-Dunning, *Schurz's Pol. Career*, 363; *Cincinnati Commercial*, Sept. 22, 1875.

[132] *Schurz's Writings*, III, 161–215; *Cincinnati Commercial*, Sept. 28, 1875; *N. Y. Herald*, Sept. 28, 1875; *St. Paul Weekly Pioneer Press*, Aug. 20, 1875.

[133] *Schurz's Writings*, III, 163.

[134] Wickoff to Schurz, Oct. 26, 1875, *ibid.*, 217; C. F. Adams, Jr. to Schurz, Oct. 13, 1875, *ibid.*, 215; Bowles to Halstead, Oct. 19, 1875, Merriam, *Bowles*, II, 348; *N. Y. Herald* editorial, Oct. 14, 1875.   The *Ohio Liberal* said of the result: "It is evident now to every one that the Liberals of Ohio are the balance of power in the politics of the State. That party, in 1876, which expects to carry Ohio must have the Liberal vote, and that vote will be cast for the party which most nearly represents Liberal principles."   Quoted in *Cincinnati Commercial*, Nov. 5, 1875.   Hamilton County which gave the Democratic candidate for secretary of state in 1874 a plurality of 4,637, went for Hayes by 1,295. *Evening Journal Almanac*, 1876, p. 74.

were prominent[135] in the "Greenback" parties which developed in 1875–1876, and these parties, drawing a large part of their membership from the Republicans, like the other independent movements, worked in the Democratic interest.[136]

Thus, up to the presidential year, 1876, the independent movements in the West, in which the Liberal Republicans took such an influential part, were a decided aid in the rejuvenation of the Democracy. There were some reverses in 1875, as was to be expected after a "landslide," but in the main, the opposition in this section was well holding its ground.[137]

[135] See proceedings of state and local conventions of the "Independent Reform" party in Kansas in 1876 in which Liberals took an active part. *Kan. Commonwealth*, July 28; Aug. 26, Oct. 27, 1876. In Minnesota, Donnelly, Ayres, and Sherwood were leaders in the Independent (Greenback) party. *Industrial Age*, Sept. 23, 1876. In a Greenback convention at Grand Rapids, Michigan, in August, 1876, former Liberals were prominent. *Chicago Tribune*, Aug. 4, 1876. The state convention of the Independent (Greenback) party in Iowa in 1876, according to the *Iowa State Register* (May 19, 1876), was composed "mainly of former Democrats and Liberals," quoted in Haynes, 154. The Greenback candidate for governor in Iowa in 1877 was a former Liberal, *ibid.*, 156. Liberals, as already stated, were leaders in the Independent parties in Indiana and Illinois.

[136] Dilla, 200; *Chicago Tribune* editorials, Oct. 16, 25, 1876 (commenting on state canvasses in Indiana and Illinois).

[137] The Democratic-Liberal coalition in Wisconsin was continued in 1875 (under the name of "Reform party"), the state ticket was renominated and all reëlected but the candidate for governor. *Milwaukee News*, July 1, 17, 22; Aug. 8, Sept. 9, 12, 1875; *Annual Cyclopedia*, 1875, pp. 763 f. The Democrats and National Reformers in Michigan united on the same candidates this year. Dilla, 183. In Minnesota a Liberal was named for lieutenant governor by the Democratic convention. *Chicago Tribune*, July 8, 1875. "The Democrats, Liberal Republicans, and Anti-Monopolists of the State of Iowa" continued to act together in 1875. *Chicago Tribune*, June 25, 1875. The *Milwaukee Sentinel* (June 26, 1875) characterized the Iowa opposition as the "three witches." The Independent party in California (whose connections with the Liberals, as already pointed out, was not

4. THE EAST

In the East, with the early withdrawal of a large portion
of the independent reform group, the Liberal activities, for
the most part, degenerated into the schemings of predatory
politicians to secure favors from one or the other of the old
parties.   In the South the desire for home-rule was driving
all of the conservatives into the opposition; in the West
there were sincere, if erratic, efforts at economic reforms of
which the Liberal and other independent political movements were an expression; but in the East in this period
there was no such widespread popular zeal for independent
political action.

In New England the Liberal organizations were continued
in several states.   In New Hampshire, where the usual
closeness of the vote gave an independent movement an
especial significance,[138] the Liberals held a state convention
in the spring of 1873 attended largely by members of the
state committee.   Candidates for state, district and county
offices were nominated.[139]   It was charged that the organization was working in the interest of the Democrats to
throw the election into the legislature.[140]   The Liberal
ticket secured less than 700 votes out of a total of 67,000,
with but three members of the lower house, and the Republicans carried the state by a narrow majority.[141]   The next
year the Liberal organization was abandoned, and the most
prominent members acted in future with the Democrats,
the party being referred to for a time as "Democratic-

very direct) by running a separate ticket enabled the straight Democratic candidates to win by a good plurality.   *Annual Cyclopedia*, 1875,
pp. 99–101.

[138] See Lyford, *Rollins*, 11.

[139] *Ibid.*, 294; *Annual Cyclopedia*, 1873, p. 533.   Leaders of the late
Labor Reform party took part in this convention.

[140] See editorials in *Chicago Tribune*, Feb. 20, 1873, and *Milwaukee
Sentinel*, Mar. 14, 1873.

[141] *Annual Cyclopedia*, 1873, p. 534; Lyford, 299.

Liberal."[142]   The Connecticut Democratic-Liberal coalition proved most successful in carrying elections.[143]   The
Liberals were well represented in the state convention of
1873, one of their number was made temporary chairman,
and the candidates for lieutenant-governor and treasurer
were taken from Liberal ranks.[144]   The successful canvass
of this year[145] was repeated in the three following years, the
Liberal officials being kept on the ticket, and special pains
being taken in other ways to conciliate that element.[146]
The Liberal members in the legislature acted with the Democrats, and one of their number was chosen speaker in 1875.[147]
The year before the legislature had chosen a Liberal for one

[142] *N. Y. Tribune*, Mar. 11, 1874.   The Democrats carried the state
in 1874 and the Liberal vote may have contributed to that result.

[143] See reference to the cordial attitude of the Democrats toward the
Liberals in that state in the campaign of 1872.   Above, ch. V, note 59.

[144] *Annual Cyclopedia*, 1873, p. 239; *N. Y. Tribune*, Feb. 20, 1873;
N. Y. World, Feb. 20, 1873.   The principles of the Cincinnati platform
were reaffirmed and Greeley was eulogized in the resolutions.   For the
most cordial and conciliatory attitude of the Democrats toward their
Liberal allies in the campaign, see the quotations from the Connecticut
Democratic papers in the *N. Y. Tribune*, Sept. 2, 1873.

[145] *Annual Cyclopedia*, 1873, p. 240.   The N. Y. *World* considered the
election of the Democratic-Liberal state ticket of great significance.
Editorial, Apr. 8, 1873.   About a dozen town officials were classed as
"Liberals."   See list in *Mass. Weekly Spy*, Oct. 17, 1873.

[146] *Annual Cyclopedia*, 1874, pp. 240 f; 1875, pp. 218 f.; 1876, pp.
205 f.   The *N. Y. Tribune* in reporting the success of the coalition ticket
in 1874 said (Apr. 7): "The Union between the Democrats and Liberals
in this state has been fostered by the conciliatory utterances of the leading Democratic newspapers and the disposition to give the Liberals
recognition in the nominations.   In consequence of this, the Liberals
have everywhere acted in concert with the Democrats, and will have a
fair sprinkling of representatives in both branches of the legislature."
The *Hartford Times* said that the success of the ticket in 1875 was aided
materially by the Liberals whose aid had been welcomed and recognized
by nominations for state offices and for the legislature where they would
be well represented.   "The Radicals abuse the Liberals, the Democrats
are proud to act with them."   Quoted in *N. Y. Tribune*, Apr. 15, 1875.

[147] *N. Y. Tribune*, May 6, 1875.

of the judges of the Superior Court.[148]   Prominent Liberals
were named for Congress, in normally Republican districts,[149] and D. A. Wells was spoken of for United States
senator in 1874.[150]   Massachusetts Liberals did not call a
convention in 1873, and finally decided not even to issue an
address.[151]   The campaign of 1874 in Massachusetts with
its election of independent congressmen and retirement of
objectionable politicians was regarded as a decided triumph
for the element who had revolted in 1872.[152]   The next
year C. F. Adams was supported for the United States
Senate by the Democrats and independent Republicans,[153]
and later in the year the leading Liberals issued an address
formally uniting with the Democrats.[154]   The Liberal element was represented in the Democratic state convention
that year and given two places on the ticket.[155]

[148] N. Y. *World*, June 12, 1874.

[149] Judge Foster in 1875 and D. A. Wells in 1876.   The *World* (Apr.
7, 1875) attributed Foster's defeat to the apathy of the Liberals.

[150] Also in 1876, but apparently always by Liberal or independent
papers.   See N. Y. *World*, May 7, 1874; *N. Y. Tribune*, Apr. 11, 1876.

[151] They had at first intended to issue an address setting forth their
views.   *N. Y. Tribune*, Sept. 17, Oct. 11, 1873.   General Banks was
elected to the state senate this year as an independent.   *Mass. Weekly
Spy*, Oct. 31, Nov. 7, 1873.

[152] Merriam, II, 273.   A widespread Republican defection was threatened this year in case of the success of Banks for the gubernatorial nomination.   Norton to Lowell, Mar. 13, 1874, Norton, *Letters*, II, 37.
The Boston Advertiser urged C. F. Adams for Sumner's successor.
Weekly Advertiser, Mar. 19, 1874.

[153] *Chicago Tribune*, Jan. 21, 1875.

[154] *Annual Cyclopedia*, 1875, p. 477.

[155] *Ibid.*, p. 478; *Mass. Weekly Spy*, Sept. 24, 1875.   W. F. Bartlett,
the Liberal who was named for lieutenant governor, finally declined.
Palfrey, *Bartlett*, 276; Merriam, II, 347 f.   A "National Union Party"
was organized in Boston in 1875 with General Banks as the chief mover,
but it apparently never secured a following.   *Annual Cyclopedia*, 1875,
p. 477; *Nation*, Aug. 26, 1875, p. 125.   A Liberal county convention
was reported at Bangor, Maine, in 1873, with a small attendance.
N. Y. *World*, Aug. 15, 1873.   No Liberal activities, after 1872, in Vermont or Rhode Island have been noted.

Pennsylvania Democrats seem not to have taken a very tactful course toward their Liberal recruits. The old-time leaders of the party were put forward in a most uncompromising fashion.[156]   But, for all that, the Liberals were more in sympathy with the Democrats than with the administration party in the state and probably contributed considerably to Democratic success in 1874, especially in the local and congressional elections.[157]   In 1875, however, the inflationist policy of the Democrats here, as in Ohio, completely alienated the best portion of the Liberals.[158]

The New York Liberals maintained a separate organization down to the campaign of 1876, and at times controlled enough votes to hold a balance between the regular parties. But, for the most part, the organization had degenerated into a band of politicians whose chief aim was to extort patronage or other recognition from one or the other of the old parties, and to drive the best bargains before they returned to party regularity.[159]   Chief among these political traders was John Cochrane, the chairman of the state committee.

In 1873 Cochrane's band of political guerrillas began their manoeuvring with an invitation to the Democratic committee to unite with the Liberals in issuing their call for a

[156] Editorials in *N. Y. Herald*, Aug. 29, 1873; *Philadelphia Enquirer*, Nov. 9, 1874.

[157] *Philadelphia Enquirer*, Nov. 9, 1874.

[158] *N. Y. Tribune*, Sept. 23, 1875; *Mass. Weekly Spy*, Oct. 1, 1875. The Democratic convention this year in its resolutions "cordially invite the Liberal Republicans and all other men, without regard to past party affiliation, to coöperate with us." *Annual Cyclopedia*, 1875, p. 618. Colonel McClure was the only representative of his faction in the legislature. McClure, *Old Time Notes*, II, 359.

[159] The *N. Y. Herald* well characterized the organization (Sept. 24, 1875) as "A kind of blackmailing business, a combination of office-seekers who meant to strike either side for place and to keep on striking until they were all provided." See also criticisms of Cochrane's policy in *Cincinnati Commercial*, Sept. 11, 22, 1873.

state convention.[160]   The Democratic committee had no
thought of such an alliance,[161] but considered the advisa-
bility of increasing the delegation from each assembly district from one to three so that the Liberals might have a
better chance to be represented in the convention.   The
committee was divided as to the wisdom of this proposal and
it was not adopted.[162]   There was much dissatisfaction in
the party, especially up-state, with the committee's decision, as it was regarded as highly expedient to retain the
Liberal vote which in some sections seemed of respectable
size.[163]   In some counties Liberal delegates were chosen
by the Democratic conventions.[164]   In the Democratic
state convention there were a considerable number of former
Liberals, who were welcomed by the chairman but given to
understand that henceforth the coalition was to be on a
strictly Democratic basis.[165]   The platform recognized in
the Liberals "worthy coadjutors," invited their coöperation in seeking reforms,[166] and, as a more direct bid for
votes, renominated Thomas Raines, the Liberal state
treasurer.[167]   But the Liberal committee decided to hold
their own convention, explaining in their call that the needed

[160] *N. Y. Tribune*, Aug. 25, 1873.

[161] See the *World's* indignant editorial on Cochrane's proposition.
Aug. 26, 1873.   The *World* was opposed to continuing an alliance with
the Liberal organization as such.   See editorials, Nov. 9, 1872, June
27, 1873.

[162] N. Y. *World*, Sept. 1, 3, 4, 1873;   *N. Y. Herald*, Sept. 4, 1873.
The amendment was apparently defeated through the influence of
John Kelly who feared that it would aid the Apollo Hall faction in the
City.

[163] Democratic papers quoted in N. Y. *World*, Aug. 25, Sept. 3,
1873, and in *N. Y. Tribune*, Sept. 4, 6, 1873;   *Albany Argus*, Sept. 2, 3,
1873.   The *Argus* (Sept. 2) chided the *World* for its injustice to "Our
Liberal Allies."

[164] *N. Y. Herald*, Sept. 29, 1873.

[165] *Argus*, Oct. 3, 1873;   *N. Y. Tribune*, Oct. 3, 1873.

[166] *Annual Cyclopedia*, 1873, p. 550.

[167] *Argus*, Oct. 3, 1873.

reforms could not be expected from the Republicans "identified with public abuses" nor from the Democrats "whose state committee has refused to unite with us in repressing them."[168]   The convention, after listening to long speeches and adopting resolutions denouncing the evils of the time and expressing their zeal for reform, endorsed the Democratic candidates with the exception of those for comptroller and prison-inspector, for whom they substituted the Republican nominees.[169]   In the election the Democratic candidates supported by the Liberals were elected by pluralities of from 10,000 to 14,000; while the Republican-Liberal nominees won by about 4,000.[170]   It was clear, as all sides had to admit, that, with the old parties in the state so evenly matched, the Liberals held the balance of power.[171]

General Cochrane and kindred spirits would doubtless have been content to hold this balance as long as it promised to yield spoils, but Liberals with more ability and a higher ambition were anxious to get back into regular party lines; and most of them took advantage of the state and congressional elections of 1874 to make this transition.   At a preliminary conference of the leading Liberals in May it was finally decided that the Liberals would "in the future as in the past keep their organization intact," and that the committee should call a state convention.[172]   Their convention met early in September, before the other conventions, obviously to secure some advantage from one of the regular

[168] N. Y. Tribune, Sept. 12, 1873.

[169] Annual Cyclopedia, 1873, p. 551; N. Y. Tribune, Oct. 9, 1873. There were 164 delegates in attendance from 22 counties.

[170] Evening Journal Almanac, 1874, pp. 71-73. Local Democratic tickets were quite generally endorsed by the Liberals. World, Oct. 21, 27, 28, Nov. 3, 1873.

[171] N. Y. Tribune, Nov. 15, 1873; N. Y. Herald, same date; World, same date. The Democratic committee was held largely responsible for the result by its failure to increase the representation in the convention. Argus, Nov. 13, 1873; World, Nov. 18, 1873.

[172] N. Y. Tribune, May 11, 14, 1874.

organizations. Fenton at this time seems to have had some understanding with the machine element of the Democrats, who were seeking to secure Judge Church's nomination in place of Tilden, and there was an effort to have the Judge endorsed by the Liberal convention as a means of forcing him upon the Democrats. But opposition to this policy developed in the convention, and it adjourned to a later date.[173] The former Liberals were well represented in the Democratic convention, and the platform praised "the independence and patriotism of the Liberal Republicans who, preferring principles to party," would now unite with the Democrats. The Liberals claimed, as a condition of the union, the lieutenant governorship, and William Dorsheimer, one of the most able of the Liberal element in the state, was selected over the regular Democratic aspirant.[174] No less than eight Democratic congressional nominations were also tendered to Liberals.[175] On the other side, prominent Liberals rejoined the Republicans.[176] During the campaign the predominant Liberal sentiment was considered to be for the Democratic ticket headed by Tilden. The adjourned Liberal convention had taken no definite action, but there was much sentiment expressed for endorsing the Demo-

[173] Alexander, *Pol. Hist. of N. Y.*, III, 312; Bigelow, *Tilden*, I, 221, 222, 225, 336; *N. Y. Herald*, Sept. 9, 10, 1874; *World*, Sept. 10, 1874.

[174] *World*, Sept. 18, 1874; *N. Y. Tribune*, same date. The call for the convention was issued to "the Democratic and Liberal Republican electors." *World*, Aug. 22, 1874. The *World* headed its account of the convention "unanimous nominations by Democrats and Liberals."

[175] *World*, Oct. 23, 28, 29, 1874. Two of these candidates subsequently declined the nominations, and of the remaining six, four were elected.

[176] Such as Depew, Hiscock, and Merritt. Fenton's position was in doubt. His speech at the Liberal convention was entirely non-committal and it was charged that he was seeking to secure the election of enough Liberals to the legislature to bargain with one of the parties for his return to the Senate. *N. Y. Herald*, Sept. 10, 1874; *Nation*, Sept. 10, 1874, p. 164.

cratic nominees.[177]   The opposition was now referred to as
"Democratic-Liberals"[178] and special appeals were made
by Tilden's supporters to the latter element.[179]   The campaign of 1874 marked the end of the New York Liberals
as a faction with any capable or reputable leaders and
with any certain voting strength.   There was apparently
little to be gained by holding together the disintegrating
following and some of the local organizations were opposed to meeting the expenses of primaries.   The efforts
of Cochranites to secure state patronage had been most
disappointing, though they had secured a few city positions
through an alliance with Mayor Havemeyer.[180]   The
Evening Post remarked that the organization had been
"kept alive solely to see what it could make.   Now, however, it has obtained everything that it can get from Democrats and Republicans and may as well be disbanded."[181]

But the hard-fought state election of 1875 gave a renewed importance to Cochrane's little band whose following
was eagerly sought after by both parties.   The Republicans
for the first time now made open bids for Liberal support.[182]

[177] *World*, Sept. 30, 1874.   The *N. Y. Herald*, Oct. 15, 1874 said the
N. Y. Liberals had largely merged with the Democrats.

[178] The *World* so designated the ticket throughout the campaign.
A campaign lithograph of Tilden was labelled "Democratic and Liberal
Candidate for Governor."   See reproduction in Buckman, *Tilden
Unmasked*, 72.

[179] *World*, Aug. 21, Oct. 12, 31, 1874.   The *N. Y. Tribune* favored
Tilden, see editorial Sept. 18, 1874; Reid to Bigelow, Nov. 7, 1874,
Bigelow, *Retrospection*, V, 170.

[180] *N. Y. Herald*, June 2, 1874; *N. Y. Tribune*, May 11, 1874.

[181] *Evening Post*, Sept. 24, 1875.   The Liberals secured four assemblymen and two senators, but as the Democrats had a majority on joint
ballot without them, they were not able to "hold the balance."   See
World, Dec. 11, 1874.   The Liberal members, however, held a separate
caucus and named candidates, *ibid.*, Jan. 6, 1875.

[182] The *Springfield Republican* predicted that the Liberal "leaders"
in New York would sell out their vote to the Republicans and "be
unable to deliver the goods."   Quoted in *N. Y. Tribune*, Aug. 11, 1875.

16

Their call was worded to include all straying members who would return,[183] and such bolters as appeared in the convention were cordially welcomed. General Merritt, a Liberal who had returned to the party the previous year, was named for state treasurer.[184] Fenton, whose reconciliation with the President had been reported some time previous,[185] was now able to act with the Republicans as they had, in his opinion, become "liberalized."[186] The "Democratic-Liberal" state convention also named a Liberal candidate,[187] and Liberal organizations in various parts of the state pledged their continued support of Tilden's reform work.[188] In the Liberal state convention the Governor's policy was formally endorsed, and strong efforts were made to secure a coalition on the state ticket.[189] But this was prevented by Cochrane,[190] who openly opposed the Democrats and advocated a reunion of the Republican factions.[191] It was evident that the New York Liberals were far from unified, and would soon split up between the old parties.

The *Tribune* said on the eve of the Republican convention (Sept. 8) that there was "every disposition to extend a hand to the Liberals," and that "there was little doubt that almost any place on the state ticket might have been theirs had they chosen to ask for it."

[183] *N. Y. Tribune*, Aug. 12, 1875.

[184] *N. Y. Tribune*, Sept. 9, 1875.

[185] Fenton lunched with the President in August. *Chicago Tribune*, Aug. 20, 1875.

[186] See his letter to the Republican state chairman in *N. Y. Tribune*, Oct. 9, 1875.

[187] For inspector of state prisons. His nomination was urged "chiefly in recognition of the Liberals." *World*, Sept. 18, 1875.

[188] *N. Y. Tribune*, Sept. 23, 1875. The *Tribune* strongly favored the Democratic ticket. See editorials, Oct. 29, 30, 1875.

[189] *World, Tribune, Herald*, Sept. 23, 1875.

[190] *N. Y. Times*, Sept. 23, 1875.

[191] N. Y. correspondent of *Chicago Journal*, quoted in *Wis. State Journal*, July 27, 1875. Ethan Allen was said to be willing to join the Republicans if he could secure office from them and prominent up-state Liberals were returning to the old parties. *Idem; N. Y. Herald*, Oct. 17, 1875.

5. THE LIBERALS IN THE CAMPAIGN OF 1876

The strength of the Democratic party, both numerically and morally, in 1876 was vastly superior to what it had been four years before. Many factors contributed to its increased vitality, such as the anti-monopoly movements in the West, the financial depression, and the numerous and widespread abuses uncovered in the Republican administration. But, as the foregoing review of local conditions has shown, considerable weight must be given to the influence of the Liberal element, both in adding directly to the Democratic vote and in increasing the party's reputation for loyalty and integrity. The party had not in all cases shown a sufficiently conciliatory and tactful attitude toward the exacting allies, and in some states the dominance of the Bourbon element had frightened away the newcomers, but, in the main, the influence of the Republican bolters of 1872 had worked decidedly for Democratic success.

Republicans viewed with no little anxiety the increasing success of the coalition, especially in the election of 1874, and tried to attract back their seceded members. Independent leaders, like Schurz, were referred to in a respectful and even appreciative manner by the administration press.[192] The bugaboo of the old unreconstructed Democracy was still utilized. The coalition, it was held, instead of advancing the Liberal cause, was simply aiding the old-time Bourbon Democrats to reintrench themselves in office.[193] After all, the best way of securing real reforms, the Liberals were reminded, was in the good old party and their return before the next presidential election was con-

[192] See *Cincinnati Semi-Weekly Gazette*, Dec. 29, 1874; *St. Paul Weekly Pioneer-Press*, Aug. 20, 1875, Apr. 20, 1876.

[193] *Milwaukee Sentinel*, May 23, 1874, June 8, 1875; *Cincinnati Semi-Weekly Gazette*, Nov. 20, 1874.

fidently predicted.[194]   Henry Wilson, in an interview in the
spring of 1875, confessed frankly that the party had made
a great blunder in forcing out the Liberals in '72, and that
now all conciliatory measures possible should be adopted to
get them back, though he realized that some were hopelessly
lost to the Democrats.[195]   Even the President took pains
to make peace with Liberal leaders.[196]

The independent leaders who had started the national
Liberal movement, and whom their organs still designated
as "Liberals," planned to make an attempt in 1876 to retrieve what they had lost in 1872.[197]   To Halstead and
Bowles, the chief editorial champions of the cause of the
independents, E. B. Washburne, as the regular Republican candidate, had seemed for a time the best possibility;[198]
but they soon came back to their first love, C. F. Adams.[199]

[194] *Wis. State Journal*, Dec. 8, 1874, July 27, 1875; *Milwaukee Sentinel*, May 16, 1874; *St. Paul Weekly Pioneer-Press*, Oct. 1, 1875; *Boston
Weekly Advertiser*, July 22, 1875.

[195] Interview in *N. Y. Tribune*, June 5, 1875, and letter replying to
criticism of his statements in *Boston Weekly Advertiser*, July 1, 1875.
In April Wilson was reported as saying to F. A. Conkling that the
Liberal Republicans held the political balance of power and they would
decide the presidential election of 1876.   N. Y. *Sun*, quoted in *Industrial
Age*, May 1, 1875.

[196] Grant appeared in company with the leader of the New York
City Liberals and a close friend of Fenton's when he paid a visit to the
city in June, 1874, and it was reported that he had made up with the
Senator.   *N. Y. Herald*, June 7, 1874.   His lunch with the Senator a
year later was taken as a sign of complete reconciliation.   *Chicago
Tribune*, Aug. 20, 1875.   In December, 1874, the President offered a
position in the Baltimore custom-house to A. W. Bradford, the leading
Liberal of the state.   N. Y. *World*, Dec. 28, 1874.

[197] Cf. Schurz to Grosvenor, July 16, 1875, *Schurz's Writings*, III, 155 f.

[198] W. H. Huntington to Bigelow, Oct. 17, 1874, Bigelow, *Retrospection*, V, 167.

[199] Bowles, to Halstead, Oct. 19, 1875, Mar. 4, 1876, Merriam, II,
348 f; *Chicago Tribune*, May 3, 1875 (reprinting Halstead's interview
in N. Y. *Sun*); *Cincinnati Commercial*, May 8, 1875; see also Bancroft-
Dunning, 361 f.

A council of the independents to consider their future action was held, under the guise of a banquet to Schurz, in New York City in April, 1875.[200]   Schurz advised that the independents agree upon some plan of concerted action for the approaching campaign.[201]   The independents now had high hopes of concessions from the Republicans if the party reverses continued, and the fall election in Ohio was considered a good test of party strength.   But much as the reformers desired to have the old organization at their mercy, they felt compelled, in view of the inflationist platform of the Democrats, to lend a decisive support to the Republican ticket.[202]

In the national campaign the independents were determined to support none but an approved reform candidate.   As their ultimatum to the regular parties, the "Independents" or "Liberals," as they were variously termed, under the management of Schurz and Bowles,[203] held a conference in New York, in May, 1876, which was watched with much attention by the politicians of both parties.   Candidates were not discussed by name, but the statement in their address of the sort of candidates that the independents would not support restricted the choice to a very small group.[204]   It was generally understood that Bristow—respected by the reformers for his work against the whiskey ring[205] of the suggested Republican candidates,

[200] Schurz to H. A. Brown, Apr. 16, 1875, *Schurz's Writings*, III, 153.
[201] N. Y. *World*, Apr. 28, 1875.
[202] So stated in *Cincinnati Commercial* editorial, June 2, 1876.
[203] See Schurz's letters to Bowles and others on the subject, *Writings*, III, 217–220, 230 f., 232 f., 233–239.   The invitation to the conference, signed by Bryant, Woolsey, Bullock, White, and Schurz, is given in *ibid.*, 228 f.
[204] *Ibid.*, 240–248; *Annual Cyclopedia*, 1876, pp. 779 f.
[205] Bowles to Halstead, Mar. 4, 1876, Merriam, II, 349; Schurz-Bristow correspondence, *Schurz's Writings*, III, 220, 221, 226.

and Tilden, of the Democratic possibilities, were strongly favored.[206]

The national Liberal organization after 1872 had apparently had no existence except in the occasional statements of Ethan Allen, its national chairman.[207] But with the approach of another national campaign, Allen saw fit to revive his old dignity and summon a national conference which met at New York on May 9, with representatives from about thirty states. It was determined that a national Liberal convention should be held at Philadelphia on July 26, but since the Liberals did not favor "causeless independent action," it was provided that, if, after the regular conventions, one or both of the old parties in the judgment of the national chairman had responded to the principles and aims of the Liberal Republican organization "both in measures and men" Allen was authorized to annul the call.[208]

In the campaign much attention was given to the attitude of the former Liberals. There was a considerable representation of ex-Liberals in both of the national conventions.[209] The nomination by both parties of candidates with strong reform tendencies divided the independent support. The inflationist views of the Democratic candidate for vice-president decided some for the Republicans,[210]

[206] For accounts of the meeting and lists of the leading participants, see *Annual Cyclopedia*, 1876, pp. 779 f.; Merriam, *Bowles*, II, 254; Bancroft-Dunning, 367; *N. Y. Herald*, May 16, 17, 1876; *N. Y. Tribune*, same dates; *Chicago Tribune*, same dates; *Cincinnati Commercial*, same dates and June 14 (gives list of those taking part or endorsing the movement); Koerner, II, 599–602.

[207] See interviews with Allen in *N. Y. Herald*, Aug. 1, Sept. 6, 1873.

[208] *N. Y. Herald*, May 9, 1876; *N. Y. Tribune*, same date.

[209] See lists of delegates in the official proceedings of the two national conventions, and appeals to Liberals in the Democratic convention by Doolittle and Gratz Brown. *Official Proceedings National Dem. Con.*, *1876*, pp. 88, 91.

[210] Reid to Bigelow, July 9, 1876, Tilden, *Letters*, II, 439; Godkin to Norton, July 14, 1876. Ogden, *Godkin*, II, 112.

while Tilden's standing as a reformer, and the failure of the
Republicans to name Bristow determined others for the
Democrats.[211] Schurz came out strongly for Hayes and
was a leading adviser in the campaign.[212] His course was
condemned by fellow independents of Democratic leanings,
who held that the generally assumed understanding of the
New York conference committed him to the support of
Tilden.[213] The greater number of the independent journals,
after some hesitation, also supported Hayes.

Allen, who for some time had been seeking to ingratiate
himself with the Republican organization, issued a letter in
July stating that, after conferring with the members of the
national committee, the decision was practically unanimous
that the call for the national Liberal convention should be
annulled and that Hayes and Wheeler should be endorsed in
the name of the Liberal Republicans of the United States.
He thought it the logical result of the Liberal movement
that it should support the Republican candidate who stood
for civil service reform, an early return to specie payment,

[211] Godwin to Bigelow, Aug. 28, 1876, Tilden, *Letters*, II, 451; Bryant to Bigelow, Sept. 21, 1876, *ibid.*, 466; Wells to Tilden, May 6,
1876, *ibid.*, 404; [C. F. Adams, Jr., probably] "The Independents in the
Canvass," *North American Review*, Oct., 1876, pp. 426–467; list of leading Ohio Liberals supporting Tilden in *Cincinnati Commercial*, June 30,
July 9, 1876; Koerner, II, 605; F. W. Bird's letter to Allen, quoted
in N. Y. *World*, May 15, 1876; Julian, *Later Speeches*, 108 ff.; Palfrey, 292; Brinkerhoff, 223–225.

[212] Schurz's correspondence with Hayes in *Schurz's Writings*, III,
248–257, 280–282, 286, 289–290. See a campaign speech, *ibid.*, 290–
337. Schurz's explanation of his course is given in his letter to C. F.
Adams, Jr., *ibid.*, 259.

[213] Bancroft-Dunning, 369; Koerner, II, 611 f. For Schurz's public
defence of his course, see his letter to Oswald Ottendorfer in his *Writings*, III, 261–280. Schurz had previously declared that Adams and
Bristow were the only Republican candidates that he would support.
See his letter to Cahoon in March, *ibid.*, 223. The *Cincinnati Commercial* (May 29, 1876) predicted that Schurz would support Tilden in
preference to Hayes.

and one term for the president. "If the Liberals of 1872," he urged, "sustained Horace Greeley, who was the foremost Republican of his day, because he was an unselfish patriot and an honest man, they must now sustain General Hayes for the same reason and to do otherwise would be inconsistent action. The opposition of the 'Liberals' has never been against the Republican party of which they formed a part, but rather against those who, unfortunately for it and the nation, had control of its destiny." If anything was lacking to complete the utter ridiculousness of the Liberal organization as a project of reform after it had been captured by the politicians, it was furnished by the closing statement of Allen's valedictory: "The Liberal movement will be remembered as an evidence that when the hour demands it the people are capable of making party managers subservient to their will."[214]

In state conventions of both parties efforts were made to influence the Liberal vote. Kansas Democrats cordially welcomed the large number of Liberals in their state convention and gave them a good representation on their state and local tickets.[215] The Democrats also entered into a coalition with the Independent party on their state ticket.[216] The Republican platform in the same state invited "the coöperation of all men, whether called 'Liberal' or 'Independent,' to whom 'reform' is something more than an empty name."[217] In Iowa the opposition convention termed itself the "Liberal Democratic party."[218] In Illinois the Democrats coalesced with the Greenbackers and

[214] Allen's letter addressed to the "Liberal Republicans of the United States" appeared in the *N. Y. Tribune*, July 21, 1876. The letter was also addressed to the *N. Y. Times*, same date.

[215] *Kan. Commonwealth*, May 19, Aug. 24, Oct. 27, 1876.

[216] *Ibid.*, Aug. 24.

[217] *Annual Cyclopedia*, 1876, p. 437. For prominent Kansas Liberals acting with the Republicans in the campaign, see *Kan. Commonwealth*, Aug. 17, Oct. 27, Nov. 3, 1876.

[218] *Annual Cyclopedia*, 1876, p. 414.

their state ticket contained at least two former Liberals.[219]
Other prominent Liberals appeared at a meeting of the
Republican state committee and represented that their
faction in Illinois was for the most part coming back to the
old party.[220]   Indiana Democrats had two former Liberals
on their ticket.[221]   In the Connecticut spring election the
"Democratic-Liberal party" renominated the old ticket,
including the Liberals,[222] and a nomination to fill a vacancy
in one of the congressional districts was given to David A.
Wells.[223]   But the Massachusetts Democrats made the
strongest bid for the independent, Liberal vote by the nomination of C. F. Adams for governor.[224]

In New York the relations of the allies in the Democratic
convention was far from harmonious.   Dorsheimer, the
Liberal lieutenant governor, now aspired to the governor-

[219] *Chicago Tribune*, July 28, 1876.   With the issue of Nov. 9, 1874,
Joseph Medill resumed the editorship of the *Chicago Tribune* and it became Republican again.

[220] *Ibid.*, July 20, 21.

[221] *Cincinnati Semi-Weekly Gazette*, Apr. 21, 1876.   A dispatch to the
same paper from Madison, Indiana, earlier in the year (Feb. 9) said of a
convention to choose delegates to the state convention: "Grangers,
Liberals, and the disaffected generally, came into the meeting, and old
feuds have been buried, and perfect harmony and enthusiasm pervade
the mind of all."   In Wisconsin, this year the opposition was called
simply "Democratic." *Milwaukee Sentinel*, Aug. 22, 1876 (editorial
calling attention to the dropping of the designation, "Reform Party");
see also the use of the old party name in *Madison Democrat*, June 6–8,
Aug. 12, 29, and passim, 1876.   The Michigan Liberal State Committee
met in July and unanimously endorsed the Democratic national candidates.   N. Y. *World*, July 20, 1876.

[222] *Annual Cyclopedia*, 1876, pp. 205 f.

[223] *Ibid.*, p. 206.

[224] *Ibid.*, pp. 513 f.; *Nation*, Sept. 14, 1876, p. 160.   The *Springfield
Republican* supported Hayes for president and Adams for governor.
Merriam, II, 277.   Tilden used his influence to secure Adams' nomina-
tion against the wishes of influential Massachusetts Democrats.   See F.
O. Prince to Tilden, *Tilden's Letters*, II, 451; C. F. Adams Jr. to Tilden,
ibid., 452 f.; Curran, *Collins*, 39 f.

ship and his candidacy was most bitterly opposed by the
old-time party leaders.[225]   So much feeling was aroused that
it was thought that Dorsheimer could not even secure a
renomination for the second place,[226] but this concession was
finally made to appease the Liberal recruits.[227]   Additional trouble came to the party through their new adherents.   Their candidate for governor, ex-Governor Seymour, refusing to run, Lucius Robinson, a man known for
political independence, was substituted and it was now
widely charged by the Republican press that the New York
Democrat leaders were so fearful of the result that they had
been forced to place a second Liberal Republican candidate
on the ticket,[228] though it was shown conclusively that
Robinson, after acting with the Union Republicans, had
rejoined the Democratic party in 1865, seven years before
the Liberal movement.[229]   The New York Liberal organization, the sole remnant of the party as such, could not survive
a presidential election.   Cochrane now sought to use his
organization to aid the machine element of the Republicans.
At a meeting of the state committee in April he secured the
adoption of resolutions favoring that party and urged that
Liberals attend the Republican national convention and
work for the desired "reforms."   An effort was also made
at this time to secure the endorsement of Blaine as the

[225] *World*, Aug. 31, 1876; N. J. Waterbury to Tilden, Sept. 1, 1876,
Tilden, *Letters*, II, 462.   There were other causes of opposition to Dorsheimer than his Liberal antecedents. See Hudson, *Randon Recollections*, 62–64.

[226] So stated in dispatch in *World*, Aug. 31, 1876.

[227] *Ibid.*, Sept. 1.

[228] *N. Y. Tribune*, Sept. 15, 1876; *N. Y. Herald*, same date; *Cincinnati Semi-Weekly Gazette*, Sept. 15, 1876.

[229] See interview with Hiram Gray in *World*, Sept. 11, 1876, and also
on Robinson's political record, Alexander, III. The *World* said
(Sept. 2, 1876) that as Robinson had once been a Liberal he "could not
be placed on the ticket with Lieutenant Governor Dorsheimer."

Liberal choice for president.[230]   It only remained for Cochrane to unite in the best manner possible with the Republican state organization and this he hastened to do.   The
Liberal convention assembled at Saratoga at the same time
as the Republican, and promptly endorsed the Republican
national ticket and platform.   Their decision was reported
to the regular convention which resolved, amid applause,
to admit the Liberal delegates to seats in their body.   But
there were several contesting delegations to the Liberal convention who, being refused admittance, held a convention
by themselves and passed resolutions praising Governor
Tilden's work, and advising "all true Liberals of the country to cordially support the St. Louis nominees as the best
means of lifting the country out of the ruin which threatens
it."[231]

In the campaign direct appeals were made to the Liberals
by both parties.   Both represented that the bulk of this
element was with them,[232] and lists of former Liberal
leaders were presented to substantiate these rival claims.[233]
Probably the greater number of Liberal voters went back

[230] *N. Y. Tribune*, Apr. 7, 1876.   Cochrane and Fenton attended the
national convention in Blaine's interest.   Convention correspondence
in *Kan. Commonwealth*, June 14, 1876.

[231] *N. Y. Tribune*, Aug. 24, 1876; *World*, same date.

[232] For the Republican side, see *Boston Advertiser*, July 20, 1876; *Chicago Tribune*, Sept. 26, 1876; *Wis. State Journal*, Aug. 15, Sept. 5, Oct.
17, 1876; *Kan. Commonwealth*, June 15, 17, Aug. 12, 1876; *N. Y. Tribune*, July 15, 1876; and for the Democrats, N. Y. *World*, Sept. 15, 1876;
Julian, *Later Speeches*, 108 ff.; Koerner's address to Liberal Republicans, quoted in *N. Y. Tribune*, July 10, 1876; Parke Godwin's letter to
N. Y. Tribune, July 22, 1876; speeches of prominent Liberals at Democratic ratification meeting in Cincinnati. *Cincinnati Commercial*,
July 9, 1876; address of Chicago German Liberals for Tilden published in
leading German Democratic papers.   See *Chicago Tribune*, Aug. 15, 1876.

[233] For most extended lists of Liberals supporting Tilden, see N. Y.
World, Sept. 15, 1876; Clinton (Iowa) *Age*, Sept. 29, 1876, cited in
Haynes, note 76.   Individual Liberal recruits were reported by both
sides throughout the campaign.

to the old party,[234] but the leaders were pretty evenly divided. Schurz's work and influence in the campaign were so highly regarded by Hayes that he was given a seat in the cabinet,[235] much to the gratification of the independents.[236] Tilden, on his side, was seriously considering for his official advisers Liberal leaders like Adams, Trumbull and Wells.[237] So in various ways this campaign tended to vindicate the policy of the independents.

In later years most of the prominent Liberals secured high recognition from one or the other of the old parties,[238] and

[234] Cf. Haworth, *Hayes-Tilden Election*, 10; Williams, I, 472; Curtis, *Hist. Rep. Party*, II, 59; Smalley, *Hist. Rep. Party*, 55.

[235] See Schurz's correspondence with Hayes following the election. *Schurz's Writings*, III, 339, 376–383, 389–397, 403–405.

[236] See correspondence on his appointment with members of this group. *Ibid.*, 397–399, 402, 408, 409. Halstead used all of his influence with Hayes for Schurz's appointment. *Ibid.*, 402. Haynes (*Third Party Movements*, 41) says, on the authority of Iowa papers, that four members of Hayes' cabinet, Evarts, Devins and Key, in addition to Schurz, "had supported Mr. Greeley in 1872." Evarts was in Europe during the campaign as one of the American counsel before the Geneva Tribunal (See Hackett, *Reminiscences of Geneva Tribunal*, 277 f. and the Earl of Selborne's *Memorials*, Part II, vol. II, pp. 285 f.) and I have found no reference to his support of the Liberal candidate. Haynes says that Devins had once run for Congress on a Democratic ticket but there is no mention of this in J. C. Ropes' Memoir in Devins' *Orations and Addresses*. In 1872 he was serving as Judge of the Superior Court of Massachusetts by the appointment of a Republican governor and the following year he was promoted to the Supreme Court by another Republican executive. I have failed to find any evidence of a support of the Liberal movement on his part. Key, as a southern Democrat, undoubtedly supported the coalition ticket, as he did the Democratic in 1876.

[237] Bigelow's diary, entry for Feb. 9, 1877. *Retrospection*, V, 299. Bigelow thought Tilden was "quite settled" in regard to Trumbull. Of Adams for secretary of state, Bigelow remarked that Tilden did not seem "to incline that way much." O'Connor, according to Bigelow, was the choice for attorney-general, and the Liberal members might thus have been associated with a "Straight-Out."

[238] See Pierce, IV, 547; Du Bois and Mathews, *Grow*, 274, 275, 279, 283; Church, *Rep. Party in Ill.*, 118; and the indices to such political histories as Powell, *Dem. Party of Ohio* and Alexander, *Pol. Hist. of N. Y.*

there seems seldom to have been a question of their good standing in the organization.[239] The Republicans, with a strong opposition to combat {from this time on, were glad to welcome back all party workers of any influence and ability, while the Democrats profited by new leaders whose adherence was a standing testimonial to the party's loyalty and good character.

<h2 style="text-align:center">CONCLUSION</h2>

The period of the seventies was one of transition from the problems and interests of the Civil War to those of a new economic and social era. These new interests are reflected in the political movements of the decade. The election of 1872 saw a national labor and a national prohibition party in the field, and an attempt to launch a woman's rights party. During the next four years a series of "independent" political organizations sprang up in the West, demanding various economic and social "reforms," the more radical merging in the National Independent or "Greenback" party of 1876. But the Liberal Republican movement was of much greater importance in the political disintegration and transition of the period, owing to its direct influence on the two leading parties. The Liberal movement marks the definite break-up of the Union Republican party through the withdrawal of the conservative leaders. A disintegrating tendency had manifested itself soon after the war; it was shown in the National Union movement of 1866, in the conflict over Johnson's impeachment, and in the opposition by conservative Republicans in Congress to radical reconstruction legislation. But the final break came only with the organized opposition in '72. The Liberal movement also marks the withdrawal from party allegiance of the independent group who, during the next quarter of a century, were to be both hated and feared by the regular

[239] For cases where objections of this sort were raised, see Lyford, 320, 326; Connelley, *Plumb*, 227.

party managers. The Liberals, by demanding, on the one hand, a final settlement of the issues growing out of the war and, on the other, a recognition of the new economic problems confronting the country, peculiarly typified the new post-bellum age. Constituted as it was of the most divergent elements of opposition, it was inevitable that the Liberal movement should meet defeat in the national election and that it should fail to develop a permanent political party. The movement being something more than a mere third-party agitation for a single reform, and offering at first good prospects of success, soon attracted disappointed and rapacious politicians, whose aims could in no way be reconciled with those of the reformers. But even among those engaging in the movement from sincere motives of public good there was a lack of common purpose and understanding. The eastern reformers, as usual, were far in advance of the general public sentiment. In the South the great issue was home rule and in the struggle for that all of the opposition was concentrated. Western Liberals were in the front ranks of the anti-monopoly movements, seeking what they regarded as very real reforms, but to the eastern reformers their leaders seemed little better than outlaws.[240] The radical Liberals who joined the green-backers were directly opposed to the fundamental principles of the organizers of the national Liberal movement. A group of reformers with such diverse aims could hold together only so long as their activities were purely nega-

[240] The *Nation* said of the argument of the Wisconsin Attorney-General (who was the Liberal state chairman) in favor of the Potter law that "Nothing more monstrous in the way of a definition of a right was probably ever heard outside of a buccaneer's cave." In the same editorial the *Nation* thus commented on the Liberal policy in Wisconsin: "In the matter of railroads, leading Liberal Republican papers and orators fanned the flame of hostility to the roads, in the belief that it would result in the promotion of a powerful opposition to the Republican party. We always denounced this as a wretched delusion." *Nation*, July 9, 1874, p. 17.

tive; they were bound to disintegrate so soon as they attempted anything positive or constructive. But the Liberal movement in all of its diverse manifestations worked decidedly for the interest of the Democrats. That party's alliance with the Liberals was in no sense an amalgamation but merely a temporary coalition. There was never any other intent on the part of the ablest and most trusted Democratic leaders. The formation of a new opposition party was out of the question, and, as usual in such combinations, the well established organization was the chief gainer. Of the offices secured by coalition the Democrats obtained the lion's share. Some of the most able leaders of the Republican party during the war passed permanently into the Democratic ranks. Most important of all, the acceptance of the Liberal platform and candidates, attesting as nothing else could the complete reconstruction of the old Democracy, assisted it ere long in regaining control of the national government.[241] The Liberal movement thus stands as an important influence in the political transition of the seventies, contributing so largely as it did to the creation of the reformer, "mugwump" group, to the consolidation of the southern opposition, to the development of the western "independent" movements, and to the reconstruction and rejuvenation of the national Democratic party.

[241] Cf. Julian, *Pol. Recollections*, 349; Hill, *Hill*, 65.

BIBLIOGRAPHY

I. MANUSCRIPT SOURCES

The following manuscript collections of correspondence have been examined in the preparation of this study:

In Harvard University Library:
> The Charles Sumner Papers.

In the Library of Congress:
> The Salmon P. Chase Papers.
> The Andrew Johnson Papers.
> The Lyman Trumbull Papers.
> The Elihu B. Washburne Papers.

The papers of William Allen, Hugh McCulloch and Edward McPherson in the same library were examined, but contain nothing of value for this study.

In the Minnesota State Historical Society Library:
> The Ignatius Donnelly Papers.

II. LETTERS AND COLLECTED WORKS

Blaine, James G. Political Discussions, Legislative, Diplomatic, and Popular. 1855–1886. Norwich, Conn., 1887.

Blaine, Mrs. James G. Letters. Edited by Harriet S. Blaine Beale. 2 vols., New York, 1908.

Booth, Newton. Speeches and Addresses. Edited by Lauren E. Crane. New York, 1894.

Chase, Salmon P. Diary and Correspondence. *Annual Report American Historical Association*, 1902, vol. II, Washington, 1903.

Garfield, James A. Works. Edited by Burke A. Hinsdale. 2 vols., Boston, 1882.

General Grant's Letters to a Friend [E. B. Washburne] 1861–1880. Edited by James Grant Wilson. New York, 1897. Also in *North American Review*, CLXV.

Greeley on Lincoln, with Mr. Greeley's Letters to Charles A. Dana and a Lady Friend to which are added Reminiscences of Horace Greeley. Edited by Joel Benton. New York, 1893.

Julian, George W. Later Speeches on Political Questions. Edited by Grace Julian Clarke. Indianapolis, 1889.

Lowell, James Russell. Letters. Edited by Charles Eliot Norton. 2 vols., New York, 1894.

Morrill, Justin S. "Notable Letters from My Political Friends," *Forum*, XXIV, 405–412, Dec., 1897.

Motley, John Lothrop. Correspondence. Edited by G. W. Curtis. 2 vols., New York, 1889.

Norton, Charles Eliot. Letters. Edited with biographical comment by Sara Norton and M. A. de Wolfe Howe. 2 vols., Boston, 1913.

Phillips, Wendell. Speeches, Lectures, and Letters. Second series, Boston, 1891.

Robinson, William S. "Warrington" Pen Sketches. Boston, 1877.

Schurz, Carl. Speeches, Correspondence and Political Papers. Selected and edited by Frederic Bancroft. 6 vols., New York, 1913. [Cited as "Schurz's Writings."]

Sherman, General W. T. Home Letters. Edited by M. A. de Wolfe Howe. New York, 1909.

Sherman Letters. The Correspondence between General and Senator Sherman from 1837 to 1891. Edited by Rachel Sherman Thorndike. New York, 1894.

Sumner, Charles. Works. 15 vols., Boston, 1875–1883.

Tilden, Samuel J. Letters and Literary Memorials. Edited by John Bigelow. 2 vols., New York, 1908.

Trumbull, Lyman. Correspondence, *Mississippi Valley Historical Review*, I, 106–108.

Tyler, Moses Coit. Selections from his Letters and Diaries. Edited by Jessie T. Austen. New York, 1911.

Worth, Jonathan. Correspondence. Collected and edited by J. G. de R. Hamilton. 2 vols., Raleigh, 1909.

III. NEWSPAPERS AND PERIODICALS

Advance. Chicago, 1872.

Albany Evening Journal. 1872.

Argus. Albany, 1872–1873.

Atlantic Monthly. Boston, 1872.

Boston Daily Advertiser. 1872.

Boston Weekly Advertiser. 1873–1876.

Central Presbyterian. Richmond, Va., Sept.–Oct., 1872.

Chicago Daily News. July–Oct., 1872.

Chicago Times. 1872.

Chicago Daily Tribune. 1872–1876.

Christian Advocate. New York, 1872.

Cincinnati Commercial. Jan.–June, 1871; 1873–1876.

Cincinnati Semi-Weekly Gazette. 1871–1876.
Commonwealth. Boston, 1871; Jan.–Aug., 1872.
Evening Bulletin. San Francisco, 1872–1876.
Evening News. Minneapolis, June–Nov., 1872.
Evening Post (Semi-Weekly edition). New York, 1872–1876.
Farmer's Union. Minneapolis, 1873.
Galaxy. New York, 1871–1872.
Golden Age. New York, 1871–1872.
Greenville (S. C.) Enterprise. Jan.–Oct., 1872.
Harper's Weekly. New York, 1870–1874.
Independent. New York, 1871–1872.
Industrial Age. Chicago, 1873–1876.
Kansas Daily Commonwealth. Topeka, 1872–1876.
Lakeside Monthly. Chicago, 1872.
Leslie's Illustrated Newspaper. New York, 1871–1872.
Lippincott's Magazine. Philadelphia, 1872.
Madison (Wis.) Daily Democrat. 1872–1876.
Maryland Union. Frederick, 1872.
Massachusetts Weekly Spy. Worcester, 1871–1876.
Memphis (Tenn.) Daily Appeal. Jan.–Mar., 1872.
Milwaukee News. 1872–1876.
Milwaukee Daily Sentinel. 1873–1876.
Milwaukee Weekly Sentinel. 1872.
Missouri Democrat. St. Louis, 1869; Jan.–June, 1870; 1871–1872.
Missouri Republican. St. Louis, 1870–1874.
Nation. New York, 1870–1876.
National Quarterly Review. New York, 1872.
National Republican. Washington, odd numbers, Jan., Sept., Oct., Nov., 1872.
New Orleans Republican. Jan.–May, Oct.–Nov., 1872.
New York Observer. 1872.
New York Herald. 1871–1876.
New York Times. 1871–1876.
New York Tribune. 1870–1876.
North American Review. New York, 1870–1876.
Old and New. Boston, 1872.
Patriot. Washington, May–Nov., 1872.
People's Tribune. Jefferson City, Mo., 1869–1874.
Philadelphia Inquirer. 1873–1874.
Pomeroy's Democrat. New York, 1872.
Press. Philadelphia, July–Dec., 1871.
Richmond Whig and Advertiser (semi-weekly edition). 1872 (incomplete file).

St. Paul Weekly Pioneer. 1873–1874.
St. Paul Weekly Pioneer-Press. Apr.–Dec., 1875, 1876.
St. Paul Weekly Press. 1871–1874.
Southern Recorder. Milledgeville, Ga., Jan.–July, 1872.
Spirit of the Times. New York, 1872.
Springfield Weekly Republican. 1871–1872.
Standard. Chicago, 1872.
Wisconsin Weekly State Journal. Madison, 1872–1876.
World. New York, 1871–1876.

IV. POLITICAL DOCUMENTS

American Annual Cyclopedia. New York, 1869–1876.
Appleton's Annual Cyclopedia. New York, 1877.
Buckman, B. E. Samuel J. Tilden Unmasked. New York, 1876.
Budlong, Pharaoh (Perkins, Frederick B.). President Greeley, President Hoffman, and the Resurrection of the Ring. A History of the Next Four Years. Boston, 1872.
Chamberlin, Everett. The Struggle of '72 and Issues and Candi-dates of the Present Political Campaign, etc., Chicago, 1872.
Congressional Globe, 41–42 Congresses. Washington, 1869–1873.
Congressional Record. 43–44 Congresses. Washington, 1873–1876.
Conkling, Roscoe. The Presidential Battle of 1872. Grant and his Defamers; Deeds against Words. Speech at Cooper Institute, New York, July 23, 1872.
Cross, N. The Modern Ulysses LL.D. His Political Record. New York, 1872.
Evening Journal Almanac, 1873–1876. Albany, 1873–1876.
Fleming, W. L. Documentary History of Reconstruction. 2 vols., Cleveland, 1906–1907.
Greeley's (Mr.) Letters from Texas and the Lower Mississippi to which are added His Address to the Farmers of Texas and His Speech on His Return to New York, June 12, 1871. New York, Tribune Office, 1871.
Greeley's (Mr.) Record on the Questions of Amnesty and Recon-struction from the Hour of Gen. Lee's Surrender. New York, June, 1872.
Life and Public Services of Horace Greeley and of B. Gratz Brown. Proceedings of the Cincinnati Convention, etc., Chicago, 1872.
McKee, T. H. The National Conventions and Platforms of all parties. 6th edition, Baltimore, 1906.
McPherson, Edward. A Hand Book of Politics for 1872. Wash-ington, 1872. Same for 1874. Washington, 1874.

Official Proceedings of the National Democratic Convention held at Baltimore, July 9, 1872. Boston, 1872.

Official Proceedings of the National Democratic Convention at St. Louis, June 27–29, 1876. St. Louis, 1876.

Proceedings of the Liberal Republican Convention in Cincinnati, May 1, 2, 3, 1872. Horace Greeley's Letter of Acceptance. Address of the New York State Committee to their Fellow Citizens. New York (1872).

Proceedings of the National Union Republican Convention held at Philadelphia, June 5 and 6, 1872. Francis H. Smith, official reporter. Washington, 1872.

Proceedings of the Republican National Convention at Cincinnati, Ohio, June 14–16, 1876. Reported by M. A. Clancy and Wm. Nelson. Concord, N. H., 1876.

Reform Movement, The. A National Convention called to meet at Cincinnati, May 1, 1872—Resolutions of the Liberal Republican State Convention of Missouri—Speech by Governor B. Gratz Brown—Letter from Senator Carl Schurz—Indorsement by Ex-Secretary J. D. Cox, Hon. Stanley Matthews, Judge George Hoadly and Judge J. B. Stallo of Ohio. Washington, 1872. [Proceedings of the Missouri Liberal State Convention at Jefferson City, Jan. 24, 1872.]

Tribune Almanac, 1873–1874. New York, 1873–74.

World Almanac, 1873–75. New York, 1873–75.

Welch, F. G. That Convention or Five Days a Politician. New York and Chicago, 1872.

V. RECOLLECTIONS

Barnum, P. T. Struggles and Triumphs or Forty Years' Recollections. Rev. ed. Buffalo, 1874.

Bigelow, John. Retrospections of an Active Life. 5 vols., New York, 1909–1913.

Blaine, James G. Twenty Years of Congress. 2 vols., Norwich, Conn., 1886.

Boutwell, George S. Reminiscences of Sixty Years in Public Affairs. 2 vols., New York, 1902.

Brinkerhoff, General Roeliff. Recollections of a Lifetime. Cincinnati, 1900.

Butler, Benjamin F. Butler's Book. Boston, 1892.

Carr, Clark E. My Day and Generation. Chicago, 1908.

Childs, George W. Recollections of General Grant. Philadelphia, 1890.

Clay, Cassius Marcellus. Life, Memoirs, Writings, and Speeches. Vol. I, Cincinnati, 1886.

Clay, Virginia Clapton. A Belle of the Fifties. Edited by Ada Sterling. New York, 1904.

Clayton, Powell. The Aftermath of the Civil War in Arkansas. New York, 1915.

Clews, Henry. Twenty-Eight Years in Wall Street. New York, 1888.

Cole, Cornelius. Memoirs. New York, 1908.

Congdon, C. T. Reminiscences of a Journalist. Boston, 1880.

Cox, J. D. "How Judge Hoar Ceased to be Attorney-General," *Atlantic Monthly,* LXXVI, 162–173.

Cox, S. S. Three Decades of Federal Legislation. Providence, 1885.

Crawford, I. C. "What the Vice President of the Confederacy thought of General Grant," *Independent,* LIX, Sept. 21, 1905.

Crawford, Samuel J. Kansas in the Sixties. Chicago, 1911.

Cullom, Shelby M. Fifty Years of Public Service. Chicago, 1911.

Douglass, Frederick. Life and Times. Hartford, 1882.

Forbes, John Murray. Letters and Recollections. Edited by Sarah Forbes Hughes. 2 vols., Boston, 1900.

Forney, John W. Anecdotes of Public Men. 2 vols., New York, 1873.

Gladden, Washington. Recollections. Boston, 1909.

Goode, John. Recollections of a Lifetime. New York, 1906.

Gouveneur, Marian. As I Remember. Recollections of American Society during the Nineteenth Century. New York, 1911.

Greeley, Horace. Recollections of a Busy Life. New York, 1868.

Grinnell, Josiah B. Men and Events of Forty Years. Boston, 1891.

Halstead, Murat. "Horace Greeley, a friendly estimate of a great career." *Cosmopaliton,* VIII, Feb., 1890. "Breakfasts with Horace Greeley," *Cosmopolitan,* XXXVI, April, 1904.

Hoar, George Frisbie. Autobiography of Seventy Years. 2 vols., New York, 1903.

Hudson, William C. Random Recollections of an Old Political Reporter. New York, 1911.

Joyce, John A. A Checkered Life. Chicago, 1883.

Julian, George W. Political Recollections. Chicago, 1884.

Koerner, Gustave. Memoirs. Edited by Thomas J. McCormack. 2 vols., Cedar Rapids, Iowa, 1909.

Lathers, Richard. Reminiscences, Sixty Years of a Busy Life in South Carolina, Massachusetts, and New York. Edited by Alvan F. Sanborn. New York, 1907.

Logan, Mrs. John A. Reminiscences of a Soldier's Wife. New York, 1913.

McClure, Alexander K. Recollections of Half a Century. Salem, Mass., 1902.

McClure, A. K. Old Time Notes of Pennsylvania. 2 vols., Philadelphia, 1905.

McClure, A. K. Our Presidents and how we make them. New York, 1900.

McCulloch, Hugh. Men and Measures of Half a Century. New York, 1888.

Massey, John E. Autobiography. Edited by Elizabeth H. Hancock. New York, 1909.

Palmer, John M. Personal Recollections. The Story of an Earnest Life. Cincinnati, 1901.

Platt, Thomas C. Autobiography. Edited by Louis J. Lang. New York, 1910.

Poore, Ben. Perley. Perley's Reminiscences. 2 vols., Philadelphia, 1886.

Pryor, Mrs. Roger A. My Day. Reminiscences of a Long Life. New York, 1909.

Schurz, Carl. Reminiscences. 3 vols., New York, 1907–1908.

Sherman, John. Recollections of Forty Years. 2 vols., Chicago, 1895.

Stevenson, Adlai E. Something of Men I have Known. Chicago, 1909.

Stewart, Senator William M. Reminiscences. Edited by George Rothwell Brown. New York, 1908.

Veteran Journalist, "Personal Reminiscences of Horace Greeley," *Bookman*, XIII, April, 1901.

Watterson, Henry. "The Humor and Tragedy of the Greeley Campaign," Comments by Whitelaw Reid and Horace White. *Century*, LXXXV, Nov., 1912.

Wheeler, Everett P. Sixty Years of American Life—Taylor to Roosevelt, 1850 to 1910. New York, 1917.

White, Andrew D. Autobiography. 2 vols., London, 1905.

VI. BIOGRAPHIES

Adams, C. F. Charles Francis Adams. Boston, 1900.

Adams, I. E. Life of Emery A. Storrs. Philadelphia, 1886.

Badeau, Adam. Grant in Peace. Hartford, Conn., 1887.

Bancroft, F. and Dunning, W. A. A Sketch of Carl Schurz's Political Career, 1869–1906 in vol. III of the Reminiscences of Carl Schurz. New York, 1908.

Barnes, T. W. Memoir of Thurlow Weed. Boston, 1884.

Bassett, J. S. Anti-Slavery Leaders of North Carolina. *Johns Hopkins Studies in Historical and Political Science.* Series XVI, No. 6. Baltimore, 1898.

Bigelow, John. Life of Samuel J. Tilden. 2 vols., New York, 1895.

Biographical Cyclopedia of Representative Men of Maryland and District of Columbia. Baltimore, 1879.

Biographical Encyclopedia of Pennsylvania of the Nineteenth Century. Philadelphia, 1874.

Blackmar, F. W. Charles Robinson, the first state governor of Kansas. Topeka, Kansas, 1902.

Brigham, Johnson. James Harlan. Iowa City, Iowa, 1913.

Cary, Edward. George William Curtis. Boston, 1894.

Connelley, W. E. The Life of Preston B. Plumb. Chicago, 1913.

Conkling, A. R. Life and Letters of Roscoe Conkling. New York, 1889.

Cox, W. Z. and Northrup, M. H. Life of Samuel Sullivan Cox. Syracuse, N. Y., 1899.

Curran, M. P. Life of Patrick A. Collins. Norwood, Mass., 1906.

Dawson, G. F. Life and Services of John A. Logan. Chicago, 1887.

Detroit Post and Tribune. Zachariah Chandler; An Outline Sketch of His Life and Public Services. Detroit, 1880.

Dingley, E. N. Life and Times of Nelson Dingley, Jr. Kalamazoo, Mich., 1902.

Dix, Morgan. Memoirs of John A. Dix. 2 vols., New York, 1883.

DuBois, J. T. and Mathews, Gertrude S. Galusha A. Grow— Father of the Homestead Law. Boston, 1917.

Ewing, J. R. Public Services of Jacob Dolson Cox. Washington, 1902.

Fielder, Herbert. A Sketch of the Life and Times and Speeches of Joseph E. Brown. Springfield, Mass., 1883.

Flower, F. A. A Life of Matthew Hale Carpenter. Madison, Wis., 1883.

Foord, John. Life and Public Services of Andrew Haswell Greene. New York, 1913.

Foord, John. Life and Public Services of Simon Sterne. London, 1903.

Foulke, W. D. Life of Oliver P. Morton. 2 vols., Indianapolis, 1899.

Frothingham, O. B. Gerrit Smith, a Biography. New York, 1879.

Garland, Hamlin. Ulysses S. Grant, His Life and Character. New York, 1898.

Garrison, Wendell P. and Francis J. William Lloyd Garrison. 4 vols., New York, 1885–1889.

George, Henry, Jr.   Life of Henry George.   New York, 1900.

Godwin, Parke.   A Biography of William Cullen Bryant.   2 vols., New York, 1883.

Hamilton, Gail.   Biography of James G. Blaine.   Norwich, Conn., 1895.

Hamlin, C. E.   Life and Times of Hannibal Hamlin.   Cambridge, 1899.

Harper, Ida Husted.   The Life and Work of Susan B. Anthony. 2 vols., Indianapolis, 1899.

Hart, A. B.   Salmon Portland Chase.   Boston, 1899.

Herrick, H. M.   Life and Public Services of William Walter Phelps. New York, 1904.

Hill, B. H., Jr.   Senator Benjamin H. Hill of Georgia, His Life, Speeches, and Writings.   Atlanta, Ga., 1891.

Holcombe, J. W. and Skinner, H. M.   Life and Public Services of Thomas A. Hendricks.   Indianapolis, 1886.

Holden, J. A. (ed.)   Proceedings at the Unveiling of a Memorial to Horace Greeley at Chappaqua, N. Y., February 3, 1914.   With reports of other Greeley celebrations related to the centennial of his birth.   February 3, 1911.   University of the State of New York, Division of Archives and History, Albany, 1915.   [Cited as "Memorial to Greeley."]

Hollister, O. J.   Life of Schuyler Colfax.   New York, 1886.

Hovey, Carl.   The Life of J. Pierpont Morgan.   New York, 1911.

Ingersoll, L. D.   The Life of Horace Greeley.   Philadelphia, 1874.

Jones, C. H.   The Life and Public Services of J. Glancy Jones.   2 vols., Philadelphia, 1910.

Kerr, W. S.   John Sherman, His Life and Public Services.   2 vols., New York, 1908.

Linn, W. A.   Horace Greeley.   New York, 1903.

Lloyd, Caro.   Henry Demarest Lloyd, A Biography.   2 vols., New York, 1912.

Lyford, J. O.   Life of Edward H. Rollins.   A Political Biography. Boston, 1906.

Martyn, Carlos.   William E. Dodge.   The Christian Merchant. New York, 1890.

Mayes, Edward.   The Life and Times of Lucius Q. C. Lamar.   Nashville, Tenn., 1896.

Merriam, George S.   The Life and Times of Samuel Bowles.   2 vols., New York, 1885.

Morehouse, Frances M. I.   Life of Jesse W. Fell.   *University of Illinois Studies in Social Sciences*, vol. V, No. 2.   Urbana, June, 1916.

Morse, J. T., Jr. The Life and Letters of Oliver Wendell Holmes. 2 vols., Boston, 1897.

Nason, Rev. Elias. The Life and Public Services of Henry Wilson. Boston, 1881.

Oberholtzer, E. P. Jay Cooke, Financier of the Civil War. 2 vols., Philadelphia, 1907.

O'Connor, Mary Doline. The Life and Letters of M. P. O'Connor. New York, 1893.

Ogden, Rollo. Life and Letters of Edwin Lawrence Godkin. · 2 vols., New York, 1907.

Orcutt, W. D. Burrows of Michigan and the Republican Party—A Biography and a History. 2 vols., New York, 1917.

Paine, A. B. Thomas Nast: His Period and His Pictures. New York, 1904.

Palfrey, F. W. Memoir of William Francis Bartlett. Boston, 1881.

Parton, James. Life of Horace Greeley. Boston, 1882.

Pelzer, Louis. Augustus Caesar Dodge. Iowa City, Iowa, 1908.

Phillips, U. B. The Life of Robert Toombs. New York, 1913.

Pierce, E. L. Memoirs and Letters of Charles Sumner. 4 vols., Boston, 1893.

Reavis, L. N. A Representative Life of Horace Greeley, with an introduction by Cassius M. Clay. New York, 1872.

Rombauer, R. E. Life of Hon. Gustavus Koerner. *Transactions of the Illinois Historical Society*, 1904. Publication No. 9, Illinois State Historical Library. Springfield, Illinois, 1904.

Salter, W. The Life of James W. Grimes. New York, 1876.

Schuckers, J. W. The Life and Public Services of Salmon Portland Chase. New York, 1874.

Sears, Lorenzo. Wendell Phillips, Orator and Agitator. New York, 1909.

Shotwell, W. G. Life of Charles Sumner. New York, 1910.

Smith, Margaret V. Virginia 1492–1892, a brief review of the discovery of the continent of North America with a History of the Executives of the Colony and Commonwealth of Virginia. Washington, 1893.

Smith, W. B. James Sidney Rollins. New York, 1891.

Spencer, Edward. An Outline of the Public Life and Services of Thomas F. Bayard, Senator of the United States from the State of Delaware 1869–1880 with Extracts from his Speeches and the Debates in Congress. New York, 1880.

Steiner, B. C. Life of Reverdy Johnson. Baltimore, 1914.

Storey, M. Charles Sumner. Boston, 1900.

Storey, Moorfield and Emerson, Edward W. Ebenezer Rockwood Hoar, A Memoir. Boston, 1911.

Taylor, Marie Hausen and Scudder, Horace. Life and Letters of Bayard Taylor. 2 vols., Boston, 1885.

Thayer, W. R. Life and Letters of John Hay. 2 vols., Boston, 1915.

Vallandigham, J. L. A Life of Clement L. Vallandigham. Baltimore, 1872.

Ward, Elizabeth P. Durbin Ward, Life, Speeches and Orations. Columbus, Ohio, 1888.

Warden, R. B. An Account of the Private Life and Public Services of Salmon Portland Chase. Cincinnati, 1874.

Washington, Booker T. Frederick Douglass. Philadelphia, 1906.

White, Horace. Life of Lyman Trumbull. Boston, 1913.

Wight, W. W. Henry Clay Payne. Milwaukee, 1907.

Williams, C. R. Life of Rutherford Birchard Hayes. 2 vols., Boston, 1914.

Wilson, J. H. The Life of Charles A. Dana. New York, 1907.

Winthrop, R. C., Jr. A memoir of Robert C. Winthrop. Boston, 1897.

Wise, Barton H. Life of Henry A. Wise of Virginia. New York, 1899.

Wister, Owen. Ulysses S. Grant. (Beacon Biographies) 2nd edition, Boston, 1901.

Zabriski, F. N. Horace Greeley, the Editor. New York, 1890.

VII. GENERAL WORKS, MONOGRAPHS AND SPECIAL STUDIES

Adams, C. F., Jr. and Henry. Chapters of Erie. New York, 1886.

Adams, Henry. Historical Essays. New York, 1901.

Alexander, D. S. Political History of the State of New York. 3 vols., New York, 1906–1909.

Andrews, E. B. The United States in Our Own Times. New York, 1903.

Anthony, Susan B. and others (eds.). History of Woman Suffrage. 4 vols., New York and Rochester, 1881–1902.

Avery, I. W. History of the State of Georgia. New York, 1881.

Bennett, F. O. Politics and politicians of Chicago, Cook County and Illinois. Chicago, 1886.

Blackmar, F. W. (ed.). Kansas, A Cyclopedia of State History. 2 vols., Chicago, 1912.

Buck, S. J. "Independent Parties in the Western States, 1873–1876," in Essays in American History dedicated to Frederick Jackson Turner. New York, 1910.

Buck, S. J. The Granger Movement. Cambridge, 1913.

Callahan, J. M. Semi-Centennial History of West Virginia. 1913.

Chandler, J. A. C. and Riley, F. L. (eds.). The South in the Building of the Nation. Parts I and II. vols., I–IV, Richmond, 1909.

Church, C. A. History of the Republican Party in Illinois, 1854–1912. Rockford, Ill., 1912.

Cooper, T. V. and Fenton, H. F. American Politics. Chicago, 1884.

Commons, J. R. "Horace Greeley and the Working-Class Origin of the Republican Party." *Political Science Quarterly*, XXIV, 468 ff.

Conrad, H. C. History of the State of Delaware. 3 vols., Wilmington, Delaware, 1908.

Crawford, J. B. The Crédit Mobilier of America. Boston, 1880.

Curtis, Francis. The Republican party, a history of its fifty years' existence and a record of its measures and leaders. 2 vols., New York, 1904.

Davis, W. J. History of Political Conventions in California, 1849–1892. Sacramento, 1892.

Davis, W. W. The Civil War and Reconstruction in Florida. *Col. Univ. Studies*, vol. 53, New York, 1913.

Dewitt, D. M. The Impeachment and Trial of Andrew Johnson. New York, 1903.

Dilla, Hariette M. The Politics of Michigan, 1865–1878. *Col. Univ. Studies*, vol. 47, No. 1. New York, 1912.

Dunning, W. A. Reconstruction, Political and Economic. New York, 1907.

Dunning, W. A. "The Second Birth of the Republican Party," *American Historical Review*, XVI, 56 ff. (Oct., 1910.)

Eckenrode, H. J. The Political History of Virginia during the Reconstruction. *Johns Hopkins Studies*, Series XXII, Nos. 6–8. Baltimore, 1904.

Fish, C. R. The Civil Service and the Patronage. New York, 1905.

Fleming, W. L. Civil War and Reconstruction in Alabama. New York, 1905.

Flower, F. A. A History of the Republican Party. Springfield, Illinois, 1884.

Fortier, A. History of Louisiana. 4 vols., New York, 1904.

Frank, J. A. The Liberal Republican Movement as Exemplified by its Progress in New York State. Master's Thesis, Cornell University. Privately printed, 1909.

Garner, J. W. Reconstruction in Mississippi. New York, 1901.

Garner, J. W. (ed.). Studies in Southern History and Politics. New York, 1914.

Greene, E. B. "Some Aspects of Politics in the Middle West, 1860–1872." *Proceedings of the Wisconsin Historical Society,* 1911. Madison, 1912.

Gue, B. F. History of Iowa from the earliest times to the beginning of the twentieth century. 4 vols., New York, 1903.

Hamilton, J. G. deR. "The Election of 1872 in North Carolina," *South Atlantic Quarterly* XI, April, 1912.

Hamilton, J. G. deR. Reconstruction in North Carolina. *Col. Univ. Studies,* Vol. LVIII. New York, 1914.

Hamilton, P. J. The Reconstruction Period. Philadelphia, 1905.

Harding, S. B. "Party struggle in Missouri during the Civil War." *American Historical Association Report,* 1900. Washington.

Harper, J. H. The House of Harper. New York, 1912.

Harrell, J. M. The Brooks and Baxter War. A History of the Reconstruction Period in Arkansas. St. Louis, 1893.

Haworth, P. L. The Hayes-Tilden Disputed Presidential Election of 1876. Cleveland, 1906.

Haynes, F. E. Third Party Movements Since the Civil War with special reference to Iowa. Iowa City, Iowa, 1916.

Herbert, H. A. (ed.). Why the Solid South? Baltimore, 1890.

Hinsdale, M. L. A History of the President's Cabinet. Ann Arbor, Mich., 1911.

Holmes, F. R. Minnesota in Three Centuries. 4 vols., Publishing Society of Minnesota, 1908.

Hopkins, J. H. A History of Political Parties in the United States. New York, 1900.

Johnson, B. S. "The Brooks-Baxter War." *Pubs. of Arkansas Historical Society.* Vol. II, pp. 122–173. Fayetteville, Ark., 1908.

Johnston, Alexander. American Political History 1763–1876, edited and supplemented by J. A. Woodburn. 2 vols., New York, 1905.

Judson, F. M. "The Administration of Governor B. Gratz Brown, 1871–1873." *Missouri Historical Society Collections,* Vol. II, No. 2. April, 1913.

Kleeberg, G. S. P. The Formation of the Republican Party as a national political organization. New York, 1911.

Lusk, D. W. Eighty years of Illinois politics and politicians. Springfield, Illinois, 1889.

McDonald, Gen. John. Secrets of the Great Whiskey Ring. Chicago, 1880.

McDougal, H. C. "A Decade of Missouri Politics, 1860–1870, From a Republican Viewpoint." *Missouri Historical Review*, III, Jan. 1909.

McNeill, G. E. The Labor Movement. Boston, 1887.

Macy, Jesse. "The Scientific Spirit in Politics," *American Political Science Review*, XI, February, 1917.

Memorial Record of Alabama. 2 vols., Madison, Wis., 1893.

Moses, John. Illinois Historical and Statistical. 2 vols., Chicago, 1889.

Myers, Gustavus. Tammany Hall. New York, 1901.

New York Typographical Union No. 6. One hundredth Anniversary of the birth of Horace Greeley, first President of Typographical Union No. 6, New York Theatre, February 5, 1911. New York, 1911.

Ostrogorski, M. Democracy and the organization of Political Parties. 2 vols., New York, 1902.

Patton, J. H. The Democratic Party: Its Political History and Influence. New York, 1884.

Pearson, C. C. The Readjuster Movement in Virginia. New Haven, 1917.

Phelps, Albert. Louisiana, a record of expansion. Boston, 1905.

Platt, G. W. A History of the Republican Party. Cincinnati, 1904.

Powell, T. E. (ed.). The Democratic Party of the State of Ohio. 2 vols., Columbus, Ohio, 1913.

Ramsdell, C. W. Reconstruction in Texas. *Col. Univ. Studies*, Vol. 36, No. 1. New York, 1910.

Reynolds, J. S. Reconstruction in South Carolina. Columbia, S. C., 1905.

Rhodes, J. F. History of the United States from the Compromise of 1850 to the restoration of home rule in the South in 1877. 7 vols., New York, 1892–1905.

Rogers, J. M. The Development of the North since the Civil War. Philadelphia, 1906.

Ross, E. D. "Horace Greeley and the South, 1865–1872," *South Atlantic Quarterly*, XVI, 324 ff. Oct., 1917.

Rowland, D. (ed.). Encyclopedia of Mississippi History. 2 vols., Madison, Wis., 1907.

Saby, R. S. Railroad Legislation in Minnesota, 1849 to 1875. Saint Paul, Minn., 1912.

Scharf, J. T. History of Maryland. 3 vols., Baltimore, 1879.

Schouler, James. History of the Reconstruction Period, being Vol. VII of the History of the United States under the Constitution. New York, 1913.

Smalley, E. V. A Brief History of the Republican Party from its organization to 1884. New York, 1884.

Smith, J. P. History of the Republican Party in Ohio. 2 vols., Chicago, 1898.

Stanwood, Edward. A History of the Presidency. Boston, 1901.

Stanwood, Edward. American Tariff controversy in the Nineteenth Century. 2 vols., Boston, 1903.

Stebbins, H. A. A Political History of the State of New York, 1865–1869. *Col. Univ. Studies*, Vol. LV, No. 1. New York, 1913.

Stocking, William. History of the Republican Party in Michigan, in Proceedings at the celebration of the fiftieth anniversary of the birth of the Republican party at Jackson, Michigan, July 6, 1904. Detroit, 1904.

Switzler, W. F. History of Missouri from 1541 to 1881. St. Louis, 1881.

Tarbell, Ida M. The Tariff in Our Own Times. New York, 1911.

Taussig, F. W. Tariff History of the United States. New York, 1910.

Townsend, G. A. ("Gath."). Washington Outside and Inside. Hartford, Conn., 1874.

Utley, H. M. and Cutcheon, B. M. Michigan as a Province, Territory and State. 4 vols., Publishing Society of Michigan, 1906.

Wallace, John. Carpetbag Rule in Florida. Jacksonville, Fla., 1888.

Watkins, Albert. History of Nebraska. 3 vols., Lincoln, 1905–1913.

Wilder, D. W. The Annals of Kansas. Topeka, Kan., 1875.

Wilson, W. L. The National Democratic Party. Baltimore, 1888.

Woodburn, J. A. Political Parties and Party Problems in the United States. 2nd edition. New York, 1914.

INDEX

Adams, C. F., Jr., on the character of the independent reformers, 4n.

Adams, C. F., Sr., and Republican nomination for president, 36; and the Liberal nomination, 82ff.; favored by the reformers, 85; strength in Cincinnati convention, 96ff.; resolution for in Reunion and Reform convention, 104; favored by Steinway Hall meeting, 113; offered Republican nomination for vice-president, 114; sentiment for in Fifth Avenue conference, 123; opposition candidate for senator, 220; choice of independents for president in 1876, 228; nominated for governor, 233; considered for Tilden's cabinet, 236.

Adams, J. Q., nominated for vice-president by Straight-Outs, declines, 147.

"Adams men," in campaign of 1872, 128.

Alabama claims, and Republican prospects, 42, 114f.

Alcorn, J. L., 23, 65.

Allen County Democracy, 200.

Allen, Ethan, chairman Liberal national committee, 104n.; calls Liberal conference in 1876, 230; announces reunion of Liberals with the Republicans, 231.

Allen, William, favors Greeley's endorsement, 132; elected governor, 203; defeated on the greenback issue, 216.

Alvord, T. G., 64.

"American Democratic-Republican party," 123.

American Free Trade League, organization, 5; activities in 1870, 14; in Cincinnati convention, 89; issues call for Steinway Hall meeting, 111;

in Fifth Avenue conference, 120; in campaign of 1872, 128.

Ames, Adelbert, 23.

Amnesty bill, 176.

Anti-Catholic issue, in campaign of 1872, 167.

Anti-Monopoly issue, in campaign of 1872, 168.

Anti-Monopoly parties, 205.

Apollo Hall, supports Straight-Outs, 148.

Arkansas, coalition movement in, 24f.; Liberal leaders in, 67f.

Ashley, J. M., 67.

Atkinson, Edward, reform writer, 3; member of Free Trade League, 5; a Liberal organizer, 64; in Cincinnati convention, 94f.; in Steinway Hall meeting, 113.

Atlantic Monthly, for political reform, 3; favors independent reformers, 50; in campaign of 1872, 127; on election prospects in 1872, 179.

Baltimore, Democratic convention of 1872 in, 140ff.

Banks, N. P., Liberal leader, 64; in the campaign of 1872, 155; retained on committee in House, 194; returns to Republicans, 196n.

Barclay, David, 65.

Barney, Hiram, 64.

Bayard, T. F., opposes Greeley's endorsement by Democrats, 139; opposes Liberal platform in Baltimore convention, 141; supports Greeley in campaign of 1872, 144.

Beauregard, General, 51.

Belmont, August, advises Liberals to nominate Adams, 84; favors Democratic endorsement of Greeley, 136; in Baltimore convention, 140.